Spiritual-elevation is the golden key to exploring the inner-strength, that lies dormant, inside the soul, and which needs to be tapped, by the aspirant, in order to lead a fulfilled life.

A HUMBLE OBEISANCE

At The Lotus-Feet

Of the

"ONLY OMNISCIENT-ONE"

who bestowed upon me

the gracious blessings of my revered mother,

SARDARNI ISHWAR KAUR,

Whose sweet memory I cherish, so very fondly,

And,

the inspiring guidance of my father,

SARDAR KARTAR SINGH,

Both of whom led me on to the Perfect- Guru,

Who gave me the Courage-of-Conviction,

To stand up for "TRUTH",

And to continue beleiving in the

" POWER OF PRAYER "

Table of Contents

Acknowledgements

I wish to acknowledge, with a deep sense of gratitude, all help and guidance, that was abundantly forthcoming from several quarters, towards the accomplishment of this onerous task. I wish to place, on record, my sincerest appreciation to the following God-loving aspirants.

Singh Sahib Giani Jagtaar Singh 'Jaachak', Head Priest at Gurdwara Sahib, Plainview NY, for his esteemed guidance, at odd hours. His comprehensive knowledge of the scriptures, coupled with an extensive study of comparative religions, was a great help. He is the ex-Head Priest of Harmandir Sahib (Golden Temple), Amritsar, the highest spiritual center of the Sikhs. He is the recipient of the International Sikh Missionary Award (1996) instituted by the Shiromani Gurdwara Prabandhak Committee (SGPC), the highest policy-making body of the Sikhs.

Mr. Amarjit Singh Anand (New York) for the extremely sincere and zealous fervor displayed during the stupendous commissioned research for this publication. I really appreciate his devotion towards the Creator and his undwindling faith in the word of the Gurus. That trust blessed him with the requisite knowledge, and his natural capabilities unfolded. It was God's benevolence that I came into contact with this humble Sikh.

Dr. Surinder Singh Kohli (London), is an eminent author of more than 100 books on Sikh Gurus, religion, philosophy, history, and culture. He has been responsible for editing this book, so painstakingly, despite his preoccupation with several ongoing projects of his own. He received his Ph.D. in the study of the Guru Granth Sahib, from University of Delhi. He is the former Head of Department, Punjabi Studies, Punjab University, Chandigarh.

I congratulate Singh Sahib Sant Singh Khalsa, M.D. (Tucson, Arizona), for the momentous effort he has put into the compilation of the English transliteration of the Sri Guru Granth Sahib, which has been a great help.

Thanks are also due to Mr. Jaswant Singh, and Mr. Tarlochan Singh, both of whom have been responsible for the compilation of a computer CD, which was a ready reference for our work.

I am indebted to Professor Kahan Singh Nabha (renowned author), Giani Sant Singh 'Maskeen' (esteemed preacher), and Sardar Pritam Singh Gill (eminent author) all of whose thoughts proved to be excellent guidance.

I am thankful to my publisher, Mr. Baljit Singh Gill (Canada), for his expedient and excellent work, and for designing the entire art-work. His sense of devotion, to the Lord and Gurus, is really admirable.

Last, but not least, I am thankful to my son, Gunit Singh, for devoting long hours on the computer, taking time off from his studies, to keep up the momentum of this work, thus enabling me to meet deadlines. I must appreciate the analytical criticism and proof-reading done by my daughter Ms. Punit Kaur, and my son Pavit Singh. My thanks are due to my wife Dr. Satnam Kaur, whose ever-smiling countenance, coupled with her constructive and critical assessment, proved to be a constant source of inspiration, all my life.

Dr. Harsimran Singh

foreword

It was, indeed, a great pleasure reading THE DIVINE TRUTH, which is an exemplary work, that incorporates some of the really fundamental spiritual thoughts, to benefit humanity. It is in conjunction with our organizational objectives, of promoting trust and goodwill amongst the adherents of divergent viewpoints of the various great Living-Religions (Christianity, Islam, Hinduism, Judaism, Sikhism, and several other Faiths).

The Central-Theme of the book, is that the Cult-of-Materialism, that has captured humanity, in it's octopus-like-tentacles, needs to be, effectively and expeditiously, tackled, head on, by the forces of Spiritualism.

The significance of the linkage, between PRAYER & MIRACLE, is highlighted, due to the fact that it is borne out of the personal experiences, of the Author, and is not, merely, an exercise in philosophical preaching. It is of great import, that the Publisher, in all his wisdom, appended the Press-Clipping, that illustrates the point, speaking volumes of the manifestations of the Power called GOD.

The diverse subjects, covered in the Book, have been most appropriately allocated under catchy Section-heads, and all of them are of topical-interest, to humanity, at large, irrespective of Faith or Religious affiliations, or linguistic / social-class barriers.

The English transliteration (of the Words of Enlightenment, by the Great Sufis, the Mystical Spiritual Leaders: Sikh Gurus, Hindu Saints, and Muslim Pirs, from the Gurmukhi-Scripture: SRI GURU GRANTH SAHIB), and the Commentary, are of a high literary-order.

This unique and sincere effort is bound to become a harbinger, towards fostering a sense of Amity, Harmony, Peace, Tolerance, and Understanding, amongst all human-beings. It, certainly, adds one more vociferous voice against religious-fanaticism, ritualistic-practices, and all other such discords, which endanger peaceful co-existence.

Edward White
Director,
UNITY IN DIVERSE-RELIGIONS, N.Y.

April 1998

Preface

'PRAYER': AN INSPIRATIONAL POWER

It all began with a feeling of guilt: Why should God's abode be smaller than that of some of his devotees'?

Having a house-of-worship, which gets tremendously over-crowded, especially during festivities, disturbed me. This realization gave birth to a fervent prayer, that later became a collective one. And the prayer resulted in the community becoming the proud owners of one of the largest Sikh-Temples in the world, spread over a sprawling 15 acres, with a built-up area covering over 30,000-sq. ft., in Glen Cove, NY. And the City of Glen Cove being proclaimed the "SISTER-CITY" of Amritsar, home of the holiest Sikh-Shrine. "The fragrance, emanating from the Golden Temple, shall abound here, in the U.S.A.", writes the Mayor of City of Glen Cove.

Later, these achievements were transformed into a powerful inspiration that widened my horizons. Why should not the humanistic teachings of Guru Granth Sahib be revealed, to the larger humanity, well beyond the confines of this newly acquired complex?

But how? Should I wield the pen? I am not a writer. Who would want to buy my book?

All fear was dispelled when I recalled that Guru Harkrishan had blessed an illiterate, mute person to become an enlightened scholarly orator. All my inhibitions were vanquished with this single answer that all knowledge emanates from Him, and that the words of spiritual wisdom (compiled in the form of Guru Granth Sahib, by the prophets themselves, hailing from diverse religions) were too invaluable for a price tag.

I implore the readers to help in spreading the universal message of fraternity, peace, and harmony, as enunciated by the mystical prophets, irrespective of religious leanings.

Harsimran Singh, Ph.D.

Please note: In some places, in this book, the literal meanings of the quotations, taken from the Sri Guru Granth Sahib (referred to as A.G. or Aadi Granth) have been summarized or elaborated, so as to give the reader a clear understanding of the context.

SECTION : 1

THE ONLY ONE

God is One, His Name is Truth, He is the Creator, He is the Fearless One, He does not bear animosity towards anyone, He is beyond the cycle of birth and death, and He is the Benevolent Grace. [1]

God is, simultaneously, transcendent and immanent, is supreme in His Excellence, and is independent of all experiences, such as birth and death: The Lord, of Himself, created Himself.

God is an *experience* of affirmation of Hope and Peace, of a blissful Radiance and Fragrance. *God is serene tranquility.*

He has no form, no shape, no color; God is beyond the three qualities. They alone understand Him, O Nanak, with whom He is pleased. [2]

You are beyond the limitations of form or shape, or of social class or race. These humans believe that You are distant; but You are quite obviously and apparently very close (in fact you reside within each creature). You enjoy Yourself in every heart, and no filth sticks to You, and You are blemishless. You are the blissful and infinite Primal Lord; Your Light is all-pervading. Among all divine beings, You are the most divine, O Creator-architect, Rejuvenator of all. How can my single tongue worship and adore You? You are the eternal, imperishable Entity. One whom You Yourself unite with the True Guru — all his generations are redeemed. All Your servants serve You, and Nanak is the most humble servant at Your Door. [3]

---

[1] ੧ਓ ਸਤਿ ਨਾਮੁ ਕਰਤਾ ਪੁਰਖੁ ਨਿਰਭਉ ਨਿਰਵੈਰੁ ਅਕਾਲ ਮੂਰਤਿ ਅਜੂਨੀ ਸੈਭੰ ਗੁਰ ਪ੍ਰਸਾਦਿ ॥

(from : The JAPJI-SAHIB: Pg.1 of The Aadi Granth)

[2] ਰੂਪੁ ਨ ਰੇਖ ਨ ਰੰਗੁ ਕਿਛੁ ਤ੍ਰਿਹੁ ਗੁਣ ਤੇ ਪ੍ਰਭ ਭਿੰਨ ॥ ਤਿਸਹਿ ਬੁਝਾਏ ਨਾਨਕਾ ਜਿਸੁ ਹੋਵੈ ਸੁਪ੍ਰਸੰਨ ॥ ੧ ॥ (Pg.283 A.G.)

[3] ਤੁਧੁ ਰੂਪੁ ਨ ਰੇਖਿਆ ਜਾਤਿ ਤੂ ਵਰਨਾ ਬਾਹਰਾ ॥ ਏ ਮਾਣਸ ਜਾਣਹਿ ਦੂਰਿ ਤੂ ਵਰਤਹਿ ਜਾਹਰਾ ॥ ਤੂ ਸਭਿ ਘਟ ਭੋਗਹਿ ਆਪਿ ਤੁਧੁ ਲੇਪੁ ਨ ਲਾਹਰਾ ॥ ਤੂ ਪੁਰਖੁ ਅਨੰਦੀ ਅਨੰਤ ਸਭ ਜੋਤਿ ਸਮਾਹਰਾ ॥ ਤੂ ਸਭ ਦੇਵਾ ਮਹਿ ਦੇਵ ਬਿਧਾਤੇ ਨਰਹਰਾ ॥ ਕਿਆ ਆਰਾਧੇ ਜਿਹਵਾ ਇਕ ਤੂ ਅਬਿਨਾਸੀ ਅਪਰਪਰਾ ॥ ਜਿਸੁ ਮੇਲਹਿ ਸਤਿਗੁਰੁ ਆਪਿ ਤਿਸ ਕੇ ਸਭਿ ਕੁਲ ਤਰਾ ॥ ਸੇਵਕ ਸਭਿ ਕਰਦੇ ਸੇਵ ਦਰਿ ਨਾਨਕੁ ਜਨੁ ਤੇਰਾ ॥ ੫ ॥ (Pg.1096 A.G.)

As much as the Word of God is in the mind, so much is Your melody; as much as the form of the universe is, so much is Your body, Lord. You Yourself are the tongue, and You Yourself are the nose. Do not speak of any other, O my mother. My Lord and Master is One (GOD). He is the One and Only; He is the One alone, proclaims Nanak. [4]

The various gods and goddesses, in various religions and cultures are, in reality, only mere manifestations of the One and ONLY God. He Himself is the Doer of deeds. [5]

The One and Only Creator of the Universe is All-pervading. All shall once again merge into the One. His One Form has one, and many colors; He leads all according to His One Word. [6]

Describe the Lord as the One, the One and Only. How rare are those who know the taste of this essence. The Glories of the Lord of the Universe cannot be known, proclaims Nanak, He is totally amazing and wonderful! [7]

In the one and in the many, He is pervading and permeating; within the range of my vision, there He is. And, beyond, too, for I can experience Him, always. God is everywhere. God is everything. Without God, there is nothing at all. As one thread holds hundreds and thousands of beads, He is woven into the textures and fibres of all His creations. The waves of the water, the foam and bubbles, are not distinct from the water. This manifested world is the playful game of

---

[4] ਜੇਤਾ ਸਬਦੁ ਸੁਰਤਿ ਧੁਨਿ ਤੇਤੀ ਜੇਤਾ ਰੂਪੁ ਕਾਇਆ ਤੇਰੀ ॥ ਤੂੰ ਆਪੇ ਰਸਨਾ ਆਪੇ ਬਸਨਾ ਅਵਰੁ ਨ ਦੂਜਾ ਕਹਉ ਮਾਈ ॥ ੧ ॥ ਸਾਹਿਬੁ ਮੇਰਾ ਏਕੋ ਹੈ ॥ ਏਕੋ ਹੈ ਭਾਈ ਏਕੋ ਹੈ ॥ ੧ ॥ ਰਹਾਉ ॥ (pg. 350 A.G.)
[5] ਬ੍ਰਹਮਾ ਬਿਸਨੁ ਮਹੇਸ ਇਕ ਮੂਰਤਿ ਆਪੇ ਕਰਤਾ ਕਾਰੀ ॥ ੧੨ ॥ (pg. 908 A.G.)
[6] ਓਅੰਕਾਰਿ ਏਕੋ ਰਵਿ ਰਹਿਆ ਸਭੁ ਏਕਸ ਮਾਹਿ ਸਮਾਵੈਗੋ ॥ ਏਕੋ ਰੂਪੁ ਏਕੋ ਬਹੁ ਰੰਗੀ ਸਭੁ ਏਕਤੁ ਬਚਨਿ ਚਲਾਵੈਗੋ ॥ ੪ ॥ (Pg.1310 A.G.)
[7] ਏਕੋ ਏਕੁ ਬਖਾਨੀਐ ਬਿਰਲਾ ਜਾਣੈ ਸ੍ਵਾਦੁ ॥ ਗੁਣ ਗੋਬਿੰਦ ਨ ਜਾਣੀਐ ਨਾਨਕ ਸਭੁ ਬਿਸਮਾਦੁ ॥ ੧੧ ॥ (Pg.299 A.G.)

the Supreme Lord God; Doubts and dreams, illusions and superstitions, ambitions and aspirations, all of them man believes to be true, whence it is all a mirage or an oasis. The Guru has instructed me to try to perform good deeds, and my awakened mind has accepted this. Says Naam Dev : See the Creation of the Lord, and reflect upon it in your heart. In each and every heart, and deep within the very nucleus of all, is the One Lord. [8]

Says Saint Kabeer : the One True Lord abides in all; by His making, everything is made (for He is the Master Architect, Engineer, Planner and Mason, all rolled into One. Whoever realizes the effect of His Command, knows the One Lord. He alone is said to be the Lord's Devotee. The Lord is Invisible, and can, yet, be seen with the Third Eye, obtained by His Grace. [9]

The emphasis is on the message of One GOD. Hence, the various manifestations of the Powers of GOD cannot be misconstrued as being God. They only represent certain attributes of GOD, which emanate from Him, and could never be an independent 'persona' or entity.

---

[8] ਏਕ ਅਨੇਕ ਬਿਆਪਕ ਪੂਰਕ ਜਤ ਦੇਖਉ ਤਤ ਸੋਈ ॥ ਮਾਇਆ ਚਿਤੁ ਬਚਿਤੁ ਬਿਮੋਹਿਤ ਬਿਰਲਾ ਬੂਝੈ ਕੋਈ ॥ ੧ ॥ ਸਭੁ ਗੋਬਿੰਦੁ ਹੈ ਸਭੁ ਗੋਬਿੰਦੁ ਹੈ ਗੋਬਿੰਦ ਬਿਨੁ ਨਹੀ ਕੋਈ ॥ ਸੂਤੁ ਏਕੁ ਮਣਿ ਸਤ ਸਹੰਸ ਜੈਸੇ ਓਤਿ ਪੋਤਿ ਪ੍ਰਭੁ ਸੋਈ ॥ ੧ ॥ ਰਹਾਉ ॥ ਜਲ ਤਰੰਗ ਅਰੁ ਫੇਨ ਬੁਦਬੁਦਾ ਜਲ ਤੇ ਭਿੰਨ ਨ ਹੋਈ ॥ ਇਹੁ ਪਰਪੰਚੁ ਪਾਰਬ੍ਰਹਮ ਕੀ ਲੀਲਾ ਬਿਚਰਤ ਆਨ ਨ ਹੋਈ ॥ ੨ ॥ ਮਿਥਿਆ ਭਰਮੁ ਅਰੁ ਸੁਪਨ ਮਨੋਰਥ ਸਤਿ ਪਦਾਰਥੁ ਜਾਨਿਆ ॥ ਸੁਕ੍ਰਿਤ ਮਨਸਾ ਗੁਰ ਉਪਦੇਸੀ ਜਾਗਤ ਹੀ ਮਨੁ ਮਾਨਿਆ ॥ ੩ ॥ ਕਹਤ ਨਾਮਦੇਉ ਹਰਿ ਕੀ ਰਚਨਾ ਦੇਖਹੁ ਰਿਦੈ ਬੀਚਾਰੀ ॥ ਘਟ ਘਟ ਅੰਤਰਿ ਸਰਬ ਨਿਰੰਤਰਿ ਕੇਵਲ ਏਕ ਮੁਰਾਰੀ ॥ ੪ ॥ ੧ ॥ (Pg.485 A.G.)

[9] ਸਭ ਮਹਿ ਸਚਾ ਏਕੋ ਸੋਈ ਤਿਸ ਕਾ ਕੀਆ ਸਭੁ ਕਛੁ ਹੋਈ ॥ ਹੁਕਮੁ ਪਛਾਨੈ ਸੁ ਏਕੋ ਜਾਨੈ ਬੰਦਾ ਕਹੀਐ ਸੋਈ ॥ ੩ ॥ (Pg.1350 A.G.)

All instructions and understandings are Yours; the mansions and sanctuaries are Yours as well. Without You, I know no other, O my Lord and Master; I continually sing Your Glorious Praises. All beings and creatures seek the Protection of Your Sanctuary; all thought of their care rests with You. That which pleases Your Will is good; this alone is Nanak's prayer.[10]

You are my Father, and You are my Mother. You are my Relative, and You are my Brother. You are my Protector everywhere; why should I feel any fear or anxiety? By Your Grace, I recognize You. You are my Shelter, and You are my Honour. Without You, there is no other; the entire Universe is the Arena of Your Play. You have created all beings and creatures. As it pleases You, You assign tasks to one and all. All Actions are Your Handiwork; we can do nothing, by ourselves. Meditating on Your Name, I have rediscovered (after experiencing the phase of being separated, from You) GREAT PEACE & SOLACE. Singing the Glorious Praises of the Lord, my mind is cooled and soothed. Through the Perfect Guru, congratulations are pouring in— Nanak is victorious on the arduous battlefield of life! [11]

God is the Paramount Power, the Insurmountable. He is beyond the experiences of Life & Death, of Joy & Sorrow, of Victory & Defeat. And, *God* is beyond the realms of Human Knowledge and Comprehension. He is attainable by Virtue of His Own Grace (if that

---

[10] ਅਗਮ ਅਗੋਚਰ ਅਲਖ ਅਪਾਰਾ ਚਿੰਤਾ ਕਰਹੁ ਹਮਾਰੀ ॥ ਜਲਿ ਥਲਿ ਮਹੀਅਲਿ ਭਰਿਪੁਰਿ ਲੀਣਾ ਘਟਿ ਘਟਿ ਜੋਤਿ ਤੁਮਾਰੀ ॥ ੨ ॥ ਸਿਖ ਮਤਿ ਸਭ ਬੁਧਿ ਤੁਮਾਰੀ ਮੰਦਿਰ ਛਾਵਾ ਤੇਰੇ ॥ ਤੁਝ ਬਿਨ ਅਵਰੁ ਨ ਜਾਣਾ ਮੇਰੇ ਸਾਹਿਬਾ ਗੁਣ ਗਾਵਾ ਨਿਤ ਤੇਰੇ ॥ ੩ ॥ ਜੀਅ ਜੰਤ ਸਭਿ ਸਰਣਿ ਤੁਮਾਰੀ ਸਰਬ ਚਿੰਤ ਤੁਧੁ ਪਾਸੇ ॥ ਜੋ ਤੁਧੁ ਭਾਵੈ ਸੋਈ ਚੰਗਾ ਇਕ ਨਾਨਕ ਕੀ ਅਰਦਾਸੇ ॥ ੪ ॥ ੨ ॥ (pg. 795 A.G.)

[11] ਤੂੰ ਮੇਰਾ ਪਿਤਾ ਤੂੰਹੈ ਮੇਰਾ ਮਾਤਾ ॥ ਤੂੰ ਮੇਰਾ ਬੰਧਪੁ ਤੂੰ ਮੇਰਾ ਭ੍ਰਾਤਾ ॥ ਤੂੰ ਮੇਰਾ ਰਾਖਾ ਸਭਨੀ ਥਾਈ ਤਾ ਭਉ ਕੇਹਾ ਕਾੜਾ ਜੀਉ ॥ ੧ ॥ ਤੁਮਰੀ ਕ੍ਰਿਪਾ ਤੇ ਤੁਧੁ ਪਛਾਣਾ ॥ ਤੂੰ ਮੇਰੀ ਓਟ ਤੂੰਹੈ ਮੇਰਾ ਮਾਣਾ ॥ ਤੁਝ ਬਿਨ ਦੂਜਾ ਅਵਰੁ ਨ ਕੋਈ ਸਭੁ ਤੇਰਾ ਖੇਲੁ ਅਖਾੜਾ ਜੀਉ ॥ ੨ ॥ ਜੀਅ ਜੰਤ ਸਭਿ ਤੁਧੁ ਉਪਾਏ ॥ ਜਿਤੁ ਜਿਤੁ ਭਾਣਾ ਤਿਤੁ ਤਿਤੁ ਲਾਏ ॥ ਸਭ ਕਿਛੁ ਕੀਤਾ ਤੇਰਾ ਹੋਵੈ ਨਾਹੀ ਕਿਛੁ ਅਸਾੜਾ ਜੀਉ ॥ ੩ ॥ ਨਾਮੁ ਧਿਆਇ ਮਹਾ ਸੁਖੁ ਪਾਇਆ ॥ ਹਰਿ ਗੁਣ ਗਾਇ ਮੇਰਾ ਮਨੁ ਸੀਤਲਾਇਆ ॥ ਗੁਰਿ ਪੂਰੈ ਵਜੀ ਵਾਧਾਈ ਨਾਨਕ ਜਿਤਾ ਬਿਖਾੜਾ ਜੀਉ ॥ ੪ ॥ ੨੪ ॥ ੩੧ ॥ (pg. 103 A.G.)

is forthcoming from Him) being bestowed on a devotee. He cannot be reached by persistence & penance. Meditation is the Sunlit-Path to the Glorious Destination.

God is Omnipotent, Omnipresent & Omniscient. He is all-pervasive, in creations and creatures, in all the mass and matter, in space and in water, on land and in the air. He is, in essence, in each particle, and in each atom. Therefore, the inference is that God is Transcendental & Immanent, both, at once, simultaneously.

Pilgrimages, austere discipline, compassion and charity—these, by themselves, bring only an iota of merit. Listening and believing with love and humility in your mind, cleanse yourself with the Name, at the sacred shrine deep within. All virtues are Yours, Lord, I have none at all. Without virtue, there is no devotional worship. I bow to the Lord of the World, to His Word. He is Beautiful, True and Eternally Joyful. What was that time, and what was that moment? What was that day, and what was that date? What was that season, and what was that month, when the Universe was created? The Pundits, the religious scholars, cannot find that time, even if it is written in the scriptures, for none has the ability to decipher the Lord's coded limits. That time is not known to the Qazis, who study the Koran. The day and the date are not known to the Yogis, nor is the month or the season. The Creator who created this creation—only He Himself knows. How can we speak about Him? How can we praise Him? How can we describe Him? How can we know Him? Everyone speaks of Him, each one wiser than the rest, but all fail to comprehend the Infinite. Great is the Master, Great is His Name. Whatever happens is according to His Will. One who claims to know everything shall not be decorated in the world hereafter. [12]

Now, to realize and to know Truth, the exact nature of Falsehood needs to be understood, in the correct perspective.

False are body, wealth, and all relations. False are ego, possessiveness and Maya (Illusion). False are power, youth, wealth

---

[12] ਤੀਰਥੁ ਤਪੁ ਦਇਆ ਦਤੁ ਦਾਨੁ ॥ ਜੇ ਕੋ ਪਾਵੈ ਤਿਲ ਕਾ ਮਾਨੁ ॥ ਸੁਣਿਆ ਮੰਨਿਆ ਮਨਿ ਕੀਤਾ ਭਾਉ ॥ ਅੰਤਰਗਤਿ ਤੀਰਥਿ ਮਲਿ ਨਾਉ ॥ ਸਭਿ ਗੁਣ ਤੇਰੇ ਮੈ ਨਾਹੀ ਕੋਇ ॥ ਵਿਣੁ ਗੁਣ ਕੀਤੇ ਭਗਤਿ ਨ ਹੋਇ ॥ ਸੁਅਸਤਿ ਆਥਿ ਬਾਣੀ ਬਰਮਾਉ ॥ ਸਤਿ ਸੁਹਾਣੁ ਸਦਾ ਮਨਿ ਚਾਉ ॥ ਕਵਣੁ ਸੁ ਵੇਲਾ ਵਖਤੁ ਕਵਣੁ ਕਵਣ ਥਿਤਿ ਕਵਣੁ ਵਾਰੁ ॥ ਕਵਣਿ ਸਿ ਰੁਤੀ ਮਾਹੁ ਕਵਣੁ ਜਿਤੁ ਹੋਆ ਆਕਾਰੁ ॥ ਵੇਲ ਨ ਪਾਈਆ ਪੰਡਤੀ ਜਿ ਹੋਵੈ ਲੇਖੁ ਪੁਰਾਣੁ ॥ ਵਖਤੁ ਨ ਪਾਇਓ ਕਾਦੀਆ ਜਿ ਲਿਖਨਿ ਲੇਖੁ ਕੁਰਾਣੁ ॥ ਥਿਤਿ ਵਾਰੁ ਨਾ ਜੋਗੀ ਜਾਣੈ ਰੁਤਿ ਮਾਹੁ ਨਾ ਕੋਈ ॥ ਜਾ ਕਰਤਾ ਸਿਰਠੀ ਕਉ ਸਾਜੇ ਆਪੇ ਜਾਣੈ ਸੋਈ ॥ ਕਿਵ ਕਰਿ ਆਖਾ ਕਿਵ ਸਾਲਾਹੀ ਕਿਉ ਵਰਨੀ ਕਿਵ ਜਾਣਾ ॥ ਨਾਨਕ ਆਖਣਿ ਸਭੁ ਕੋ ਆਖੈ ਇਕ ਦੂ ਇਕੁ ਸਿਆਣਾ ॥ ਵਡਾ ਸਾਹਿਬੁ ਵਡੀ ਨਾਈ ਕੀਤਾ ਜਾ ਕਾ ਹੋਵੈ ॥ ਨਾਨਕ ਜੇ ਕੋ ਆਪੌ ਜਾਣੈ ਅਗੈ ਗਇਆ ਨ ਸੋਹੈ ॥ ੨੧ ॥ (pg. 4 A.G)

and property. *False are sexual desire and wild anger. False are chariots, elephants, horses and expensive clothes. False is the love of gathering wealth, and revelling in its marvels. False are deception, emotional attachment and egotistical pride. False is self-conceit. Only devotional worship is Permanent, Constant and it is the TRUTH. Nanak lives by meditating, on the Lotus Feet of the Lord. False are the ears which listen to the slander of others. False are the hands which steal the wealth of others. False are the eyes which gaze, stealthily, upon the beauty of another's wife. False is the tongue which enjoys delicacies and external tastes. False are the feet which run to do evil to others. False is the mind which covets the wealth of others. False is the body which does not do good to others. False is the nose that inhales polluted oxygen. Without understanding, everything is false. Blessed is that body, says Nanak, that remembers the Lord's Name.*[13]

The Supreme **One** is a Reality. Truth or Fact or Reality exists at two planes : Mental and Material. Mind observes the Universe through the medium of the Senses, and all that is observed is considered to being a Reality. Furthermore, Matter, too, is a Realistic-Entity. And, Human-beings are a combination of Mind & Matter, and Spirit & Intelligence. All of these, together, constitute Truth.

GOD, alone, is the undisputed, unchallenged Truth.

---

[13] ਮਿਥਿਆ ਤਨੁ ਧਨੁ ਕੁਟੰਬੁ ਸਬਾਇਆ ॥ ਮਿਥਿਆ ਹਉਮੈ ਮਮਤਾ ਮਾਇਆ ॥ ਮਿਥਿਆ ਰਾਜ ਜੋਬਨ ਧਨ ਮਾਲ ॥ ਮਿਥਿਆ ਕਾਮ ਕ੍ਰੋਧ ਬਿਕਰਾਲ ॥ ਮਿਥਿਆ ਰਥ ਹਸਤੀ ਅਸ੍ਵ ਬਸਤ੍ਰਾ ॥ ਮਿਥਿਆ ਰੰਗ ਸੰਗਿ ਮਾਇਆ ਪੇਖਿ ਹਸਤਾ ॥ ਮਿਥਿਆ ਧ੍ਰੋਹ ਮੋਹ ਅਭਿਮਾਨੁ ॥ ਮਿਥਿਆ ਆਪਸ ਊਪਰਿ ਕਰਤ ਗੁਮਾਨੁ ॥ ਅਸਥਿਰੁ ਭਗਤਿ ਸਾਧ ਕੀ ਸਰਨ ॥ ਨਾਨਕ ਜਪਿ ਜਪਿ ਜੀਵੈ ਹਰਿ ਕੇ ਚਰਨ ॥ ੪ ॥ ਮਿਥਿਆ ਸ੍ਰਵਨ ਪਰ ਨਿੰਦਾ ਸੁਨਹਿ ॥ ਮਿਥਿਆ ਹਸਤ ਪਰ ਦਰਬ ਕਉ ਹਿਰਹਿ ॥ ਮਿਥਿਆ ਨੇਤ੍ਰ ਪੇਖਤ ਪਰ ਤ੍ਰਿਅ ਰੂਪਾਦ ॥ ਮਿਥਿਆ ਰਸਨਾ ਭੋਜਨ ਅਨ ਸ੍ਵਾਦ ॥ ਮਿਥਿਆ ਚਰਨ ਪਰ ਬਿਕਾਰ ਕਉ ਧਾਵਹਿ ॥ ਮਿਥਿਆ ਮਨ ਪਰ ਲੋਭ ਲੁਭਾਵਹਿ ॥ ਮਿਥਿਆ ਤਨ ਨਹੀ ਪਰਉਪਕਾਰਾ ॥ ਮਿਥਿਆ ਬਾਸੁ ਲੇਤ ਬਿਕਾਰਾ ॥ ਬਿਨੁ ਬੂਝੇ ਮਿਥਿਆ ਸਭ ਭਏ ॥ ਸਫਲ ਦੇਹ ਨਾਨਕ ਹਰਿ ਹਰਿ ਨਾਮ ਲਏ ॥ ੫ ॥
(pg. 268 A.G.)

By His Nature we see, by His Nature we hear; by His Nature we have fear, and the essence of happiness. By His Nature the nether worlds exist, and the ethereal ones; by His Nature the entire creation exists. By His Nature the Holy Scriptures of the Hindu, Jewish, Christian and Islamic religions are compiled. By His Nature all deliberations are held. By His Nature we eat, drink and dress; by His Nature all love exists. By His Nature come the species of all kinds and colors; by His Nature the living beings of the world exist. By His Nature virtues exist, and by His Nature vices exist. By His Nature come honour and dishonour. By His Nature wind, water and fire exist; by His Nature earth and dust exist. Everything is in Your Nature, Lord; You are the All-Powerful Creator. Your Name is the Holiest of the Holy. Says Nanak, through the Command of His Will, He beholds and pervades the creation; He is absolutely unrivalled. [14]

He Himself created Himself; He Himself assumed His Name. Secondly, He fashioned the creation; seated within the creation, He beholds it with delight. You Yourself are the Giver and the Creator; by Your Pleasure, You bestow Your Mercy. You are the Knower of all; You give life, and take it away, again with a Single-Word (Command). Seated within the creation, You behold it with delight. [15]

You Yourself are the Creator. Everything that happens is Your Doing. There is none except You. You created the creation; You behold it and

---

[14] ਕੁਦਰਤਿ ਦਿਸੈ ਕੁਦਰਤਿ ਸੁਣੀਐ ਕੁਦਰਤਿ ਭਉ ਸੁਖ ਸਾਰੁ ॥ ਕੁਦਰਤਿ ਪਾਤਾਲੀ ਆਕਾਸੀ ਕੁਦਰਤਿ ਸਰਬ ਆਕਾਰੁ ॥ ਕੁਦਰਤਿ ਵੇਦ ਪੁਰਾਣ ਕਤੇਬਾ ਕੁਦਰਤਿ ਸਰਬ ਵੀਚਾਰੁ ॥ ਕੁਦਰਤਿ ਖਾਣਾ ਪੀਣਾ ਪੈਨ੍ਣੁ ਕੁਦਰਤਿ ਸਰਬ ਪਿਆਰੁ ॥ ਕੁਦਰਤਿ ਜਾਤੀ ਜਿਨਸੀ ਰੰਗੀ ਕੁਦਰਤਿ ਜੀਅ ਜਹਾਨ ॥ ਕੁਦਰਤਿ ਨੇਕੀਆ ਕੁਦਰਤਿ ਬਦੀਆ ਕੁਦਰਤਿ ਮਾਨੁ ਅਭਿਮਾਨੁ ॥ ਕੁਦਰਤਿ ਪਉਣੁ ਪਾਣੀ ਬੈਸੰਤਰੁ ਕੁਦਰਤਿ ਧਰਤੀ ਖਾਕੁ ॥ ਸਭ ਤੇਰੀ ਕੁਦਰਤਿ ਤੂੰ ਕਾਦਿਰੁ ਕਰਤਾ ਪਾਕੀ ਨਾਈ ਪਾਕੁ ॥ ਨਾਨਕ ਹੁਕਮੈ ਅੰਦਰਿ ਵੇਖੈ ਵਰਤੈ ਤਾਕੋ ਤਾਕੁ ॥ ੨ ॥ (pg. 464 A.G.)

[15] ਆਪੀਨੈ ਆਪੁ ਸਾਜਿਓ ਆਪੀਨੈ ਰਚਿਓ ਨਾਉ ॥ ਦੁਯੀ ਕੁਦਰਤਿ ਸਾਜੀਐ ਕਰਿ ਆਸਣੁ ਡਿਠੋ ਚਾਉ ॥ ਦਾਤਾ ਕਰਤਾ ਆਪਿ ਤੂੰ ਤੁਸਿ ਦੇਵਹਿ ਕਰਹਿ ਪਸਾਉ ॥ ਤੂੰ ਜਾਣੋਈ ਸਭਸੈ ਦੇ ਲੈਸਹਿ ਜਿੰਦੁ ਕਵਾਉ ॥ ਕਰਿ ਆਸਣੁ ਡਿਠੋ ਚਾਉ ॥ ੧ ॥ (pg. 463 A.G.)

understand it. Says servant Nanak, the Lord is revealed to the aspirirant-soul, who is God-loving, the Living Expression of the Guru's Word. [16]

---

[16] ਤੂ ਆਪੇ ਕਰਤਾ ਤੇਰਾ ਕੀਆ ਸਭੁ ਹੋਇ ॥ ਤੁਧੁ ਬਿਨੁ ਦੂਜਾ ਅਵਰੁ ਨ ਕੋਇ ॥ ਤੂ ਕਰਿ ਕਰਿ ਵੇਖਹਿ ਜਾਣਹਿ ਸੋਇ ॥ ਜਨ ਨਾਨਕ ਗੁਰਮੁਖਿ ਪਰਗਟੁ ਹੋਇ ॥ ੪ ॥ ੨ (Pg.12 A.G.)

True is the Master, True is His Name—speak it with infinite love. People beg and pray, and the Great Giver distributes His Gifts, so very magnanimously, and in abundance. So, what offering can we place before Him, by which we might have an Exclusive Audience, with HIM? What words can we speak to evoke His Love? In the ambrosial hours before dawn, chant the True Name, and contemplate upon His Glorious Greatness. By the karma of past actions, the magnificently exquisite robe (this physical body) is obtained. By His Grace, the Gate of Liberation is found. Know this well: the True One Himself is All. [17]

His Blessings are so abundant that there can be no written account of them. The Great Giver does not hold back anything. There are so many great, heroic warriors begging at the Door of the Infinite Lord. So many contemplate and dwell upon Him, that they cannot be counted. So many perish, engaged in corruption. So many enjoy HIS Bounties, and then deny receiving. So many foolish consumers keep on consuming. So many endure distress, deprivation and constant abuse. Even these are Your Gifts, O Great Giver! Liberation from bondage comes only by Your Will. No one else has any say. If some fool should presume that he does, he shall learn, and feel the effects of his folly. He Himself knows, He Himself gives. Few, and rarest of the rare are those who acknowledge this. [18]

---

[17] ਸਾਚਾ ਸਾਹਿਬੁ ਸਾਚੁ ਨਾਇ ਭਾਖਿਆ ਭਾਉ ਅਪਾਰੁ ॥ ਆਖਹਿ ਮੰਗਹਿ ਦੇਹਿ ਦੇਹਿ ਦਾਤਿ ਕਰੇ ਦਾਤਾਰੁ ॥ ਫੇਰਿ ਕਿ ਅਗੈ ਰਖੀਐ ਜਿਤੁ ਦਿਸੈ ਦਰਬਾਰੁ ॥ ਮੁਹੌ ਕਿ ਬੋਲਣੁ ਬੋਲੀਐ ਜਿਤੁ ਸੁਣਿ ਧਰੇ ਪਿਆਰੁ ॥ ਅੰਮ੍ਰਿਤ ਵੇਲਾ ਸਚੁ ਨਾਉ ਵਡਿਆਈ ਵਿਚਾਰੁ ॥ ਕਰਮੀ ਆਵੈ ਕਪੜਾ ਨਦਰੀ ਮੋਖੁ ਦੁਆਰੁ ॥ ਨਾਨਕ ਏਵੈ ਜਾਣੀਐ ਸਭੁ ਆਪੇ ਸਚਿਆਰੁ ॥ ੪ ॥ (pg. 2 A.G.)

[18] ਬਹੁਤਾ ਕਰਮੁ ਲਿਖਿਆ ਨਾ ਜਾਇ ॥ ਵਡਾ ਦਾਤਾ ਤਿਲੁ ਨ ਤਮਾਇ ॥ ਕੇਤੇ ਮੰਗਹਿ ਜੋਧ ਅਪਾਰ ॥ ਕੇਤਿਆ ਗਣਤ ਨਹੀ ਵੀਚਾਰੁ ॥ ਕੇਤੇ ਖਪਿ ਤੁਟਹਿ ਵੇਕਾਰ ॥ ਕੇਤੇ ਲੈ ਲੈ ਮੁਕਰੁ ਪਾਹਿ ॥ ਕੇਤੇ ਮੂਰਖ ਖਾਹੀ ਖਾਹਿ ॥ ਕੇਤਿਆ ਦੂਖ ਭੂਖ ਸਦ ਮਾਰ ॥ ਏਹਿ ਭਿ ਦਾਤਿ ਤੇਰੀ ਦਾਤਾਰ ॥ ਬੰਦਿ ਖਲਾਸੀ ਭਾਣੈ ਹੋਇ ॥ ਹੋਰੁ ਆਖਿ ਨ ਸਕੈ ਕੋਇ ॥ ਜੇ ਕੋ ਖਾਇਕੁ ਆਖਣਿ ਪਾਇ ॥ ਓਹੁ ਜਾਣੈ ਜੇਤੀਆ ਮੁਹਿ ਖਾਇ ॥ ਆਪੇ ਜਾਣੈ ਆਪੇ ਦੇਇ ॥ ਆਖਹਿ ਸਿ ਭਿ ਕੇਈ ਕੇਇ ॥(pg. 5 A.G.)

All happiness comes, when God is pleased. The Feet of the Perfect Guru dwell in my mind. I am intuitively absorbed in introspective meditation. My Lord and Master is Inaccessible and Unfathomable. Deep within each and every heart, He dwells near and close at hand. He is always detached; How rare is that person who understands his own self. This is the sign of Communion with God: in the mind, the Command of the True Lord is recognized. Intuitive peace and poise, contentment, enduring satisfaction and bliss come through the Pleasure of the Master's Will. God, the Great Giver, has given me His Hand. He has eliminated all sickness and misery, all doubt and penury, all pain and fear, of birth and death. Says Nanak, those whom God has made His Chosen-ones, rejoice in the pleasure of singing the Hymns of the Lord's Praises.[19]

This, then, is the Life-Divine. And, it is made available, to only a select and chosen few, by the Lord, who showers all the bounties at His disposal, on his devotees.

---

[19] ਸਭੇ ਸੁਖ ਭਏ ਪ੍ਰਭ ਤੁਠੇ ॥ ਗੁਰ ਪੂਰੇ ਕੇ ਚਰਣ ਮਨਿ ਵੁਠੇ ॥ ਸਹਜ ਸਮਾਧਿ ਲਗੀ ਲਿਵ ਅਮਤਰਿ ਸੋ ਰਸੁ ਸੋਈ ਜਾਣੈ ਜੀਉ ॥ ੧ ॥ ਅਗਮ ਅਗੋਚਰੁ ਸਾਹਿਬੁ ਮੇਰਾ ॥ ਘਟ ਘਟ ਅੰਤਰਿ ਵਰਤੈ ਨੇਰਾ ॥ ਸਦਾ ਅਲਿਪਤੁ ਜੀਆ ਕਾ ਦਾਤਾ ਕੋ ਵਿਰਲਾ ਆਪੁ ਪਛਾਣੈ ਜੀਉ ॥ ੨ ॥ ਪ੍ਰਭ ਮਿਲਣੈ ਕੀ ਏਹ ਨੀਸਾਣੀ ॥ ਮਨਿ ਇਕੋ ਸਚਾ ਹੁਕਮੁ ਪਛਾਣੀ ॥ ਸਹਜਿ ਸੰਤੋਖਿ ਸਦਾ ਤ੍ਰਿਪਤਾਸੇ ਅਨਦੁ ਖਸਮ ਕੈ ਭਾਣੈ ਜੀਉ ॥ ੩ ॥ ਹਥੀ ਦਿਤੀ ਪ੍ਰਭਿ ਦੇਵਣਹਾਰੈ ॥ ਜਨਮ ਮਰਣ ਰੋਗ ਸਭਿ ਨਿਵਾਰੇ ॥ ਨਾਨਕ ਦਾਸ ਕੀਏ ਪ੍ਰਭਿ ਅਪੁਨੇ ਹਰਿ ਕੀਰਤਨਿ ਰੰਗ ਮਾਣੇ ਜੀਉ ॥ ੪ ॥ ੩੫ ॥ ੪੨ ॥ (pg. 106 A.G.)

Do not blame the Sovereign Lord; when someone grows old, his intellect leaves him. The blind man talks and babbles, and then falls into the ditch. All that the Perfect Lord does is perfect; there is not too little, or too much. Says Nanak, the God-loving Person merges into the Perfect Lord. [20]

(Do not become like the infirm or the blind, while you have all faculties, intact, to reason out issues).

This Unison & Harmonious Blend, between God & Man, is termed 'communion'. In such a state, one does not criticize God's decisions and refrains from denying His existence.

The Supreme Lord, the Transcendent Lord, the True Guru, saves all. Hence, it is unbecoming to criticize God's decisions, his ways and his works. Says Nanak, without the Guru, no one crosses over the turbulent life-ocean; this is the perfect essence of all contemplation. [21]

---

[20] ਦੋਸੁ ਨ ਦੇਅਹੁ ਰਾਇ ਨੋ ਮਤਿ ਚਲੈ ਜਾਂ ਬੁਢਾ ਹੋਵੈ ॥ ਗਲਾਂ ਕਰੇ ਘਣੇਰੀਆ ਤਾਂ ਅੰਨੇ ਪਵਣਾ ਖਾਤੀ ਟੋਵੈ ॥ ੩੨ ॥ ਪੂਰੇ ਕਾ ਕੀਆ ਸਭ ਕਿਛੁ ਪੂਰਾ ਘਟਿ ਵਧਿ ਕਿਛੁ ਨਾਹੀ ॥ ਨਾਨਕ ਗੁਰਮੁਖਿ ਐਸਾ ਜਾਣੈ ਪੂਰੇ ਮਾਂਹਿ ਸਮਾਂਹੀ ॥ ੩੩ ॥ (pg. 1412 A.G.)

[21] ਨਿੰਦਉ ਨਾਹੀ ਕਾਹੂ ਬਾਤੈ ਏਹੁ ਖਸਮ ਕਾ ਕੀਆ ॥ ਜਾ ਕਉ ਕ੍ਰਿਪਾ ਕਰੀ ਪ੍ਰਭਿ ਮੇਰੈ ਮਿਲਿ ਸਾਧਸੰਗਤਿ ਨਾਉ ਲੀਆ ॥ ੩ ॥ ਪਾਰਬ੍ਰਹਮ ਪਰਮੇਸੁਰ ਸਤਿਗੁਰ ਸਭਨਾ ਕਰਤ ਉਧਾਰਾ ॥ ਕਹੁ ਨਾਨਕ ਗੁਰ ਬਿਨੁ ਨਹੀ ਤਰੀਐ ਇਹੁ ਪੂਰਨ ਤਤੁ ਬੀਚਾਰਾ ॥ ੪ ॥ ੯ ॥ (Pg.611 A.G.)

All are within Your mind; You see and move them under Your Glance of Grace, O Lord. You Yourself grant them glory, and You Yourself cause them to act. The Lord is the greatest of the great; great is His world. He assigns them their tasks. If he should cast an angry glance, He can transform Kings into gardeners. Even though they may beg from door to door, no one will give them charity.[22]

On the contrary, God, during His pleasure, may grant the boon of a Kingdom, to a penniless devotee, who is Truth-Incarnate.

I cannot comprehend the confines of Your Royal-Abode, neither do I have the requisite faculties to understand Your Powers. I am the humble slave of Your Saints. One who goes laughing, returns crying, and the one who goes crying returns laughing. What is inhabited becomes deserted, and what is deserted becomes inhabited. And, all of it happens by Your Orders. The rivers dry out, into a desert, the desert turns into a well, and the well turns into a mountain, and mountains crumble under their own weight. From the earth, the mortal is exalted to the Ethereal-Worlds (realms); and from the ethers on high, he plunges down. The beggar is transformed into a king, and the king into a pauper. The idiotic fool is transformed into a Pandit, a religious scholar, and the Pandit into a fool. The woman is transformed into a man, and the man into woman. Says Kabeer : God is the Beloved of the Holy Saints. I am a sacrifice to His image. [23]

---

[22] ਚਿਤੈ ਅੰਦਰਿ ਸਭੁ ਕੋ ਵੇਖਿ ਨਦਰੀ ਹੇਠਿ ਚਲਾਇਦਾ ॥ ਆਪੇ ਦੇ ਵਡਿਆਈਆ ਆਪੇ ਹੀ ਕਰਮ ਕਰਾਇਦਾ ॥ ਵਡਹੁ ਵਡਾ ਵਡ ਮੇਦਨੀ ਸਿਰੇ ਸਿਰਿ ਧੰਧੈ ਲਾਇਦਾ ॥ ਨਦਰਿ ਉਪਠੀ ਜੇ ਕਰੇ ਸੁਲਤਾਨਾ ਘਾਹੁ ਕਰਾਇਦਾ ॥ ਦਰਿ ਮੰਗਨਿ ਭਿਖ ਨ ਪਾਇਦਾ ॥ ੧੬ ॥ (pg. 472 A.G.)

[23] ਰਾਜਾਸ੍ਰਮ ਮਿਤਿ ਨਹੀ ਜਾਨੀ ਤੇਰੀ ॥ ਤੇਰੇ ਸੰਤਨ ਕੀ ਹਉ ਚੇਰੀ ॥ ੧ ॥ ਰਹਾਉ ॥ ਹਸਤੋ ਜਾਇ ਸੁ ਰੋਵਤੁ ਆਵੈ ਰੋਵਤੁ ਜਾਇ ਸੁ ਹਸੈ ॥ ਬਸਤੋ ਹੋਇ ਹੋਇ ਸੋ ਊਜਰੁ ਊਜਰੁ ਹੋਇ ਸੁ ਬਸੈ ॥ ੧ ॥ ਜਲ ਤੇ ਥਲ ਕਰਿ ਥਲ ਤੇ ਕੂਆ ਕੂਪ ਤੇ ਮੇਰੁ ਕਰਾਵੈ ॥ ਧਰਤੀ ਤੇ ਆਕਾਸਿ ਚਢਾਵੈ ਚਢੇ ਆਕਾਸਿ ਗਿਰਾਵੈ ॥ ੨ ॥ ਭੇਖਾਰੀ ਤੇ ਰਾਜੁ ਕਰਾਵੈ ਰਾਜਾ ਤੇ ਭੇਖਾਰੀ ॥ ਖਲ ਮੂਰਖ ਤੇ ਪੰਡਿਤੁ ਕਰਿਬੋ ਪੰਡਿਤ ਤੇ ਮੁਗਧਾਰੀ ॥ ੩ ॥ ਨਾਰੀ ਤੇ ਜੋ ਪੁਰਖੁ ਕਰਾਵੈ ਪੁਰਖਨ ਤੇ ਜੋ ਨਾਰੀ ॥ ਕਹੁ ਕਬੀਰ ਸਾਧੂ ਕੋ ਪ੍ਰੀਤਮੁ ਤਿਸੁ ਮੂਰਤਿ ਬਲਿਹਾਰੀ ॥ ੪ ॥ ੨ ॥ (Pg. 1252 A.G.)

Tigers, hawks, falcons and eagles—the Lord could make them eat grass. And those animals which eat grass—He could make them eat meat. He could radically alter anyone's life. He could raise dry land from the rivers, and turn the deserts into bottomless oceans. He could annoint a measly worm as a king, and reduce an army to ashes. All beings and creatures live by breathing, but He could keep us alive, even without the breath. Says Nanak : As it pleases the True Lord, He sustains all.[24]

---

[24] ਸੀਹਾ ਬਾਜਾ ਚਰਗਾ ਕੁਹੀਆ ਏਨਾ ਖਵਾਲੇ ਘਾਹ ॥ ਘਾਹੁ ਖਾਨਿ ਤਿਨਾ ਮਾਸੁ ਖਵਾਲੇ ਏਹਿ ਚਲਾਏ ਰਾਹ ॥ ਨਦੀਆ ਵਿਚਿ ਟਿਬੇ ਦੇਖਾਲੇ ਥਲੀ ਕਰੇ ਅਸਗਾਹ ॥ ਕੀੜਾ ਥਾਪਿ ਦੇਇ ਪਾਤਿਸਾਹੀ ਲਸਕਰ ਕਰੇ ਸੁਆਹ ॥ ਜੇਤੇ ਜੀਅ ਜੀਵਹਿ ਲੈ ਸਾਹਾ ਜੀਵਾਲੇ ਤਾ ਕਿ ਅਸਾਹ ॥ ਨਾਨਕ ਜਿਉ ਜਿਉ ਸਚੇ ਭਾਵੈ ਤਿਉ ਤਿਉ ਦੇਇ ਗਿਰਾਹ ॥ ੧ ॥ (Pg.144 A.G.)

Those who take pleasure in God's Will, doubt shall be eliminated from within them. Know Him as the True Guru, who unites all with the Lord. Meeting with the True Guru, they receive the fruits of their destiny, and egotism is driven out from within. The pain of evil-mindedness is eliminated; good fortune radiates on their foreheads.[25]

Sayeth Sheikh Farid, a Muslim Seer:-
Treat Sorrow and Happiness, as the same par value, and conquer the vices, and banish them from your heart and soul, forever. Allah (GOD) appreciates such people and they are honoured in HIS court[26]

He alone obeys Your Will, O Lord, on whom You decide to bestow Your Gracious Vision. That alone is devotional worship, which is pleasing to Your Will. You are the Nourisher of all beings. O my Sovereign Lord, You are the Support of the Saints. Whatever pleases You, they accept. You are the sustenance of their minds and bodies. [27]

Naked we come, and naked we go. This is by the Lord's Command; what else can we do? All objects belongs to Him; He shall take them away (life and death are under His Will). One who loves Him, accepts God's Will; he intuitively drinks in the Lord's sublime-essence. Says Nanak : Praise the Giver of peace, forever; with your tongue, savor the Lord's Name, always.[28]

---

[25] ਜਿਨਾ ਭਾਣੇ ਕਾ ਰਸੁ ਆਇਆ ॥ ਤਿਨ ਵਿਚਹੁ ਭਰਮੁ ਚੁਕਾਇਆ ॥ ਨਾਨਕ ਸਤਿਗੁਰੁ ਐਸਾ ਜਾਣੀਐ ਜੋ ਸਭਸੈ ਲਏ ਮਿਲਾਇ ਜੀਉ ॥ ੧੦ ॥ ਸਤਿਗੁਰਿ ਮਿਲਿਐ ਫਲੁ ਪਾਇਆ ॥ ਜਿਨਿ ਵਿਚਹੁ ਅਹਕਰਣੁ ਚੁਕਾਇਆ ॥ ਦੁਰਮਤਿ ਕਾ ਦੁਖੁ ਕਟਿਆ ਭਾਗੁ ਬੈਠਾ ਮਸਤਕਿ ਆਇ ਜੀਉ ॥ ੧੧ ॥ (pg. 72 A.G.)

[26] ਫਰੀਦਾ ਦੁਖ ਸੁਖ ਇਕੁ ਕਰਿ ਦਿਲ ਤੇ ਲਾਹਿ ਵਿਕਾਰੁ ॥ ਅਲਹ ਭਾਵੈ ਸੋ ਭਲਾ ਤਾਂ ਲਭੀ ਦਰਬਾਰੁ ॥ ੧੦੮ ॥ (pg. 1383 A.G.)

[27] ਤੇਰਾ ਭਾਣਾ ਤੂਹੈ ਮਨਾਇਹਿ ਜਿਸ ਨੋ ਹੋਹਿ ਦਇਆਲਾ ॥ ਸਾਈ ਭਗਤਿ ਜੋ ਤੁਧੁ ਭਾਵੈ ਤੂੰ ਸਰਬ ਜੀਆ ਪ੍ਰਤਿਪਾਲਾ ॥ ੧ ॥ ਮੇਰੇ ਰਾਮ ਰਾਇ ਸੰਤਾ ਟੇਕ ਤੁਮਾਰੀ ॥ ਜੋ ਤੁਧੁ ਭਾਵੈ ਸੋ ਪਰਵਾਣੁ ਮਨਿ ਤਨਿ ਤੂਹੈ ਅਧਾਰੀ ॥ ੧ ॥ (Pg.747 A.G.)

[28] ਨਾਂਗੇ ਆਵਣਾ ਨਾਂਗੇ ਜਾਣਾ ਹਰਿ ਹੁਕਮੁ ਪਾਇਆ ਕਿਆ ਕੀਜੈ ॥ ਜਿਸ ਕੀ ਵਸਤੁ ਸੋਈ ਲੈ ਜਾਇਗਾ

Meditate, continually and constantly, on the Name of the Lord within your heart. Thus you shall save all your companions and associates, alongwith yourself. My Guru is always with me, near at hand. Meditating, and reminiscing about Him, I cherish Him forever. Your actions seem so sweet to me. Nanak begs for the treasure of the Naam, the Name of the Lord. [29]

ਰੋਸੁ ਕਿਸੈ ਸਿਉ ਕੀਜੈ ॥ ਗੁਰਮੁਖਿ ਹੋਵੈ ਸੁ ਭਾਣਾ ਮੰਨੇ ਸਹਜੇ ਹਰਿ ਰਸੁ ਪੀਜੈ ॥ ਨਾਨਕ ਸੁਖਦਾਤਾ ਸਦਾ ਸਲਾਹਿਹੁ ਰਸਨਾ ਰਾਮੁ ਰਵੀਜੈ ॥ ੨ ॥ (Pg.1246 A.G.)

[29] ਹਰਿ ਕਾ ਨਾਮੁ ਰਿਦੈ ਨਿਤ ਧਿਆਈ ॥ ਸੰਗੀ ਸਾਥੀ ਸਗਲ ਤਰਾਂਈ ॥ ੧ ॥ ਗੁਰੁ ਮੇਰੈ ਸੰਗਿ ਸਦਾ ਹੈ ਨਾਲੇ ॥ ਸਿਮਰਿ ਸਿਮਰਿ ਤਿਸੁ ਸਦਾ ਸਮੑਾਲੇ ॥ ੧ ॥ ਰਹਾਉ ॥ ਤੇਰਾ ਕੀਆ ਮੀਠਾ ਲਾਗੈ ॥ ਹਰਿ ਨਾਮੁ ਪਦਾਰਥੁ ਨਾਨਕੁ ਮਾਂਗੈ ॥ ੨ ॥ ੪੨ ॥ ੯੩ ॥ (Pg.394 A.G.)

NOTES

IT 'S A SIN TO CORRUPT INNOCENT MINDS

Let's not, only, blame the boy, aged eleven, who wields the gun, as a 'toy', and the thirteen-year-old girl, who becomes pregnant, without realizing the consequences.

The society must share the accountability, for letting the media portray explicit violence and sex, corrupting the innocent minds, which are exposed to the onslaught, day in and day out.

SECTION : 2

CHANGE YOUR LIFE

The three pillars of the Rock-like steadfast "Monument of Prayer" are: **Service, Meditation, and Total Surrender of one's ego.**

He confers solace and fearlessness. Prayer is an essential ingredient of the "Faith-in-God" Doctrine, which emphasizes that God is, always, right. Doubt should not be permitted to creep in, on this count. Hence, one must pray to God, the Source and the Light, at all times, day or night, in joy or sorrow, and on all significant occasions, like birth, naming-ceremony, wedding, death, commencement of educational or business ventures,

PRAY to God, at all times, in prosperity or adversity. The concept of Prayer is engrained in the Sikh Psyche and Belief-Structure. It says that God is not a Law of Nature, alone, nor of Karma, or of Pre-Determination, alone. It is, in essence, all of these, together, and even much more. If HIS Grace is to be bestowed on one, HIS NEGATIVE WRIT may be modified or amended to rescue the bereaved one, who is, now, praying in agony, and wailing for help. The Savior is Omnipresent and All-Pervasive. Hence, we see that God is Transcendental and Immanent, both, at once. After crossing the Barriers, Hindrances and Obstacles of Physical Desires, Material Gains and Mental Traumas, one is forced to (there's no alternative available, there's no other strategy to be employed) pray to the Lord, for express grant of Sublime and Pristine Grace. This, then, is the finality of spiritual elevation.

Prayer, when coupled with sincere Meditative-Contemplation, becomes an extremely potent force, that could radically alter the prevailing scenario, thereby bringing about a positive transformation, in the life of the devotee. The deity is in the heart and soul, and is not to be searched, anywhere else. One needs to remind oneself, constantly, not to let fear and failure creep in, after praying for strength, otherwise the entire purpose Prayer shall stand defeated. While offering prayers, one must experience Celestial-Bliss, forgetting about all the mundane affairs of life. One must visualize oneself as begging before the Munificent-Power, seated on the Eternal-Throne, in Paradise. Each day should commence with a Prayer for strength (moral and physical) to wade through the rough tides of life, and one must retire, at night, after an exercise in self-analysis. Int times of upheaval, one must remind oneself that the prayer made earlier cannot go in vain, and hence one should not let weakness and doubt creep in.

Mortals may go to the heavenly realms, but because of their hypocrisy, insincerity, and nefarious- prayers, they must undergo the torture of rebirth. What should I ask for? Nothing lasts forever. Enshrine the Lord's Name within your mind. Fame and glory, power, wealth and glorious greatness — none of these will go with you or help you in the end. Children, spouse, and wealth and prestige — who has ever obtained peace from these? Answers Kabeer, nothing else is of any use. Within my mind is the TRUE wealth of the Lord's Name.[30]

Selfless prayers are always granted by the Lord because such prayers are made for the betterment of others.

O God, please save me! By myself, I cannot do anything, O my Lord and Master; by Your Grace, please bless me with Your Name. Family and worldly affairs are an ocean of fire. Through doubt, emotional attachment and ignorance, we are enveloped in darkness. Prestige and status, pleasure and pain trouble this tormented soul. Hunger and thirst are not satiated. The mind is engrossed in passion, and the disease of corruptible-vices. The five thieves (Lust, Anger, Greed, Attachment and Ego) my companions, are totally incorrigible. The beings and souls and wealth of the world are all Yours. Declares Nanak : Know that the Lord is always near at hand.[31]

---

[30] ਇੰਦੁ ਲੋਕ ਸਿਵ ਲੋਕਹਿ ਜੈਬੋ ॥ ਓਛੇ ਤਪ ਕਰਿ ਬਾਹੁਰਿ ਐਬੋ ॥ ੧ ॥ ਕਿਆ ਮਾਂਗਉ ਕਿਛੁ ਥਿਰੁ ਨਾਹੀ ॥ ਰਾਮ ਨਾਮ ਰਖੁ ਮਨ ਮਾਹੀ ॥ ੧ ॥ ਰਹਾਉ ॥ ਸੋਭਾ ਰਾਜ ਬਿਭੈ ਬਡਿਆਈ ॥ ਅੰਤਿ ਨ ਕਾਹੂ ਸੰਗ ਸਹਾਈ ॥ ੨ ॥ ਪੁਤੁ ਕਲਤੁ ਲਛਮੀ ਮਾਇਆ ॥ ਇਨ ਤੇ ਕਹੁ ਕਵਨੈ ਸੁਖੁ ਪਾਇਆ ॥ ੩ ॥ ਕਹਤ ਕਬੀਰ ਅਵਰ ਨਹੀ ਕਾਮਾ ॥ ਹਮਰੈ ਮਨ ਧਨ ਰਾਮ ਕੋ ਨਾਮਾ ॥ ੪ ॥ ੪ ॥ (pg. 692 A.G.)

[31] ਹਾ ਹਾ ਪ੍ਰਭ ਰਾਖਿ ਲੇਹੁ ॥ ਹਮ ਤੇ ਕਿਛੁ ਨ ਹੋਇ ਮੇਰੇ ਸੁਆਮੀ ਕਰਿ ਕਿਰਪਾ ਅਪੁਨਾ ਨਾਮੁ ਦੇਹੁ ॥ ੧ ॥ ਰਹਾਉ ॥ ਅਗਨਿ ਕੁਟੰਬ ਸਾਗਰ ਸੰਸਾਰ ॥ ਭਰਮ ਮੋਹ ਅਗਿਆਨ ਅੰਧਾਰ ॥ ੧ ॥ ਉਚ ਨੀਚ ਸੁਖ ਦੁਖ ॥ ਪ੍ਰਾਪਸਿ ਨਾਹੀ ਤ੍ਰਿਸਨਾ ਭੁਖ ॥ ੨ ॥ ਮਨਿ ਬਾਸਨਾ ਰਚਿ ਬਿਖੈ ਬਿਆਧਿ ॥ ਪੰਚ ਦੂਤ

20

O True Guru, I have come to Your Refuge. Grant me the peace and glory of the Lord's Name, and eliminate all my anxieties and worries. I cannot see any other Sanctuary; I have grown weary, and collapsed at Your door. Please ignore my account; only then may I be saved. I am worthless — please, save me! You are always forgiving, and always merciful; You lend support to all. Slave Nanak follows the Path of the Saints; save him, O' Lord, this time.[32]

Please go to: ' A Note From The Publisher ', followed by a 'Press-Clipping ', appended at the end of the book.....

..... publisher

ਸੰਗਿ ਮਹਾ ਅਸਾਧ ॥ ੩ ॥ ਜੀਅ ਜਹਾਨੁ ਪ੍ਰਾਨ ਧਨੁ ਤੇਰਾ ॥ ਨਾਨਕ ਜਾਨੁ ਸਦਾ ਹਰਿ ਨੇਰਾ ॥ ੪ ॥ ੧ ॥ ੧੯ ॥ (Pg.675 A.G.)

[32] ਸਤਿਗੁਰ ਆਇਓ ਸਰਣਿ ਤੁਹਾਰੀ ॥ ਮਿਲੈ ਸੂਖੁ ਨਾਮੁ ਹਰਿ ਸੋਭਾ ਚਿੰਤਾ ਲਾਹਿ ਹਮਾਰੀ ॥ ੧ ॥ ਰਹਾਉ ॥ ਅਵਰ ਨ ਸੂਝੈ ਦੂਜੀ ਠਾਹਰ ਹਾਰਿ ਪਰਿਓ ਤਉ ਦੁਆਰੀ ॥ ਲੇਖਾ ਛੋਡਿ ਅਲੇਖੈ ਛੂਟਹ ਹਮ ਨਿਰਗੁਨ ਲੇਹੁ ਉਬਾਰੀ ॥ ੧ ॥ ਸਦ ਬਖਸਿੰਦੁ ਸਦਾ ਮਿਹਰਵਾਨਾ ਸਭਨਾ ਦੇਇ ਅਧਾਰੀ ॥ ਨਾਨਕ ਦਾਸ ਸੰਤ ਪਾਛੈ ਪਰਿਓ ਰਾਖਿ ਲੇਹੁ ਇਹ ਬਾਰੀ ॥ ੨ ॥ ੪ ॥ ੯ ॥ (Pg.713 A.G.)

Without the Grace of God, and meditation upon His Name, the Wild Horses, of this Mind, shall never rest in tranquility and peace.

If I were to become a Siddha, and work miracles, summon wealth and become invisible and visible at will, so that people would hold me in awe and esteem, I might go astray and forget You, and Your Name would not reside in my mind.[33]

All miracles are the maids of Noumenon. Having the ability to succeed in performing miracles, on a superficial-plane, does not have any linkages with being a spiritually-inclined and/or a religiously-oriented individual.

Impure souls have, often, resorted to, and taken recourse to, adopting mean and cheap tricks and techniques, for mastering the arts and crafts of performing miracles, with a view to gaining wealth, power, women (forcibly overpowering the thought-processes of others' wives, for fulfillment of lust), or to subjugate or kill someone. Some of these miracle-masters would produce ash out of the palm of their hand, or present fruits, out of thin air.

The recitation of Vedas and Mantras (Hymns & Verses from the ancient Scriptures, from the earliest human civilizations, including India) have been used as a means to invoke the innumerable and myriad so-called Gods & Goddesses, according to the references from the mythological folk-lore, of yore, from the nation of India, on the Continent of Asia.

Walking the surface of water, swallowing fire, enhancing one's own life-span or increasing one's youthful vigor and vitality are some of the instances for which miracles have been deployed and employed. Some

---

[33] ਸਿਧੁ ਹੋਵਾ ਸਿਧਿ ਲਾਈ ਰਿਧਿ ਆਖਾ ਆਉ ॥ ਗੁਪਤੁ ਪਰਗਟੁ ਹੋਇ ਬੈਸਾ ਲੋਕੁ ਰਾਖੈ ਭਾਉ ॥ ਮਤੁ ਦੇਖਿ ਭੂਲਾ ਵੀਸਰੈ ਤੇਰਾ ਚਿਤਿ ਨ ਆਵੈ ਨਾਉ ॥ ੩ ॥ (pg. 14 A.G.)

miracles are just performed to gain public attention, by influencing the layman's mind, by playing on his guile, while others are performed to satiate the lust for power, wealth or sex.

On the positive side, the usage of the Adept-Art of Miracle-Performance, has been in the sphere of curing patients, ailing from a variety of diseases, and problems. Also, significantly, miracles have been known to wash-out the effects of poison, on the body, whether by eating something or as a result of snake-bites etc.

The Spiritual-Power of performing miracles, has been used by the Great Masters, over the ages, all over the world, for the spread of the Gospel and the Word of God, and the Universal Message of Love & Compassion, Peace & harmony. Healing of the tormented Mind and the haunted Soul, too, has been an important field, where the Real Godheads and pious Ones have worked wonders, without expecting recognition or reward, power or position for themselves. It was meant to be selfless-service, commanded by their Creator & Mentor, Philosopher & Guide, the ALL-IN-ONE, GOD (the ONE-in-all). This classification of Miracles is, therefore, the one required by humanity, in this, the Age of Struggle and Hatred, infested and ridden with Violence and Greed.*

*All the Sikh-Gurus, Hindu Saints and Muslim Pirs, whose verses have been included in the Sri Guru Granth Sahib, as also other mystical-spiritual leaders were vociferously against the negative forms of miracles. They did not subscribe to the school of thought that someone possessing miraculous powers would, necessarily, be an enlightened soul.

23

Primarily, its an admittance and acceptance of the fact that the Universe and the Creator were, are, and, always, shall be, a mystery "par excellence", that shall never be completely solved by the limited range/domain of the human intellect, whose advances in science and technology have crossed innumerable landmarks.

Sayeth Guru Nanak, about the complexity of the Universe :

Endless are His Praises, endless are those who speak them. Endless are His Actions, endless are His Gifts. Endless is His Vision, endless is His Hearing. What is the Mystery of His Mind? Its limits here and beyond cannot be perceived. HE is incomprehensible. The more you say about HIS limits, infinitely more there still remains to be said. Great is the Master, High is His Heavenly Home. Highest of the High, above all is His Name. Only one as Great and as High as God can know His Lofty and Exalted State. Only He Himself is that Great. He Himself knows Himself. Reassures Nanak : by His Gracious Glance, He bestows His Benediction.[34]

The negative feeling of Life-Negation should not, and must not, be given any leverage, whatsoever. One must strive to lead a worthy life in all respects : Work for subsistence & sustenance, pray and meditate for spiritual-elevation, bear an exemplary moral character, abiding by the Code of Ethics (relating to adultery, fraudulent practices, oppression & tyranny, helping the deserving and needy), and never to renounce the world to become a reclusive-entity (thereby becoming a burden on the society).

---

[34] ਅੰਤੁ ਨ ਸਿਫਤੀ ਕਹਣਿ ਨ ਅੰਤੁ ॥ ਅੰਤੁ ਨ ਕਰਣੈ ਦੇਣਿ ਨ ਅੰਤੁ ॥ ਅੰਤੁ ਨ ਵੇਖਣਿ ਸੁਣਣਿ ਨ ਅੰਤੁ ॥ ਅੰਤੁ ਨ ਜਾਪੈ ਕਿਆ ਮਨਿ ਮੰਤੁ ॥ ਅੰਤੁ ਨ ਜਾਪੈ ਕੀਤਾ ਆਕਾਰੁ ॥ ਅੰਤੁ ਨ ਜਾਪੈ ਪਾਰਾਵਾਰੁ ॥ ਅੰਤ ਕਾਰਣਿ ਕੇਤੇ ਬਿਲਲਾਹਿ ॥ ਤਾ ਕੇ ਅੰਤ ਨ ਪਾਏ ਜਾਹਿ ॥ ਏਹੁ ਅੰਤੁ ਨ ਜਾਣੈ ਕੋਇ ॥ ਬਹੁਤਾ ਕਹੀਐ ਬਹੁਤਾ ਹੋਇ ॥ ਵਡਾ ਸਾਹਿਬੁ ਊਚਾ ਥਾਉ ॥ ਊਚੇ ਉਪਰਿ ਊਚਾ ਨਾਉ ॥ ਏਵਡੁ ਊਚਾ ਹੋਵੈ ਕੋਇ ॥ ਤਿਸੁ ਊਚੇ ਕਉ ਜਾਣੈ ਸੋਇ ॥ ਜੇਵਡੁ ਆਪਿ ਜਾਣੈ ਆਪਿ ਆਪਿ ॥ ਨਾਨਕ ਨਦਰੀ ਕਰਮੀ ਦਾਤਿ ॥ ੨੪ ॥ (pg. 5 of AG)

Great emphasis has been laid on virtue & morality, as against the hitherto prevalent stress on The Law of KARMA, alone, according to which : " Worthy deeds shall bear good and tasty fruits (respect, glory, health & prosperity), while evil deeds shall bring forth or reap misery/pain, in the form and shape of disease, poverty, and the Victory-of-Vice, in general.   An amalgamation of   VIRTUE and KARMA (Deed /Action) is advocated.

The world is not an illusionary concept: It is a reality.

True are Your worlds, True are Your solar Systems. True are Your realms, True is Your creation. True are Your actions, and all Your deliberations. True is Your Command, and True is Your Court. True is the Command of Your Will, True is Your Order. True is Your Mercy, True is Your Insignia. Hundreds of thousands and millions call You True. In the True Lord is all the power vested, and so is all the Might. True is Your Praise, True is Your Adoration. True is Your almighty creative power, O' True King. Says Nanak, true are those who meditate on the True One.[35]

The goal should be to live life, in an exemplary fashion, and not to resort to escapism, or not to shun struggle, by adopting short cuts to success, thereby harming the interests of others. Simultaneous with living a good life, one must strive towards perfection, in order to achieve the Ultimate Goal of attaining Emancipation, during this very lifetime, itself, here and now, on this our own planet, without having to carry the burdensome thought of worrying about Heaven or Hell, in the subsequent birth/s.

---

[35] ਸਚੇ ਤੇਰੇ ਖੰਡ ਸਚੇ ਬ੍ਰਹਮੰਡ ॥ ਸਚੇ ਤੇਰੇ ਲੋਅ ਸਚੇ ਆਕਾਰ ॥ ਸਚੇ ਤੇਰੇ ਕਰਣੇ ਸਰਬ ਬੀਚਾਰ ॥ ਸਚਾ ਤੇਰਾ ਅਮਰੁ ਸਚਾ ਦੀਬਾਣੁ ॥ ਸਚਾ ਤੇਰਾ ਹੁਕਮੁ ਸਚਾ ਫੁਰਮਾਣੁ ॥ ਸਚਾ ਤੇਰਾ ਕਰਮੁ ਸਚਾ ਨੀਸਾਣੁ ॥ ਸਚੇ ਤੁਧੁ ਆਖਹਿ ਲਖ ਕਰੋੜਿ ॥ ਸਚੈ ਸਭਿ ਤਾਣਿ ਸਚੈ ਸਭਿ ਜੋਰਿ ॥ ਸਚੀ ਤੇਰੀ ਸਿਫਤਿ ਸਚੀ ਸਾਲਾਹ ॥ ਸਚੀ ਤੇਰੀ ਕੁਦਰਤਿ ਸਚੇ ਪਾਤਿਸਾਹ ॥ ਨਾਨਕ ਸਚੁ ਧਿਆਇਨਿ ਸਚੁ ॥ ਜੋ ਮਰਿ ਜੰਮੇ ਸੁ ਕਚੁ ਨਿਕਚੁ ॥ ੧ ॥ (pg. 463 of A. G.)

In the Primal Void, the Infinite Lord assumed His Power. He Himself is unattached, infinite and incomparable. He Himself exercises His Creative Power, and He gazes upon His creation; from the Primal Void, He formed the Void. From this Primal Void, He fashioned air and water. He created the universe, and the fortress-like body. Your Light pervades fire, water and souls; Your Power rests in the Primal Void. This Primal Void is pervasive throughout all the ages. That humble being who contemplates this state is perfect; doubt is dispelled, from within him. From this Primal Void, the seven seas were established. That human being who becomes a God-loving person, who bathes in the pool of Truth, does not have to suffer the agony and ignominy of commencing life, in the mother's womb, again. From this Primal Void, came the moon, the sun and the earth. His Light pervades all the three worlds. The Lord of this Primal Void is unseen, infinite and immaculate; He is absorbed in the Primal Trance of Deep Meditation. From this Primal Void, the earth and the Ethers were created. He supports them without any visible support, by exercising His True Power. He fashioned the three worlds, and the rope of Illusion; He Himself creates and destroys. From this Primal Void, came the source of creation, and the power of speech. They were created from the Void, and they will merge into the Void. The Supreme Creator created the play of Nature; through the Word of His Holy hymns, He stages His Wondrous Show. From this Primal Void, He made both night and day; creation and destruction, pleasure and pain. The God-loving person is immortal, untouched by pleasure and pain. None of the Scriptures can describe His worth. We speak as He inspires us to speak. From the Primal Void, He created the seven nether regions. From the Primal Void, He established this world to lovingly dwell upon Him. The Infinite Lord Himself created the creation. Everyone acts as You make them act, Lord. Your Power is diffused through the deficiencies and vices, or the positive qualities. Through egotism, they suffer the pains of birth and death. Those blessed by His Grace become God-loving people; they attain the fourth state of Redemption. From the Primal Void, all the incarnations welled up. Creating the Universe, He made the expanse. He fashioned the demi-gods and demons, the heavenly heralds and celestial musicians; everyone acts according to their past karma. The God-loving person understands, and does not suffer the disease. How rare are those who understand the intricacies of the Path, leading to the Guru. Throughout the ages, they are dedicated to liberation, and so they become liberated; thus they are honoured. From the Primal Void, the five elements became manifest. They joined to form the body, which engages in actions. The images of virtue and vice are inscribed on the forehead. The True Guru, like the Primal Being, is sublime and detached. Attuned to the Word of the Holy hymns, he is intoxicated with the sublime essence of the Lord. Riches, intellect, miraculous spiritual powers and spiritual wisdom are obtained from the Guru; through perfect destiny, they are received. This mind is madly obsessed with Illusion. Only a few are spiritually wise enough to understand and know this. In hope and desire, egotism and skepticism, the greedy man indulges in falsehood and deceit. From the True Guru, contemplative meditation is obtained. And then, one dwells with the True Lord in His celestial mansion, the Primal State of Absorption in Deepest Meditation. Says Nanak : the immaculate resonance of the Celestial music, and the Music of the Holy hymns resound; one merges into the True Name of the Lord.[36]

Sayeth Saint Kabir Das:

One who remains dead, while yet alive (one who treats life and death at the same par-value), will live even after death (shall attain immortality); thus he merges into the Primal Void of the Absolute Lord. Remaining pure in the midst of impurity, he will never again fall

---

[36] ਸੁੰਨ ਕਲਾ ਅਪਰੰਪਰਿ ਧਾਰੀ ॥ ਆਪਿ ਨਿਰਾਲਮੁ ਅਪਰ ਅਪਾਰੀ ॥ ਆਪੇ ਕੁਦਰਤਿ ਕਰਿ ਕਰਿ ਦੇਖੈ ਸੁੰਨਹੁ ਸੁੰਨੁ ਉਪਾਇਦਾ ॥ ੧ ॥ ਪਉਣੁ ਪਾਣੀ ਸੁੰਨੈ ਤੇ ਸਾਜੇ ॥ ਸ੍ਰਿਸਟਿ ਉਪਾਇ ਕਾਇਆ ਗੜ ਰਾਜੇ ॥ ਅਗਨਿ ਪਾਣੀ ਜੀਉ ਜੋਤਿ ਤੁਮਾਰੀ ਸੁੰਨੇ ਕਲਾ ਰਹਾਇਦਾ ॥ ੨ ॥ ਸੁੰਨਹੁ ਬ੍ਰਹਮਾ ਬਿਸਨੁ ਮਹੇਸੁ ਉਪਾਏ ॥ ਸੁੰਨੇ ਵਰਤੇ ਜੁਗ ਸਬਾਏ ॥ ਇਸੁ ਪਦ ਵੀਚਾਰੇ ਸੋ ਜਨੁ ਪੂਰਾ ਤਿਸੁ ਮਿਲੀਐ ਭਰਮੁ ਚੁਕਾਇਦਾ ॥ ੩ ॥ ਸੁੰਨਹੁ ਸਪਤ ਸਰੋਵਰ ਥਾਪੇ ॥ ਜਿਨਿ ਸਾਜੇ ਵੀਚਾਰੇ ਆਪੇ ॥ ਤਿਤੁ ਸਤ ਸਰਿ ਮਨੂਆ ਗੁਰਮੁਖਿ ਨਾਵੈ ਫਿਰਿ ਬਾਹੁੜਿ ਜੋਨਿ ਨ ਪਾਇਦਾ ॥ ੪ ॥ ਸੁੰਨਹੁ ਚੰਦੁ ਸੂਰਜੁ ਗੈਣਾਰੇ ॥ ਤਿਸ ਕੀ ਜੋਤਿ ਤ੍ਰਿਭਵਣ ਸਾਰੇ ॥ ਸੁੰਨੇ ਅਲਖ ਅਪਾਰ ਨਿਰਾਲਮੁ ਸੁੰਨੇ ਤਾੜੀ ਲਾਇਦਾ ॥ ੫ ॥ ਸਤਿਗੁਰ ਤੇ ਪਾਏ ਵੀਚਾਰਾ ॥ ਸੁੰਨ ਸਮਾਧਿ ਸਚੇ ਘਰ ਬਾਰਾ ॥ ਨਾਨਕ ਨਿਰਮਲ ਨਾਦੁ ਸਬਦ ਧੁਨਿ ਸਚੁ ਰਾਮੈ ਨਾਮਿ ਸਮਾਇਦਾ ॥ ੧੦ ॥ ੫ ॥ ੧੦ ॥ (pg. 1037 A.G.)

27

into the terrifying world-ocean. Through the Guru's Teachings, hold your mind steady and stable, and in this way, drink the Ambrosial Nectar.[37]

The unstruck melody of the sound current resounds with the vibrations of the celestial instruments. My mind is imbued with the Love of my Beloved (GOD). Night and day, my detached mind remains absorbed in the Lord, and I obtain my home in the profound trance of the celestial void. The True Guru has revealed to me the Primal Lord, the Infinite, my Beloved, the Invisible and the Invincible. The Lord's posture and His Throne are permanent; my mind is absorbed in reflective contemplation upon Him. Says Nanak : the detached ones are imbued with His Name, the unstruck melody, and the celestial vibrations.[38]

Void, or 'nothingness' is the sum-total of two opposite and equal forces. Now, considering, and accepting the fact, that Virtue & Sin act on a Human-being, with equal, but opposing, impact, if the subject of focus (HUMAN) remains in a state of equipoise, he is said to be in a state of Void. And, while resting in this posture of equilibrium, he strives to realize God. This, then, is a uniquely ideal state of dispassion, of detachment. And, now, Virtue is sure to emerge victorious over Sin.

---

[37] ਜੀਵਤ ਮਰੈ ਮਰੈ ਫੁਨਿ ਜੀਵੈ ਐਸੇ ਸੁੰਨਿ ਸਮਾਇਆ ॥ ਅੰਜਨ ਮਾਹਿ ਨਿਰੰਜਨਿ ਰਹੀਐ ਬਹੁੜਿ ਨ ਭਵਜਲਿ ਪਾਇਆ ॥ ੧ ॥ ਮੇਰੇ ਰਾਮ ਐਸਾ ਖੀਰੁ ਬਿਲੋਈਐ ॥ ਗੁਰਮਤਿ ਮਨੂਆ ਅਸਥਿਰੁ ਰਾਖਹੁ ਇਨ ਬਿਧਿ ਅੰਮ੍ਰਿਤੁ ਪੀਓਈਐ ॥ ੧ ॥ (pg. 332 A.G.)

[38] ਅਨਹਦੋ ਅਨਹਦੁ ਵਾਜੈ ਰੁਣ ਝੁਣਕਾਰੇ ਰਾਮ ॥ ਮੇਰਾ ਮਨੋ ਮੇਰਾ ਮਨੁ ਰਾਤਾ ਲਾਲ ਪਿਆਰੇ ਰਾਮ ॥ ਅਨਦਿਨੁ ਰਾਤਾ ਮਨੁ ਬੈਰਾਗੀ ਸੁੰਨ ਮੰਡਲਿ ਘਰੁ ਪਾਇਆ ॥ ਆਦਿ ਪੁਰਖੁ ਅਪਰੰਪਰੁ ਪਿਆਰਾ ਸਤਿਗੁਰਿ ਅਲਖੁ ਲਖਾਇਆ ॥ ਆਸਣਿ ਬੈਸਣਿ ਥਿਰੁ ਨਾਰਾਇਣੁ ਤਿਤੁ ਮਨੁ ਰਾਤਾ ਵੀਚਾਰੇ ॥ ਨਾਨਕ ਨਾਮਿ ਰਤੇ ਬੈਰਾਗੀ ਅਨਹਦ ਰੁਣ ਝੁਣਕਾਰੇ ॥ ੧ ॥ (pg. 436 A.G.)

With whom do I share this ecstatic feeling of peace and bliss, while I gaze upon the Blessed Vision of God's Audience. My mind sings His Songs of Joy and His Glories. I am wonderstruck, gazing upon the Wondrous Lord. The Merciful Lord is All-pervading everywhere. I drink in the Invaluable Nectar of the Naam, the Name of the Lord. Like the mute, I can only smile — I cannot speak of its flavour. As the breath is held in bondage, no one can understand its coming in and going out. So is that person, whose heart is enlightened by the Lord — his story cannot be told. As many other efforts as you can think of — I have seen them and studied them all. My Beloved, Carefree Lord has revealed Himself within the home of my own heart; thus I have realized the Inaccessible Lord. The Absolute, Formless, Eternally Unchanging, Immeasurable Lord cannot be measured. Says Nanak, whoever endures the unendurable — this state belongs to him alone.[39]

Baygumpura, 'the city without sorrow', is the name of the town. There is no suffering or anxiety there. There are no troubles or taxes on commodities there. There is no fear, blemish or downfall there. Now, I have discovered this excellent city. There is ever-lasting peace and safety there, O Siblings of Destiny. God's Kingdom is steady, stable and eternal. There is no second or third status; all are equal there. That city is populous and eternally famous. Those who live there are wealthy and contented. They stroll about freely, just as they please. They know the Mansion of the Lord's Presence, and no one blocks

---

[39] ਉਇ ਸੁਖ ਕਾ ਸਿਉ ਬਰਨਿ ਸੁਨਾਵਤ ॥ ਅਨਦ ਬਿਨੋਦ ਪੇਖਿ ਪ੍ਰਭ ਦਰਸਨ ਮਨਿ ਮੰਗਲ ਗੁਨ ਗਾਵਤ ॥ ੧ ॥ ਰਹਾਉ ॥ ਬਿਸਮ ਭਈ ਪੇਖਿ ਬਿਸਮਾਦੀ ਪੂਰਿ ਰਹੇ ਕਿਰਪਾਵਤ ॥ ਪੀਓ ਅੰਮ੍ਰਿਤ ਨਾਮੁ ਅਮੋਲਕ ਜਿਉ ਚਾਖਿ ਗੁੰਗਾ ਮੁਸਕਾਵਤ ॥ ੧ ॥ ਜੈਸੇ ਪਵਨੁ ਬੰਧ ਕਰਿ ਰਾਖਿਓ ਬੂਝ ਨ ਆਵਤ ਜਾਵਤ ॥ ਜਾ ਕਉ ਰਿਦੈ ਪ੍ਰਗਾਸੁ ਭਇਓ ਹਰਿ ਉਆ ਕੀ ਕਹੀ ਨ ਜਾਇ ਕਹਾਵਤ ॥ ੨ ॥ ਆਨ ਉਪਾਵ ਜੇਤੇ ਕਿਛੁ ਕਹੀਅਹਿ ਤੇਤੇ ਸੀਖੇ ਪਾਵਤ ॥ ਅਚਿੰਤ ਲਾਲੁ ਗ੍ਰਿਹ ਭੀਤਰਿ ਪ੍ਰਗਟਿਓ ਅਗਮ ਜੈਸੇ ਪਰਖਾਵਤ ॥ ੩ ॥ ਨਿਰਗੁਣ ਨਿਰੰਕਾਰ ਅਬਿਨਾਸੀ ਅਤੁਲੋ ਤੁਲਿਓ ਨ ਜਾਵਤ ॥ ਕਹੁ ਨਾਨਕ ਅਜਰੁ ਜਿਨਿ ਜਰਿਆ ਤਿਸੁ ਹੀ ਕਉ ਬਨਿ ਆਵਤ ॥ ੪ ॥ ੮ ॥ (pg. 1205 A.G.)

their path, or creates impediments. Says Ravi Daas, the emancipated shoe-maker: whoever is a citizen of that region, is a friend of mine. [40]

An overwhelming feeling of joy and contentment, when one wakes up, in the wee hours of the morning, to indulge in an exercise of self-analysis, is the first step towards attaining Inner-Peace, because that is the best time when one can experience a serene tranquility, all around, as everyone is in a deep-slumber, and all activity is at a standstill.

---

[40]ਬੇਗਮਪੁਰਾ ਸਹਰ ਕੋ ਨਾਉ ॥ ਦੂਖੁ ਅੰਦੋਹੁ ਨਹੀ ਤਿਹਿ ਠਾਉ ॥ ਨਾਂ ਤਸਵੀਸ ਖਿਰਾਜੁ ਨ ਮਾਲੁ ॥ ਖਉਫੁ ਨ ਖਤਾ ਨ ਤਰਸੁ ਜਵਾਲੁ ॥ ੧ ॥ ਅਬ ਮੋਹਿ ਖੂਬ ਵਤਨ ਗਹ ਪਾਈ ॥ ਊਹਾਂ ਖੈਰਿ ਸਦਾ ਮੇਰੇ ਭਾਈ ॥ ੧ ॥ ਰਹਾਉ ॥ ਕਾਇਮੁ ਦਾਇਮੁ ਸਦਾ ਪਾਤਿਸਾਹੀ ॥ ਦੋਮ ਨ ਸੇਮ ਏਕ ਸੋ ਆਹੀ ॥ ਆਬਾਦਾਨੁ ਸਦਾ ਮਸਹੂਰ ॥ ਊਹਾਂ ਗਨੀ ਬਸਹਿ ਮਾਮੂਰ ॥ ੨ ॥ ਤਿਉ ਤਿਉ ਸੈਲ ਕਰਹਿ ਜਿਉ ਭਾਵੈ ॥ ਮਹਰਮ ਮਹਲ ਨ ਕੋ ਅਟਕਾਵੈ ॥ ਕਹਿ ਰਵਿਦਾਸ ਖਲਾਸ ਚਮਾਰਾ ॥ ਜੋ ਹਮ ਸਹਰੀ ਸੁ ਮੀਤੁ ਹਮਾਰਾ ॥ ੩ ॥ ੨ ॥ (Pg.345 A.G.)

The ideals or purposes, of life, undergo a rapid transformation, in consonance with the change and variance in socio-economic and polito- religious environment & conditions, cultural background, levels of education /literacy, God-gifted talents & intelligence, and of course, with advancing age. Hence, it can be safely inferred and assumed that the purpose-of-life, for an infant, would be surely different from that of an adult, or of an aged-person. Priorities shift, automatically, in accordance with the change in scenario.

Also, another significant determining factor is that the human-species, has come of age, after millions of years of evolvement, commencing the journey from the most primitive of the creations of the Lord-Almighty. The advances achieved by humans are really commendable, but, in the process, God and spirituality have been relegated to the back-seat, with an increasing interest in materialistic values, and pleasures of the senses, which are momentary (sexual-promiscuity, addictions, an insatiable lust and appetite for wealth and power, even at the cost of the annihilating life, on earth, with a single press of a Red - Button).

Sayeth Guru Nanak :
First, the baby loves mother's milk; second, he learns of his mother and father; third, his brothers, sisters and aunts; fourth, the love of play awakens. Fifth, he runs after food and drink; sixth, in his sexual desire, he does not respect social customs. Seventh, he gathers wealth and dwells in his house; eighth, he becomes angry, and his body is consumed. Ninth, he turns grey, and his breathing becomes labored; tenth, he is cremated, and turns to ashes. His companions send him off, crying out and lamenting. The swan of the soul takes flight, and asks which way to go. He came and he went, and now, even his name has died. After he left, food was offered on leaves, and the birds were

called to come and eat. O Nanak, the self-willed egoistic persons love the darkness. Without the Guru, the world is drowning. [41]

Senses, Soul, Mind & Intellect constitute a human being. Soul is the Real Self, and the remaining three comprise the Unreal Self. The Soul is eternally awakened, is Free & Pure, whilst the Life of the Senses is Finite & Trivial.

The 3rd Nanak, Guru Amar Daas recommends the Ideal Purpose should be :

O my mind, you are the embodiment of the Divine Light — recognize your own origin. O my mind, the Dear Lord is with you; through the Guru's Teachings, enjoy His Love. Acknowledge your origin, and then you shall know your Husband Lord, and so understand death and birth. By Guru's Grace, know the One; then, you shall not love any other. Peace comes to the mind, and gladness resounds; then, you shall be acclaimed. My mind, you are the very image of the Luminous Lord; recognize the true origin of your self. [42]

Life of Knowledge should be the Cherished Ideal of a worthy and worthwhile life. Only when the intellect guides the mind, does the acquired knowledge serve the purpose of its acquisition, otherwise it, all, shall be in vain, and is equivalent to going down the drain : An exercise in futility. A life of spirit is the one where one transcends the barriers of the senses. Realization of one's Divine, Immortal Nature is

---

[41] ਪਹਿਲੈ ਪਿਆਰਿ ਲਗਾ ਥਣ ਦੁਧਿ ॥ ਦੂਜੈ ਮਾਇ ਬਾਪ ਕੀ ਸੁਧਿ ॥ ਤੀਜੈ ਭਯਾ ਭਾਭੀ ਬੇਬ ॥ ਚਉਥੈ ਪਿਆਰਿ ਉਪੰਨੀ ਖੇਡ ॥ ਪੰਜਵੈ ਖਾਣ ਪੀਅਣ ਕੀ ਧਾਤੁ ॥ ਛਿਵੈ ਕਾਮੁ ਨ ਪੁਛੈ ਜਾਤਿ ॥ ਸਤਵੈ ਸੰਜਿ ਕੀਆ ਘਰ ਵਾਸੁ ॥ ਅਠਵੈ ਕ੍ਰੋਧੁ ਹੋਆ ਤਨ ਨਾਸੁ ॥ ਨਾਵੈ ਧਉਲੇ ਉਭੇ ਸਾਹ ॥ ਦਸਵੈ ਦਧਾ ਹੋਆ ਸੁਆਹ ॥ ਗਏ ਸਿਗੀਤ ਪੁਕਾਰੀ ਧਾਹ ॥ ਉਡਿਆ ਹੰਸੁ ਦਸਾਏ ਰਾਹ ॥ ਆਇਆ ਗਇਆ ਮੁਇਆ ਨਾਉ ॥ ਪਿਛੈ ਪਤਲਿ ਸਦਿਹੁ ਕਾਵ ॥ ਨਾਨਕ ਮਨਮੁਖਿ ਅੰਧੁ ਪਿਆਰੁ ॥ ਬਾਝੁ ਗੁਰੂ ਡੁਬਾ ਸੰਸਾਰੁ ॥ ੨ ॥ (pg. 137 A..G.)

[42] ਮਨ ਤੂੰ ਜੋਤਿ ਸਰੂਪੁ ਹੈ ਆਪਣਾ ਮੂਲੁ ਪਛਾਣੁ ॥ ਮਨ ਹਰਿ ਜੀ ਤੇਰੈ ਨਾਲਿ ਹੈ ਗੁਰਮਤੀ ਰੰਗੁ ਮਾਣੁ ॥ ਮੂਲੁ ਪਛਾਣਹਿ ਤਾਂ ਸਹੁ ਜਾਣਹਿ ਮਰਣ ਜੀਵਣ ਕੀ ਸੋਝੀ ਹੋਈ ॥ ਗੁਰ ਪਰਸਾਦੀ ਏਕੋ ਜਾਣਹਿ ਤਾਂ ਦੂਜਾ ਭਾਉ ਨ ਹੋਈ ॥ ਮਨਿ ਸਾਂਤਿ ਆਈ ਵਜੀ ਵਧਾਈ ਤਾ ਹੋਆ ਪਰਵਾਣੁ ॥ ਇਉ ਕਹੈ ਨਾਨਕੁ ਮਨ ਤੂੰ ਜੋਤਿ ਸਰੂਪੁ ਹੈ ਆਪਣਾ ਮੂਲੁ ਪਛਾਣੁ ॥ ੫ ॥ (pg. 441 of A. G.)

32

of paramount significance. Spirituality is the prerogative of all humans, and the Life-Divine recognizes it.

The ultimate goal should be designated as 'the attainment of Salvation', thereby experiencing the bliss of freedom from the bondage of rebirth.

This human body has been gifted to you. This is your only chance to meet the Lord of the Universe. Nothing else will work. Participate in the Holy-Congregation, and meditate on the Jewel of the Lord's Noumenon. Make every effort to cross this terrifying world-ocean. You are squandering this life uselessly in the love and lure of Illusion. I have not practiced meditation, self-discipline, self-restraint or righteous living. I have not served the Holy; I have not acknowledged the Lord, my King. Repents Nanak : My actions are contemptible! O' Lord, I seek Your Sanctuary; please, preserve my honor! and grant me Your pardon. [43]

Serving the Guru, devotional worship is practiced. Then, this human body is obtained. Even the gods long for this human body. So make optimum utilization of this human-birth, and think of serving the Lord. Meditate on the Lord of the Universe, lest you forget Him. This is the blessed opportunity of this human incarnation. As long as the disease of old age hath not afflicted your body, and as long as death has not come and seized it, and as long as your voice has not lost its power, O mortal being, meditate on the Lord of the World. If you do not meditate on Him now, when will you, O Sibling of Destiny? When the end comes, you will not be able to meditate on Him, for you shall have no time at your disposal. Whatever you have to do — now is the opportune time to do it. Later, you shall have to regret and repent, and you shall not be ferried across the fiery life-ocean. He alone is a servant, whom the Lord enjoins to His service. He alone attains the Immaculate Divine Lord. Meeting with the True Guru, he does not have to journey again on the path of reincarnation. This is your

---

[43] ਭਈ ਪਰਾਪਤਿ ਮਾਨੁਖ ਦੇਹੁਰੀਆ॥ ਗੋਬਿੰਦ ਮਿਲਣ ਕੀ ਇਹ ਤੇਰੀ ਬਰੀਆ॥ ਅਵਰਿ ਕਾਜ ਤੇਰੈ ਕਿਤੈ ਨ ਕਾਮ ॥ ਮਿਲੁ ਸਾਧਸੰਗਤਿ ਭਜੁ ਕੇਵਲ ਨਾਮ ॥ ੧ ॥ ਸਰੰਜਾਮਿ ਲਾਗੁ ਭਵਜਲ ਤਰਨ ਕੈ॥ ਜਨਮੁ ਬ੍ਰਿਥਾ ਜਾਤ ਰੰਗਿ ਮਾਇਆ ਕੈ ॥ ੧ ॥ ਰਹਾਉ ॥ ਜਪੁ ਤਪੁ ਸੰਜਮੁ ਧਰਮੁ ਨ ਕਮਾਇਆ ॥ ਸੇਵਾ ਸਾਧ ਨ ਜਾਨਿਆ ਹਰਿ ਰਾਇਆ ॥ ਕਹੁ ਨਾਨਕ ਹਮ ਨੀਚ ਕਰੰਮਾ ॥ ਸਰਣਿ ਪਰੇ ਕੀ ਰਾਖਹੁ ਸਰਮਾ ॥ ੨ ॥ ੪ ॥ (Pg.12 A.G.)

33

chance, and this is your time. Delve deep into your own heart, and reflect on this. Says Kabeer : Victory or defeat, is your own choice. In so many different ways, I have proclaimed this loud and clear. [44]

---

[44] ਗੁਰ ਸੇਵਾ ਤੇ ਭਗਤਿ ਕਮਾਈ ॥ ਤਬ ਇਹ ਮਾਨਸ ਦੇਹੀ ਪਾਈ ॥ ਇਸ ਦੇਹੀ ਕਉ ਸਿਮਰਹਿ ਦੇਵ ॥ ਸੋ ਦੇਹੀ ਭਜੁ ਹਰਿ ਕੀ ਸੇਵ ॥ ੧ ॥ ਭਜਹੁ ਗੋਬਿੰਦ ਭੂਲਿ ਮਤ ਜਾਹੁ ॥ ਮਾਨਸ ਜਨਮ ਕਾ ਏਹੀ ਲਾਹੁ ॥ ੧ ॥ ਰਹਾਉ ॥ ਜਬ ਲਗੁ ਜਰਾ ਰੋਗੁ ਨਹੀ ਆਇਆ ॥ ਜਬ ਲਗੁ ਕਾਲਿ ਗ੍ਰਸੀ ਨਹੀ ਕਾਇਆ ॥ ਜਬ ਲਗੁ ਬਿਕਲ ਭਈ ਨਹੀ ਬਾਨੀ ॥ ਭਜਿ ਲੇਹਿ ਰੇ ਮਨ ਸਾਰਿਗਪਾਨੀ ॥ ੨ ॥ ਅਬ ਨ ਭਜਸਿ ਭਜਸਿ ਕਬ ਭਾਈ ॥ ਆਵੈ ਅੰਤੁ ਨ ਭਜਿਆ ਜਾਈ ॥ ਜੋ ਕਿਛੁ ਕਰਹਿ ਸੋਈ ਅਬ ਸਾਰੁ ॥ ਫਿਰਿ ਪਛੁਤਾਹੁ ਨ ਪਾਵਹੁ ਪਾਰੁ ॥ ੩ ॥ ਸੋ ਸੇਵਕੁ ਜੋ ਲਾਇਆ ਸੇਵ ॥ ਤਿਨ ਹੀ ਪਾਏ ਨਿਰੰਜਨ ਦੇਵ ॥ ਗੁਰ ਮਿਲਿ ਤਾ ਕੇ ਖੁਲੇ ਕਪਾਟ ॥ ਬਹੁਰਿ ਨ ਆਵੈ ਜੋਨੀ ਬਾਟ ॥ ੪ ॥ ਇਹੀ ਤੇਰਾ ਅਉਸਰੁ ਇਹ ਤੇਰੀ ਬਾਰ ॥ ਘਟ ਭੀਤਰਿ ਤੂ ਦੇਖੁ ਬਿਚਾਰਿ ॥ ਕਹਤ ਕਬੀਰੁ ਜੀਤਿ ਕੈ ਹਾਰਿ ॥ ਬਹੁ ਬਿਧਿ ਕਹਿਓ ਪੁਕਾਰਿ ਪੁਕਾਰਿ ॥ ੫ ॥ ੧ ॥ ੯ ॥(Pg.1159 A.G.)

VIII : SALVATION

(LIBERATION / EMANCIPATION / BEATITUDE)

Great emphasis has been laid upon the Doctrine of "Attunement-with-God" (entering into the realm of God-consciousness). This belief relates to the Transmigration of the Soul, and Salvation, thence, would mean Total Release from the vicious cycle of birth and death. Salvation could be attained, even in the present lifetime, here and now, on our very own planet, instead of the imaginary Heavens, after death. It is very much possible that such an ecstatic level or plane is arrived at, but the only condition is that utmost restraint is required to be exercised, over the reins of the wild -horses of the senses. "PARAMPAD" (the 4th and highest state of the mind) is, in effect, the quintessential "SALVATION". The lower three states are : the Waking-state, the Dream-state, and the Dreamless-sleeping-state.

Salvation could, also, mean Loving God, with all the intensity & faith, at one's disposal, so as to arrive in the fragrantly wonderful zone of "Communion with God". Grace & Benediction & Benevolence play a far significant role, than Karma alone, towards the realization of this objective. Emancipation is very much possible right here, provided the pleader is sincere in his prayer and approach, and inclination and motives.

One who, in his soul, loves the Will of God, is said to be liberated while yet alive. As is joy, so is sorrow to him. He experiences eternal bliss, and is not separated from God. As is gold, so is dust to him. As is ambrosial nectar, so is bitter poison to him. As is honor, so is dishonor. Such a one treats a pauper and a king alike. Whatever God ordains, is acceptable to such a person.[45]

---

[45] ਪ੍ਰਭ ਕੀ ਆਗਿਆ ਆਤਮ ਹਿਤਾਵੈ ॥ ਜੀਵਨ ਮੁਕਤਿ ਸੋਊ ਕਹਾਵੈ ॥ ਤੈਸਾ ਹਰਖੁ ਤੈਸਾ ਉਸੁ ਸੋਗੁ ॥ ਸਦਾ ਅਨੰਦੁ ਤਹ ਨਹੀ ਬਿਓਗੁ ॥ ਤੈਸਾ ਸੁਵਰਨੁ ਤੈਸੀ ਉਸੁ ਮਾਟੀ ॥ ਤੈਸਾ ਅੰਮ੍ਰਿਤੁ ਤੈਸੀ ਬਿਖੁ ਖਾਟੀ ॥ ਤੈਸਾ ਮਾਨੁ ਤੈਸਾ ਅਭਿਮਾਨੁ ॥ ਤੈਸਾ ਰੰਕੁ ਤੈਸਾ ਰਾਜਾਨੁ ॥ ਜੋ ਵਰਤਾਏ ਸਾਈ ਜੁਗਤਿ ॥ ਨਾਨਕ ਓਹੁ ਪੁਰਖੁ ਕਹੀਐ ਜੀਵਨ ਮੁਕਤਿ ॥ ੭ ॥ (from the Sukhmani : pg.275 A.G.)

Guru Nanak lays great stress on the Path of Sublime-Love (Prem-Marg). He says, real worship and devotion to God, would be getting rid of the physical-cravings.

The soul-bride is in love with her Husband Lord; she focuses her consciousness on the Word of the Guru's Holy hymns. The soul-bride is joyously embellished with the gift of intuition; her hunger and thirst are taken away.[46]

An ideal Human-being is one who exercises utmost restraint over passions, holding tightly the reigns of his mind's horses, leading a life of equipoise (SAHAJ-BHAAV), a very worldly-life, carrying out sundry duties, and tackling mundane issues and problems. Having experienced eternal bliss, inside, such a person attains humility to such an extent, that he masters the art of REFRAINING from practicing self-aggrandizement. He would masquerade in the guise of "the lowest of the lowly", for such a one does not wish to be eulogized.

One who is beyond praise and slander, who looks upon gold and iron alike — says Nanak: understand this, my mind, that such a person is liberated. One who is not affected by pleasure or pain, who looks upon friend and foe alike — says Nanak, listen, mind: know that such a person is liberated[47]

Myriads of heavens do not equal the Lord's Name. The spiritually wise forsake mere liberation. The One Universal Creator Lord is found through the True Guru. I am a sacrifice unto the Blessed Vision of the Guru's Audience. No one knows how to serve the Guru. The Guru is the unfathomable, Supreme Lord God. He alone is the Guru's servant, whom the Guru Himself links to His service, and upon whose forehead such blessed destiny is inscribed.[48]

---

[46] ਪਿਰ ਸੇਤੀ ਧਨ ਪ੍ਰੇਮੁ ਰਚਾਏ ॥ ਗੁਰ ਕੈ ਸਬਦਿ ਤਥਾ ਚਿਤੁ ਲਾਏ ॥ ਸਹਜ ਸੇਤੀ ਧਨ ਖਰੀ ਸੁਹੇਲੀ ਤ੍ਰਿਸਨਾ ਤਿਖਾ ਨਿਵਾਰੀ ਜੀਉ ॥ ੨ ॥ (pg. 993 of A.G.)

[47] ਉਸਤਤਿ ਨਿੰਦਿਆ ਨਾਹਿ ਜਿਹਿ ਕੰਚਨ ਲੋਹ ਸਮਾਨਿ ॥ ਕਹੁ ਨਾਨਕ ਸੁਨਿ ਰੇ ਮਨਾ ਮੁਕਤਿ ਤਾਹਿ ਤੈ ਜਾਨਿ ॥ ੧੪ ॥ ਹਰਖੁ ਸੋਗੁ ਜਾ ਕੈ ਨਹੀ ਬੈਰੀ ਮੀਤ ਸਮਾਨਿ ॥ ਕਹੁ ਨਾਨਕ ਸੁਨਿ ਰੇ ਮਨਾ ਮੁਕਤਿ ਤਾਹਿ ਤੈ ਜਾਨਿ ॥ ੧੫ ॥(Pg. 1427 A.G.)

[48] ਕਈ ਬੈਕੁੰਠ ਨਾਹੀ ਲਵੈ ਲਾਗੇ ॥ ਮੁਕਤਿ ਬਪੁੜੀ ਭੀ ਗਿਆਨੀ ਤਿਆਗੇ ॥ ਏਕੰਕਾਰੁ ਸਤਿਗੁਰ ਤੇ ਪਾਈਐ ਹਉ ਬਲਿ ਬਲਿ ਗੁਰ ਦਰਸਾਇਣਾ ॥ ੮ ॥ ਗੁਰ ਕੀ ਸੇਵ ਨ ਜਾਣੈ ਕੋਈ ॥ ਗੁਰੁ ਪਾਰਬ੍ਰਹਮੁ

The Vedas, the Simritees, the Shaastras   (all are names of Hindu Scriptures) and the Lord's devotees contemplate Him; liberation is attained in the Saadh Sangat, the Company of the Holy, and thus is the darkness of ignorance dispelled.   The lotus feet of the Lord are the support of His humble servants. They are his only capital and investment. The True Lord is Nanak's strength, honor and support; He alone is his protection. [49]

ਅਗੋਚਰੁ ਸੋਈ ॥ ਜਿਸ ਨੋ ਲਾਇ ਲਏ ਸੋ ਸੇਵਕੁ ਜਿਸੁ ਵਡਭਾਗ ਮਥਾਇਣਾ ॥ ੯ ॥ (Pg.1078 A.G.)
[49] ਬੇਦ ਸਿੰਮ੍ਰਿਤਿ ਕਥੈ ਸਾਸਤ ਭਗਤ ਕਰਹਿ ਬੀਚਾਰੁ ॥ ਮੁਕਤਿ ਪਾਈਐ ਸਾਧਸੰਗਤਿ ਬਿਨਸਿ ਜਾਇ ਅੰਧਾਰੁ ॥ ੩ ॥ ਚਰਨ ਕਮਲ ਅਧਾਰੁ ਜਨ ਕਾ ਰਾਸਿ ਪੂੰਜੀ ਏਕ ॥ ਤਾਣੁ ਮਾਣੁ ਦੀਬਾਣੁ ਸਾਚਾ ਨਾਨਕ ਕੀ ਪ੍ਰਭ ਟੇਕ ॥ ੪ ॥ ੨ ॥ ੨੦ ॥ (Pg.675 A.G.)

When the hands and the feet and the body are dirty, water can wash away the dirt. When the clothes are soiled and stained, soap can wash them clean. But when the intellect is stained and polluted by sin, it can only be cleansed by the Love of the Name. Virtue and vice do not come by mere words; actions repeated, over and over again, are engraved on the soul. You shall harvest what you plant. Says Nanak, by God's Command, we come and go in reincarnation.[50]

When the mind is filthy, everything is filthy; by washing the body, the mind is not cleansed. This world is deluded by doubt; hardly anyone understands this. My mind, chant the One Name. The True Guru has given me this treasure. Even if one learns the Yogic postures of the Siddhas, and holds his sexual energy in check, still, the filth of the mind is not removed, and the filth of egotism is not eliminated. This mind is not controlled by any other discipline, except the Sanctuary of the True Guru. Meeting the True Guru, one is transformed beyond description. Prays Nanak, one who dies upon meeting the True Guru, shall be rejuvenated through the Word of the Guru's Shabad. The filth of attachment and possessiveness shall depart, and the mind shall become pure.[51]

Bathing in the nectar tank of the Lord's Noumenon, the residues of all sins are erased. One becomes immaculately pure, taking this Holy bath. The Perfect Guru has bestowed this gift. God has blessed all

---

[50] ਭਰੀਐ ਹਥੁ ਪੈਰੁ ਤਨੁ ਦੇਹ ॥ ਪਾਣੀ ਧੋਤੈ ਉਤਰਸੁ ਖੇਹ ॥ ਮੂਤ ਪਲੀਤੀ ਕਪੜੁ ਹੋਇ ॥ ਦੇ ਸਾਬੂਣੁ ਲਈਐ ਓਹੁ ਧੋਇ ॥ ਭਰੀਐ ਮਤਿ ਪਾਪਾ ਕੈ ਸੰਗਿ ॥ ਓਹੁ ਧੋਪੈ ਨਾਵੈ ਕੈ ਰੰਗਿ ॥ ਪੁੰਨੀ ਪਾਪੀ ਆਖਣੁ ਨਾਹਿ ॥ ਕਰਿ ਕਰਿ ਕਰਣਾ ਲਿਖਿ ਲੈ ਜਾਹੁ ॥ ਆਪੇ ਬੀਜਿ ਆਪੇ ਹੀ ਖਾਹੁ ॥ ਨਾਨਕ ਹੁਕਮੀ ਆਵਹੁ ਜਾਹੁ ॥ ੨੦ ॥ (pg. 4 A.G.)

[51] ਮਨਿ ਮੈਲੈ ਸਭੁ ਕਿਛੁ ਮੈਲਾ ਤਨਿ ਧੋਤੈ ਮਨੁ ਹਛਾ ਨ ਹੋਇ ॥ ਇਹੁ ਜਗਤੁ ਭਰਮਿ ਭੁਲਾਇਆ ਵਿਰਲਾ ਬੁਝੈ ਕੋਇ ॥ ੧ ॥ ਜਪਿ ਮਨ ਮੇਰੇ ਤੂ ਏਕੋ ਨਾਮੁ ॥ ਸਤਿਗੁਰ ਦੀਆ ਮੋ ਕਉ ਏਹੁ ਨਿਧਾਨੁ ॥ ੧ ॥ ਰਹਾਉ ॥ ਸਿਧਾ ਕੇ ਆਸਣ ਜੇ ਸਿਖੈ ਇੰਦ੍ਰੀ ਵਸਿ ਕਰਿ ਕਮਾਇ ॥ ਮਨ ਕੀ ਮੈਲੁ ਨ ਉਤਰੈ ਹਉਮੈ ਮੈਲੁ ਨ ਜਾਇ ॥ ੨ ॥ ਇਸੁ ਮਨ ਕਉ ਹੋਰੁ ਸੰਜਮੁ ਕੋ ਨਾਹੀ ਵਿਣੁ ਸਤਿਗੁਰ ਕੀ ਸਰਣਾਇ ॥ ਸਤਗੁਰਿ ਮਿਲਿਐ ਉਲਟੀ ਭਈ ਕਹਣਾ ਕਿਛੁ ਨ ਜਾਇ ॥ ੩ ॥ ਭਣਤਿ ਨਾਨਕੁ ਸਤਿਗੁਰ ਕਉ ਮਿਲਦੋ ਮਰੈ ਗੁਰ ਕੈ ਸਬਦਿ ਫਿਰਿ ਜੀਵੈ ਕੋਇ ॥ ਮਮਤਾ ਕੀ ਮਲੁ ਉਤਰੈ ਇਹੁ ਮਨੁ ਹਛਾ ਹੋਇ ॥ ੪ ॥ ੧ ॥ (pg. 558 A.G.)

with peace and pleasure. Everything is safe and sound, as we contemplate the Word of the Guru. In the Saadh Sangat, the Company of the Holy, filth is washed off. The Supreme Lord God has become our friend and helper. Nanak meditates on the Name of the Lord. He has found God, the Primal Being. I found the Guru, the ocean of peace, and all my doubts were dispelled.[52]

Like nobody prefers to sit in close proximity to a person wearing unwashed clothes, similarly a person with a 'sullied' thought-process is shunned by all and sundry, for he would only be spreading vitriolic words around, thereby vitiating the environment.

God has blessed me in every sphere of life, and by meditating upon HIS NAME, my sagging spirits have been rejuvenated, and I've been saved. In the Saadh-Sangat (the Company of the Holy), filth is washed away. The Supreme Lord has become my companion and benefactor. Continue to meditate, and the Primal-Being is sure to become the Protector, everywhere and for all times to come.

The effects of the past-life deeds, coupled with the devastating impact of the vices, in the present life, have made the mind corrupt and polluted. Just as the rain-drop starts its downward journey, in pure form and colour, the soul, too, is pure in the beginning. But when the rain-drop is passing through atmospheric-layers, it is adulterated by the dust-particles in the air. And, finally, on falling to the earth, the mud would sully it, completely.

---

[52] ਰਾਮਦਾਸ ਸਰੋਵਰਿ ਨਾਤੇ ॥ ਸਭਿ ਉਤਰੇ ਪਾਪ ਕਮਾਤੇ ॥ ਨਿਰਮਲ ਹੋਏ ਕਰਿ ਇਸਨਾਨਾ ॥ ਗੁਰਿ ਪੂਰੈ ਕੀਨੇ ਦਾਨਾ ॥ ੧ ॥ ਸਭਿ ਕੁਸਲ ਖੇਮ ਪ੍ਰਭਿ ਧਾਰੇ ॥ ਸਹੀ ਸਲਾਮਤਿ ਸਭਿ ਥੋਕ ਉਬਾਰੇ ਗੁਰ ਕਾ ਸਬਦੁ ਵੀਚਾਰੇ ॥ ਰਹਾਉ ॥ ਸਾਧਸੰਗਿ ਮਲੁ ਲਾਥੀ ॥ ਪਾਰਬ੍ਰਹਮੁ ਭਇਓ ਸਾਥੀ ॥ ਨਾਨਕ ਨਾਮੁ ਧਿਆਇਆ ॥ ਆਦਿ ਪੁਰਖ ਪ੍ਰਭੁ ਪਾਇਆ ॥ ੨ ॥ ੧ ॥ ੬੫ ॥ ਸੋਰਠਿ ਮਹਲਾ ੫ ॥ ਜਿਤੁ ਪਾਰਬ੍ਰਹਮੁ ਚਿਤਿ ਆਇਆ ॥ ਸੋ ਘਰੁ ਦਯਿ ਵਸਾਇਆ ॥ ਸੁਖ ਸਾਗਰੁ ਗੁਰੁ ਪਾਇਆ ॥ ਤਾ ਸਹਸਾ ਸਗਲ ਮਿਟਾਇਆ ॥ ੧ ॥ (pg. 625-26 A.G.)

Do not blame anyone else; blame instead your own actions. Whatever I did, for that I have suffered; I do not blame anyone else. [53]

By His Command, bodies are created; His Command cannot be described. By His Command, souls come into being; by His Command, glory and greatness are obtained. By His Command, some are high and some are low; by His Written Command, pain and pleasure are obtained. Some, by His Command, are blessed and forgiven; others, by His Command, wander aimlessly forever. Everyone is subject to His Command; no one is beyond His Command. Says Nanak, one who understands His Command, does not speak in ego. [54]

All intuitive understanding, all Yoga, all the Scriptures, all actions, all penances, all hymns and spiritual wisdom, all intellect, all enlightenment, all sacred shrines of pilgrimage, all kingdoms, all royal commands, all joys and all delicacies, all mankind, all divinities, all meditation, all worlds, all celestial realms; all the beings of the universe, in ssence ALL creations and ALL creatures are under the Supreme Command. According to His Will, He commands them. His Pen writes out the account of their actions. Says Nanak, True is the Lord, and True is His Name. True is His Congregation and His Court. [55]

---

[53] ਦਦੈ ਦੋਸੁ ਨ ਦੇਊ ਕਿਸੈ ਦੋਸੁ ਕਰੰਮਾ ਆਪਣਿਆ ॥ ਜੋ ਮੈ ਕੀਆ ਸੋ ਮੈ ਪਾਇਆ ਦੋਸੁ ਨ ਦੀਜੈ ਅਵਰ ਜਨਾ ॥ ੨੧ ॥ (pg. 433 A.G.)

[54] ॥ ਹੁਕਮੀ ਹੋਵਨਿ ਆਕਾਰ ਹੁਕਮੁ ਨ ਕਹਿਆ ਜਾਈ ॥ ਹੁਕਮੀ ਹੋਵਨਿ ਜੀਅ ਹੁਕਮਿ ਮਿਲੈ ਵਡਿਆਈ ॥ ਹੁਕਮੀ ਉਤਮੁ ਨੀਚੁ ਹੁਕਮਿ ਲਿਖਿ ਦੁਖ ਸੁਖ ਪਾਈਅਹਿ ॥ ਇਕਨਾ ਹੁਕਮੀ ਬਖਸੀਸ ਇਕਿ ਹੁਕਮੀ ਸਦਾ ਭਵਾਈਅਹਿ ॥ ਹੁਕਮੈ ਅੰਦਰਿ ਸਭੁ ਕੋ ਬਾਹਰਿ ਹੁਕਮ ਨ ਕੋਇ ॥ ਨਾਨਕ ਹੁਕਮੈ ਜੇ ਬੁਝੈ ਤ ਹਉਮੈ ਕਹੈ ਨ ਕੋਇ ॥ ੨ ॥ (pg. 1 A.G)

[55] ਸਭੇ ਸੁਰਤੀ ਜੋਗ ਸਭਿ ਸਭੇ ਬੇਦ ਪੁਰਾਣ ॥ ਸਭੇ ਕਰਣੇ ਤਪ ਸਭਿ ਸਭੇ ਗੀਤ ਗਿਆਨ ॥ ਸਭੇ ਬੁਧੀ ਸੁਧਿ ਸਭਿ ਸਭਿ ਤੀਰਥ ਸਭਿ ਥਾਨ ॥ ਸਭਿ ਪਾਤਿਸਾਹੀਆ ਅਮਰ ਸਭਿ ਸਭਿ ਖੁਸੀਆ ਸਭਿ ਖਾਨ ॥ ਸਭੇ ਮਾਣਸ ਦੇਵ ਸਭਿ ਸਭੇ ਜੋਗ ਧਿਆਨ ॥ ਸਭੇ ਪੁਰੀਆ ਖੰਡ ਸਭਿ ਸਭੇ ਜੀਅ ਜਹਾਨ ॥ ਹੁਕਮਿ

God driveth according to His Will; The present-life circumstances/conditions, that one finds oneself embroiled in, may be attributable to, and traceable to, the innumerable acts of commission and omission, during the past life/lives. These may be construed to be in the form and shape of rewards, or penalties, as the case may be.

Virtuous deeds, in this lifetime, have the potential of presenting a human-being with the invaluably cherished gift, of being spared the agony and ignominy of undergoing Transmigration.

They have forsaken God the Primal Being, the Life of the World, and they have come to rely upon mere mortals. In the love of duality, the soul-bride is ruined; around her neck she wears the noose of Death. As you plant, so shall you harvest; your destiny is recorded on your forehead. The life-night passes away, and in the end, one comes to regret and repent, and then depart with no hope at all. Those who meet with the Holy Saints are liberated in the Court of the Lord. Show Your Mercy to me, O God; I pine for Your Blessed Vision.[56]

Fareed, the farmer plants acacia trees, and wishes for grapes. He is spinning wool, but he wishes to wear silk.[57]

Worthy Deeds (performed on the physical-plane) that are visible to the human-eye, are appreciated and recognized by God, in the form of worldly prestige and honour, that is, also apparent and obvious, to everyone. And, honourable Deeds, on the spiritual-plane (that cannot be viewed, even under the most advanced microscope, shall be credited to the account of the pious soul, who shall become the deserving recipient of magnificent accolades and encomiums, in the world, hereafter.

ਚਲਾਏ ਆਪਣੈ ਕਰਮੀ ਵਹੈ ਕਲਾਮ ॥ ਨਾਨਕ ਸਚਾ ਸਚਿ ਨਾਇ ਸਚੁ ਸਭਾ ਦੀਬਾਨੁ ॥ ੨ ॥ (pg. 1241 A.G.)

[56] ਜਗਜੀਵਨ ਪੁਰਖੁ ਤਿਆਗਿ ਕੈ ਮਾਣਸ ਸੰਦੀ ਆਸ ॥ ਦੁਯੈ ਭਾਇ ਵਿਗੁਚੀਐ ਗਲਿ ਪਈਸੁ ਜਮ ਕੀ ਫਾਸ ॥ ਜੇਹਾ ਬੀਜੈ ਸੋ ਲੁਣੈ ਮਥੈ ਜੋ ਲਿਖਿਆਸੁ ॥ ਰੈਣਿ ਵਿਹਾਣੀ ਪਛੁਤਾਣੀ ਉਠਿ ਚਲੀ ਗਈ ਨਿਰਾਸ ॥ ਜਿਨ ਕੌ ਸਾਧੂ ਭੇਟੀਐ ਸੋ ਦਰਗਹ ਹੋਇ ਖਲਾਸੁ ॥ ਕਰਿ ਕਿਰਪਾ ਪ੍ਰਭ ਆਪਣੀ ਤੇਰੇ ਦਰਸਨ ਹੋਇ ਪਿਆਸ ॥ (Pg.134 A.G.)

[57] ਫਰੀਦਾ ਲੋੜੈ ਦਾਖ ਬਿਜਉਰੀਆਂ ਕਿਕਰਿ ਬੀਜੈ ਜਟੁ ॥ ਹੰਢੈ ਉਂਨ ਕਤਾਇਦਾ ਪੈਧਾ ਲੋੜੈ ਪਟੁ ॥ ੨੩ ॥(Pg.1379 A.G.)

41

XI : SERVICE TO HUMANITY

IS

SERVICE TO GOD

You, Yourself inspire the aspirant to serve You (by believing in Your Existence). No one else can do it. He alone is Your devotee, who is pleasing to You. You bless him with Your Love. You are the Great Giver; You are so very Wise. There is no other like You. You are my All-powerful Lord and Master; I do not know how to worship You. Your Mansion is imperceptible, O my Beloved; it is so difficult to accept Your Will. Says Nanak : I have collapsed at Your Door, Lord. I am foolish and ignorant — please save me! [58]

Brahma and Vishnu, the Rishis and the silent sages, Shiva and Indra, anyone high or low, whoever obeys the Lord's Command, looks beautiful in the Court of the True Lord, while the stubborn rebels die. The wandering beggars, warriors, celibates and hermit, through the Perfect Guru, consider this: without selfless service, no one ever receives the rewards. Serving the Lord is the excellent action. [59]

That selfless servant, who lives in the Guru's household, is to obey the Guru's Commands. He is not to call attention to himself in any way. He is to meditate constantly within his heart on the Name of the Lord. One who sells his mind to the True Guru — that humble servant's affairs are resolved. One who performs selfless service, without thought of reward, shall attain his Lord and Master. He Himself grants His Grace; Says Nanak : that selfless servant practices the Guru's Teachings & Preachings. [60]

---

[58] ਤੇਰੀ ਸੇਵਾ ਤੁਝ ਤੇ ਹੋਵੈ ਅਉਰੁ ਨ ਦੂਜਾ ਕਰਤਾ ॥ ਭਗਤੁ ਤੇਰਾ ਸੋਈ ਤੁਧੁ ਭਾਵੈ ਜਿਸ ਨੋ ਤੂ ਰੰਗੁ ਧਰਤਾ ॥ ੨ ॥ ਤੂ ਵਡ ਦਾਤਾ ਤੂ ਵਡ ਦਾਨਾ ਅਉਰੁ ਨਹੀ ਕੋ ਦੂਜਾ ॥ ਤੂ ਸਮਰਥੁ ਸੁਆਮੀ ਮੇਰਾ ਹਉ ਕਿਆ ਜਾਣਾ ਤੇਰੀ ਪੂਜਾ ॥ ੩ ॥ ਤੇਰਾ ਮਹਲੁ ਅਗੋਚਰੁ ਮੇਰੇ ਪਿਆਰੇ ਬਿਖਮੁ ਤੇਰਾ ਹੈ ਭਾਣਾ ॥ ਕਹੁ ਨਾਨਕ ਢਹਿ ਪਇਆ ਦੁਆਰੈ ਰਖਿ ਲੇਵਹੁ ਮੁਗਧ ਅਜਾਣਾ ॥ ੪ ॥ ੨ ॥ ੨੦ ॥ (pg. 1185 A.G.)

[59] ਬ੍ਰਹਮਾ ਬਿਸਨੁ ਰਿਖੀ ਮੁਨੀ ਸੰਕਰੁ ਇੰਦੁ ਤਪੈ ਭੇਖਾਰੀ ॥ ਮਾਨੈ ਹੁਕਮੁ ਸੋਹੈ ਦਰਿ ਸਾਚੈ ਆਕੀ ਮਰਹਿ ਅਫਾਰੀ ॥ ਜੰਗਮ ਜੋਧ ਜਤੀ ਸੰਨਿਆਸੀ ਗੁਰਿ ਪੂਰੈ ਵੀਚਾਰੀ ॥ ਬਿਨੁ ਸੇਵਾ ਫਲੁ ਕਬਹੁ ਨ ਪਾਵਸਿ ਸੇਵਾ ਕਰਣੀ ਸਾਰੀ ॥ ੨ ॥ (pg. 992 A.G.)

[60] ਗੁਰ ਕੈ ਗ੍ਰਿਹਿ ਸੇਵਕੁ ਜੋ ਰਹੈ ॥ ਗੁਰ ਕੀ ਆਗਿਆ ਮਨ ਮਹਿ ਸਹੈ ॥ ਆਪਸ ਕਉ ਕਰਿ ਕਛੁ ਨ

42

This body is softened with the Guru's Word; you shall find peace, doing seva (selfless service). All the world continues to be affected by the force of reincarnation. Perform selfless-service, and you shall be given a place of honor in the Court of the Lord. Says Nanak: swing your arms in joy![61]

ਜਨਾਵੈ ॥ ਹਰਿ ਹਰਿ ਨਾਮੁ ਰਿਦੈ ਸਦ ਧਿਆਵੈ ॥ ਮਨੁ ਬੇਚੈ ਸਤਿਗੁਰ ਕੈ ਪਾਸਿ ॥ ਤਿਸੁ ਸੇਵਕ ਕੇ ਕਾਰਜ ਰਾਸਿ ॥ ਸੇਵਾ ਕਰਤ ਹੋਇ ਨਿਹਕਾਮੀ ॥ ਤਿਸ ਕਉ ਹੋਤ ਪਰਾਪਤਿ ਸੁਆਮੀ ॥ ਅਪਨੀ ਕ੍ਰਿਪਾ ਜਿਸੁ ਆਪਿ ਕਰੇਇ ॥ ਨਾਨਕ ਸੋ ਸੇਵਕੁ ਗੁਰ ਕੀ ਮਤਿ ਲੇਇ ॥ ੨ ॥ (pg. 286-87 A.G.)

[61] ਕਰਿ ਚਾਨਣੁ ਸਾਹਿਬ ਤਉ ਮਿਲੈ ॥ ੧ ॥ ਰਹਾਉ ॥ ਇਤੁ ਤਨਿ ਲਾਗੈ ਬਾਣੀਆ ॥ ਸੁਖੁ ਹੋਵੈ ਸੇਵ ਕਮਾਣੀਆ ॥ ਸਭ ਦੁਨੀਆ ਆਵਣ ਜਾਣੀਆ ॥ ੩ ॥ ਵਿਚਿ ਦੁਨੀਆ ਸੇਵ ਕਮਾਈਐ ॥ ਤਾ ਦਰਗਹ ਬੈਸਣੁ ਪਾਈਐ ॥ ਕਹੁ ਨਾਨਕ ਬਾਹ ਲੁਡਾਈਐ ॥ ੪ ॥ ੩੩ ॥ (pg. 25-26 A.G.)

If the noose of emotional attachment binds me, then I shall bind You, Lord, with the bonds of my devotion and love. Go ahead and try to escape, Lord; As for me, I have escaped by worshipping and adoring You. O' Lord, You know my love for You. Now, what would You do? A fish is caught, cut up, and it is cooked, in many different ways. Bit by bit, it is eaten, but still, it does not forget the water.[62]

The Power of Love has the potential of significantly changing one's overall perspective, for the betterment of self, and others. This new outlook could achieve wonders in all spheres of human-endeavour. Of all the Godly- attributes, LOVE is the chieftain. All religious and spiritual deeds, sans Love, shall be rendered tasteless, directionless and purposeless, in fact they shall be said to be exercises-in-futility .

Love develops gradually, over a period of time, in everybody's life, as per varying circumstances, experiences and conducive-environment. Various instances of Love can be cited, in the Natural-realms. The blossoming of flowers, and the buzzing around of the bumblebee, are two examples. The peacock-dance is famous, at the sighting of rain-clouds. The love-pangs emanating from the heart of the timid partridge, pining for the Full Moon, are all manifestations of the hidden love, that is sublime and pristine, elevated and selfless, true and sacred. Love is such a magnetic- force, which attracts and influences everyone. Love is a state-of-the-mind. Its born inside the human heart, grows and develops, and on attaining maturity, assumes the form of affection, and the whole personality undergoes a metamorphic sea-change. The body and the mind, the heart and the soul, all, start reverberating with spiritually gifted strains-of-mellifluous-music.

---

[62] ਜਉ ਹਮ ਬਾਂਧੇ ਮੋਹ ਫਾਸ ਹਮ ਪ੍ਰੇਮ ਬਧਨਿ ਤੁਮ ਬਾਧੇ ॥ ਅਪਨੇ ਛੂਟਨ ਕੋ ਜਤਨੁ ਕਰਹੁ ਹਮ ਛੂਟੇ ਤੁਮ ਆਰਾਧੇ ॥ ੧ ॥ ਮਾਧਵੇ ਜਾਨਤ ਹਹੁ ਜੈਸੀ ਤੈਸੀ ॥ ਅਬ ਕਹਾ ਕਰਹੁਗੇ ਐਸੀ ॥ ੧ ॥ ਰਹਾਉ ॥ ਮੀਨੁ ਪਕਰਿ ਫਾਂਕਿਓ ਅਰੁ ਕਾਟਿਓ ਰਾਂਧਿ ਕੀਓ ਬਹੁ ਬਾਨੀ ॥ ਖੰਡ ਖੰਡ ਕਰਿ ਭੋਜਨ ਕੀਨੋ ਤਊ ਨ ਬਿਸਰਿਓ ਪਾਨੀ ॥ ੨ ॥ (pg. 658 A.G.)

An unparalleled and inexplicable feeling of exhilaration engulfs the person. Anyone, who has never had this experience, this BOON, is really an unfortunate and condemned mortal. But, one must remain wary of all such people, who have a negative influence on one's life, even if those people are the closest relations or friends. One must learn to love oneself, instead of depending on a supplementary-diet of receiving regular love from others, for sustenance and happiness. Loving humanity is loving God.

My love for the Lord overwhelms me. How can I go and meet the Lord? My mind and body are so thirsty for the Blessed Vision of the Lord. Won't someone please come and lead me to Him, O Mother. The Saints are the helpers of the Lord's lovers; I fall and touch their feet. Without God, how can I find peace? There is nowhere else to go. Those who have tasted the sublime essence of His Love, remain satisfied and fulfilled. They renounce their selfishness and conceit, and they pray, "God, please attach me to the hem of Your robe." Those whom the Husband Lord has united with Himself, shall not be separated from Him again. Without God, there is no other at all. Nanak has entered the Sanctuary of the Lord. The Lord, the Sovereign King, has granted His Mercy, and they dwell in peace.[63]

This, hitherto, unknown feeling of Love brings radiance and fragrance into the life. When Love remains confined within the domains of the home, it is called Attachment. But when love's horizons get expanded, and it acquires wings, it takes the whole universe into its embrace. Now, whosoever comes within range is captured, for a lifetime, and merges into the unfathomable Ocean-of-Love. And the all-embracing and overwhelming feeling of loving-all, is equivalent to loving God, who created those "ALL". Just this, very experience, transforms the latent and dormant feeling of Love (inside) into a powerful force.

---

[63] ਅਸਟਨਿ ਪ੍ਰੇਮ ਉਮਾਹੜਾ ਕਿਉ ਮਿਲੀਐ ਹਰਿ ਜਾਇ ॥ ਮਨਿ ਤਨਿ ਪਿਆਸ ਦਰਸਨ ਘਣੀ ਕੋਈ ਆਣਿ ਮਿਲਾਵੈ ਮਾਇ ॥ ਸੰਤ ਸਹਾਈ ਪ੍ਰੇਮ ਕੇ ਹਉ ਤਿਨ ਕੈ ਲਾਗਾ ਪਾਇ ॥ ਵਿਣੁ ਪ੍ਰਭ ਕਿਉ ਸੁਖੁ ਪਾਈਐ ਦੂਜੀ ਨਾਹੀ ਜਾਇ ॥ ਜਿੰਨੀ ਚਾਖਿਆ ਪ੍ਰੇਮ ਰਸੁ ਸੇ ਤ੍ਰਿਪਤਿ ਰਹੇ ਆਘਾਇ ॥ ਆਪੁ ਤਿਆਗਿ ਬਿਨਤੀ ਕਰਹਿ ਲੇਹੁ ਪ੍ਰਭੂ ਲੜਿ ਲਾਇ ॥ ਜੋ ਹਰਿ ਕੰਤਿ ਮਿਲਾਈਆ ਸਿ ਵਿਛੁੜਿ ਕਤਹਿ ਨ ਜਾਇ ॥ ਪ੍ਰਭ ਵਿਣੁ ਦੂਜਾ ਕੋ ਨਹੀ ਨਾਨਕ ਹਰਿ ਸਰਣਾਇ ॥ ਅਸੂ ਸੁਖੀ ਵਸੰਦੀਆ ਜਿਨਾ ਮਇਆ ਹਰਿ ਰਾਇ ॥ ੮ ॥ (ਪੰਨਾ ੧੩੪ ਅੰ.ਘ.)

Like coal, after lying unexplored in the mines, for centuries together, becomes gas, eventually, so does the combination of meditation and prayer transform Attachment into LOVE, of the highest order. While the former demands sacrifice, the latter offers sacrifice, totally unconditional, without any strings attached. LOVE is sharing with, and giving away, everything, to the Beloved. Sacrifice is always made towards, and in favour of, a superior entity (material or person). A devotee sacrifices his egocentric-nature to reach/approach GOD. Similarly, man loves someone whom he considers to be greater and better, than him, in attributes, power, knowledge, et-al .

Such becomes the mental-frame of one in Love. This is the Pinnacle & Zenith of Humility & Love. In the sugarcane, if there is a knot, it would, for sure, leave a feeling of tastelessness, in the mouth. And this would mean Loss-of-Love.

If there is to be found a knot of selfishness, in the fiber-of-love, it becomes futile, as Love denotes selflessness, under all circumstances. Love between mortals (of opposite sexes) has been the subject of much heated debates, over the millennia. In the Indian sub-continent, which is a civilization dating back to several thousands of years, there lived lovers, who could rise over and above LUST, and provided a new and refreshing dimension to the deep meaning and essence of LOVE. In the process, after conquering Lust, they gave a damn for family status, prestige, and caste-barriers, and continued to Love one another. And sacrificed their lives, to uphold, and prove, the sanctity of their LOVE. It was of no consequence to them if their love could not be consummated as a natural culmination of physical intimacy. All that mattered, to them, was living and dying, in Love, and all of that, only for the sake of Love, pure and sacred and sublime, the highest Godly-attribute.

God was, is, and shall always be. He sustains and destroys all. Know that these Holy people are true, Says Nanak; they are in love with the Lord. The mortal is engrossed in sweet words and transitory pleasures which shall soon fade away. Disease, sorrow and separation afflict him; says Nanak, such a one never finds peace, even in dreams.[64]

Love purifies the heart, the mind, the soul, and the body, and the human-frame, now, assumes the super-structure of a SANCTUM SANCTORUM, where GOD loves to reside, until eternity. God can be witnessed in the radiance that emanates from the faces of such persons, whose gleam and glow illumines the darkest corridors, of the hearts of the loveless-ones.

---

[64] ਹੋਜੋ ਹੈ ਹੋਵੰਤੇ ਹਰਣ ਭਰਣ ਸੰਪੂਰਣਃ ॥ ਸਾਧੂ ਸਤਮ ਜਾਣੋ ਨਾਨਕ ਪ੍ਰੀਤਿ ਕਾਰਣੰ ॥ ੨੩ ॥ ਸੁਖੇਣ ਬੈਣ ਰਤਨੰ ਰਚਨੰ ਕਸੁੰਭ ਰੰਗਣਃ ॥ ਰੋਗ ਸੋਗ ਬਿਓਗੰ ਨਾਨਕ ਸੁਖੁ ਨ ਸੁਪਨਹ ॥ ੨੪ ॥ (pg. 1361 A.G.)

Woman and Man are complements, as well as supplements, to each other. The mutual attraction between the two magnetic fields is, but, natural, because man has certain female hormones/genes in him, and vice -versa.

The female is in the male, and the male is in the female. Understand this, O God-realized being! The meditation is in the music, and knowledge is in meditation. Become a Devotee, and speak the Language of Love, Faith and Trust (with, and in, GOD). The Light is in the mind, and the mind is in the Light. The Guru brings the five senses together, like brothers. Nanak is, forever, a sacrifice unto those who relish the love of God, and cherish God's Name. [65]

Some of the characteristics of the female are : Devotion, Faith & Trust, Hesitation, Charm, Tolerance.   And the male traits may be summarized as : Physical strength, Multi-faceted - thought- processes, Courage-of-conviction, Fearlessness. (This is a generalized statement, with the obvious possibility of exceptions).

While jealousy is the "forte" of a woman, the equivalent, in a male, is "egocentricism", which are, both, immensely, negative aspects of the human-personality.   Serious conflicts and clashes are a natural consequence of such a scenario.   When such a discord acquires fatal-proportions, relationships get torn, asunder, thereby leading to misery and self-inflicted psychological, emotional, mental, and physical problems.

The insatiable appetite for power and authority has led man to assume the leadership-roles in a variety of spheres of endeavor, namely politics, religion, business, warfare, and the larger society, in general.

---

[65] ਪੁਰਖ ਮਹਿ ਨਾਰਿ ਨਾਰਿ ਮਹਿ ਪੁਰਖਾ ਬੂਝਹੁ ਬ੍ਰਹਮ ਗਿਆਨੀ ॥ ਧੁਨਿ ਮਹਿ ਧਿਆਨੁ ਧਿਆਨ ਮਹਿ ਜਾਨਿਆ ਗੁਰਮੁਖਿ ਅਕਥ ਕਹਾਨੀ ॥ ੩ ॥ ਮਨ ਮਹਿ ਜੋਤਿ ਜੋਤਿ ਮਹਿ ਮਨੂਆ ਪੰਚ ਮਿਲੇ ਗੁਰ ਭਾਈ ॥ ਨਾਨਕ ਤਿਨ ਕੈ ਸਦ ਬਲਿਹਾਰੀ ਜਿਨ ਏਕ ਸਬਦਿ ਲਿਵ ਲਾਈ ॥ ੪ ॥ ੯ ॥ (pg. 879 of A.G.)

With the passage of time, most of the major religious-scriptures came to be authored by men, the major political-leaders were men, the world's most popular and populous religions came to be founded by men, not to mention the innumerable power-hungry invaders and tyrant rulers, all of whom happened to be men. All this had a direct, adverse bearing on the position of the female. Some thinkers and philosophers, naturally men, had the courage to classify women as "Insignificant, irrelevant ones". Women were castigated, oppressed, subjugated, tortured, exploited in all manners, possible, and were relegated to the background, in all matters.

From woman, man is born; within woman, man is conceived; to woman he is engaged and married. Woman becomes his friend; through woman, the future generations come. When his woman dies, he seeks another woman; to woman he is bound. So why call her low? From her, kings are born. From woman, woman is born; without woman, there would be no one at all. Only the True Lord is without a woman. That mouth which praises the Lord continually is blessed and beautiful. Says Nanak, those faces shall be radiant in the Court of the True Lord. [66]

This new thought brought about a radical transformation in the terrorized rank and file of the oppressed womenfolk.

Hence, the inference is that the Mother is responsible, in a majority of the cases, for the upbringing and success of her children. Therefore her contribution to the society should be recognized, and her writ should run, parallel and concurrent, to that of man.

The human -frame is a Temple, erected by God, himself, and the Home is a Temple-of-Understanding, created by Woman and Man. Only when they respect and love each other, with humility and grace, witnessing God, in each other's Body, shall their home be blessed, where peace, harmony and tranquility and serenity shall prevail.

---

[66] ਭੰਡਿ ਜੰਮੀਐ ਭੰਡਿ ਨਿੰਮੀਐ ਭੰਡਿ ਮੰਗਣੁ ਵੀਆਹੁ ॥ ਭੰਡਹੁ ਹੋਵੈ ਦੋਸਤੀ ਭੰਡਹੁ ਚਲੈ ਰਾਹੁ ॥ ਭੰਡੁ ਮੁਆ ਭੰਡੁ ਭਾਲੀਐ ਭੰਡਿ ਹੋਵੈ ਬੰਧਾਨੁ ॥ ਸੋ ਕਿਉ ਮੰਦਾ ਆਖੀਐ ਜਿਤੁ ਜੰਮਹਿ ਰਾਜਾਨ ॥ ਭੰਡਹੁ ਹੀ ਭੰਡੁ ਉਪਜੈ ਭੰਡੈ ਬਾਝੁ ਨ ਕੋਇ ॥ ਨਾਨਕ ਭੰਡੈ ਬਾਹਰਾ ਏਕੋ ਸਚਾ ਸੋਇ ॥ ਜਿਤੁ ਮੁਖਿ ਸਦਾ ਸਾਲਾਹੀਐ ਭਾਗਾ ਰਤੀ ਚਾਰਿ ॥ ਨਾਨਕ ਤੇ ਮੁਖ ਉਜਲੇ ਤਿਤੁ ਸਚੈ ਦਰਬਾਰਿ ॥ ੨ ॥ (Pg.473 A.G.)

Nobody is my enemy, and I am no one's enemy. God, who expanded His expanse, is within all; I learned this from the True Guru. I am a friend to all; I am everyone's friend. When the sense of separation was removed from my mind, then I was united with the Lord, my King. My stubbornness is gone, Ambrosial Nectar rains down, and the Word of the Guru's Holy hymns seems so sweet to me. He is pervading everywhere, in the water, on the land and in the sky; Nanak beholds the all-pervading Lord. [67]

He is your friend, your companion, your very best friend, who imparts the Teachings of the Lord. Nanak is a sacrifice to one who chants the Name of the Lord.[68]

If you make friends with the self-willed ones, O friend, how can you expect peace? Make friends with the evolved souls, and focus your consciousness on the True Guru. The root of birth and death will be cut away, and then, you shall find peace, O friend. The Lord Himself instructs those who are misguided, when He casts His Glance of Grace. Those who are not blessed by His Glance of Grace, cry and weep and wail. [69]

---

[67] ਨਾ ਕੋ ਮੇਰਾ ਦੁਸਮਨੁ ਰਹਿਆ ਨ ਹਮ ਕਿਸ ਕੇ ਬੈਰਾਈ ॥ ਬ੍ਰਹਮੁ ਪਸਾਰੁ ਪਸਾਰਿਓ ਭੀਤਰਿ ਸਤਿਗੁਰ ਤੇ ਸੋਝੀ ਪਾਈ ॥ ੨ ॥ ਸਭੁ ਕੋ ਮੀਤੁ ਹਮ ਆਪਨ ਕੀਨਾ ਹਮ ਸਭਨਾ ਕੇ ਸਾਜਨ ॥ ਦੂਰਿ ਪਰਾਇਓ ਮਨ ਕਾ ਬਿਰਹਾ ਤਾ ਮੇਲੁ ਕੀਓ ਮੇਰੈ ਰਾਜਨ ॥ ੩ ॥ ਬਿਨਸਿਓ ਢੀਠਾ ਅੰਮ੍ਰਿਤ ਵੂਠਾ ਸਬਦੁ ਲਗੋ ਗੁਰ ਮੀਠਾ ॥ ਜਲਿ ਥਲਿ ਮਹੀਅਲਿ ਸਰਬ ਨਿਵਾਸੀ ਨਾਨਕ ਰਮਈਆ ਢੀਠਾ ॥ ੪ ॥ ੩ ॥ (pg. 671 A.G.)

[68] ਸੋ ਸਾਜਨੁ ਸੋ ਸਖਾ ਮੀਤੁ ਜੋ ਹਰਿ ਕੀ ਮਤਿ ਦੇਇ ॥ ਨਾਨਕ ਤਿਸੁ ਬਲਿਹਾਰਣੈ ਹਰਿ ਹਰਿ ਨਾਮੁ ਜਪੇਇ ॥ ੨ ॥ (Pg.298 A.G.)

[69] ਮਨਮੁਖ ਸਉ ਕਰਿ ਦੋਸਤੀ ਸੁਖ ਕਿ ਪੁਛਹਿ ਮਿਤ ॥ ਗੁਰਮੁਖ ਸਉ ਕਰਿ ਦੋਸਤੀ ਸਤਿਗੁਰ ਸਉ ਲਾਇ ਚਿਤੁ ॥ ਜੰਮਣ ਮਰਣ ਕਾ ਮੂਲੁ ਕਟੀਐ ਤਾਂ ਸੁਖੁ ਹੋਵੀ ਮਿਤ ॥ ੬੬॥ ਭੁਲਿਆਂ ਆਪਿ ਸਮਝਾਇਸੀ ਜਾਕਉ ਨਦਰਿ ਕਰੇ ॥ ਨਾਨਕ ਨਦਰੀ ਬਾਹਰੀ ਕਰਣ ਪਲਾਹ ਕਰੇ ॥ ੬੭ ॥ (Pg.1421 A.G.)

In the beginning, He was pervading; in the middle, He is pervading; in the end, He will be pervading. He is the Transcendent Lord. The Saints remember in meditation the all-pervading Lord God. Says Nanak, the Lord of the Universe is the destroyer of all sins. See, hear, speak and implant the True Lord within your mind. He is all-pervading, permeating everywhere; Advises Nanak : be absorbed in the Lord's Love.[70]

Do not delay in practicing righteousness; delay in committing sins. Implant the Name of the Lord, within yourself, and abandon greed. In the Sanctuary of the Saints, the sinful residues of past mistakes are erased. The credential of righteousness is received by that person, with whom the Lord is pleased and satisfied. A person of shallow understanding withers away, in emotional attachment; he is engrossed in pursuits of sensual-pleasures, all his life. With youthful beauty and golden earrings, wondrous mansions, decorations and clothes — this is how Illusion clings onto him, and enslaves such a weak and meek person, whose resilience hath hit the lowest ebb. O'Eternal, Unchanging, Benevolent Lord, Nanak humbly prostrates before You. If there is birth, then there is death. Where there is pleasure, pain is not very distant. If enjoyment abounds, then then disease and misery should be following. If there is high, then there is low. If there is small, then there is great. If there is power, then there is pride. If there is egotistical pride, then there will be a fall. Engrossed in worldly ways, one is ruined. Meditating on the Lord of the Universe in the Company of the Holy, you shall become steady and stable. Nanak meditates on the Lord, for nothing and none else is Constant, everything being variable, fluctuating, oscillating and temporary.[71]

---

[70] ਆਦਿ ਪੂਰਨ ਮਧਿ ਪੂਰਨ ਅੰਤਿ ਪੂਰਨ ਪਰਮੇਸੁਰਹ ॥ ਸਿਮਰੰਤਿ ਸੰਤ ਸਰਬਤ੍ਰ ਰਮਣੰ ਨਾਨਕ ਅਘਨਾਸਨ ਜਗਦੀਸੁਰਹ ॥ ੧ ॥ ਪੇਖਨ ਸੁਨਨ ਸੁਨਾਵਨੋ ਮਨ ਮਹਿ ਦ੍ਰਿੜੀਐ ਸਾਚੁ ॥ ਪੂਰਿ ਰਹਿਓ ਸਰਬਤ੍ਰ ਮੈ ਨਾਨਕ ਹਰਿ ਰੰਗਿ ਰਾਚੁ ॥ ੨ ॥ (pg. 705 A.G.)

[71] ਨਹ ਬਿਲੰਬ ਧਰਮੰ ਬਿਲੰਬ ਪਾਪੰ ॥ ਦ੍ਰਿੜੰਤ ਨਾਮੰ ਤਜੰਤ ਲੋਭੰ ॥ ਸਰਣਿ ਸੰਤੰ ਕਿਲਬਿਖ ਨਾਸੰ ਪ੍ਰਾਪਤੰ ਧਰਮ ਲਖਿਣ ॥ ਨਾਨਕ ਜਿਹ ਸੁਪ੍ਰਸੰਨ ਮਾਧਵਹ ॥ ੧੦ ॥ ਮਿਰਤ ਮੋਹੰ ਅਲਪ ਬੁਧੰ ਰਚੰਤਿ ਬਨਿਤਾ ਬਿਨੋਦ ਸਾਹੰ ॥ ਜੋਬਨ ਬਹਿਕ੍ਰਮ ਕਨਿਕ ਕੁੰਡਲਹ ॥ ਬਚਿਤ੍ਰ ਮੰਦਿਰ ਸੋਭੰਤਿ ਬਸਤ੍ਰਾ ਇਤ੍ਰੰਤ ਮਾਇਆ

There is none who could lay claim to acieving perfection, for GOD is the ONLY Perfect One.

Blessed is the company of an emancipated soul. His mere glance has the potential of awarding peace and solace to a tormented being. Touching His Feet, one's conduct and lifestyle become pure. Abiding in his company, one chants the Lord's Praise, and reaches the Court of the Supreme Lord. Adhering to his teachings, one's thinking becomes revolutionized. The heart is contented, and the soul's aspirations are fulfilled. Such a Guru is perfect; his Teachings are everlasting. Beholding his Ambrosial Glance, one becomes saintly. Endless are his virtuous qualities, and his worth cannot be appraised. One who pleases him is united with Him. The tongue is one, but His Praises are countless. The True Lord of perfection is Inaccessible, Incomprehensible, balanced in the state of Nirvaana. He is not sustained by food; He has no hatred or vengeance; He is the Giver of peace. Countless devotees continually bow in reverence to Him. In their hearts, they meditate on His Lotus Feet. One must always strive to enshrine His Pure Thoughts in one's mind, to attain a blessed life..

Only GOD, does not contract or expand, does not become small or big, and, hence, is COMPLETE, TOTAL, and the only PERFECT ONE. Anything incomplete becomes an eyesore, whether it's a statue, machinery, or an item of furniture, because in that state it is of no consequence, and of no avail, for it cannot be put to any usage. Similarly, an incomplete work of music, dance, prose or poetry is futile, as it cannot be enjoyed by anybody. A musical instrument would not render the notes. if the strings and chords are not attached to the main-frame.

Likewise, an imperfect human-being is disliked by all and sundry, and by GOD Himself, who seems to like those who have adopted, and incorporated, His Attributes, into their lifestyles.

ਬ੍ਰਹਪਿਤੰ ॥ ਹੇ ਅਚੁਤ ਸਰਣਿ ਸੰਤ ਨਾਨਕ ਭੋ ਭਗਵਾਨਏ ਨਮਹ ॥ ੧੧ ॥ ਜਨਮੰ ਤ ਮਰਣੰ ਹਰਖੰ ਤ ਸੋਗੰ ਭੋਗੰ ਤ ਰੋਗੰ ॥ ਉਚੰ ਤ ਨੀਚੰ ਨਾਨ੍ਾ ਸੁ ਮੂਚੰ ॥ ਰਾਜੰ ਤ ਮਾਨੰ ਅਭਿਮਾਨੰ ਤ ਹੀਨੰ ॥ ਪ੍ਰਵਿਰਤਿ ਮਾਰਗੰ ਵਰਤੰਤਿ ਬਿਨਾਸਨੰ ॥ ਗੋਬਿੰਦ ਭਜਨ ਸਾਧ ਸੰਗੇਣ ਅਸਥਿਰੰ ਨਾਨਕ ਭਗਵੰਤ ਭਜਨਾਸਨੰ ॥ ੧੨ ॥
(pg. 1354 A.G.)

52

A human-being thinks he would become perfect, with the accumulation of wealth and property, with the acquisition of power and prestige, by looking youthful and energetic and by procreating several offsprings, and by gaining knowledge and education and skills. But the ignorant creature does not realize that the state-of-perfection can be achieved only by Meditation and Selfless-Service, and not by getting involved in religion of rituals, or wasting time in leisure and enjoyment.

This is a Once-in-a-lifetime-Opportunity, hence the best possible effort must be made to utilize it for knowing God.

A human-being remains impure and imperfect, until such time as he merges heart and soul, into the Ultimate Reality. A river attains finality on achieving unison with the vast expanses of the ocean. A seed becomes perfect and experiences the ecstasy and joy of completion/fruition, when it assumes the shape and form of a tree, yielding fruits and flowers. Man must reach the pinnacle of perfection, prior to hoping for a glimpse of the Zenith of Illumination & Glory, that GOD is.

These eyes have seen a great many leave. All are worried about themselves, and so am I bothered at my own plight, laments Fareed. If you reform yourself, you shall meet Me, and meeting Me, you shall be at peace. When you become Mine, the whole world will be yours.[72]
(The "ME" & "MINE", hereinabove, refer to GOD, and not to the composer of the Verse : SHEIKH FAREED, a mystic and thinker).

Just as man likes to have decorated, organized and beautiful objects and people, so does God want to adopt only such humans, who are disciplined, in all senses of the word. Only spiritually-inclined, truthful, just, compassionate, morally and ethically-clear people get the privilege of attaining Communion-with-GOD.

The entire Universe is functioning in consonance with the Laws & Discipline, enshrined in the Unwritten Constitution of the Nature, authored by GOD.

Bricks must be laid out, in a certain mode or array, in order that a straight wall be raised. And, all mechanisms must function in accordance with a planned structure or design, involving operations and optimum utilization and desired results.

Similarly, the human body is a very complicated example of a machine, so intricately designed and organized. Some functions are automatic, and remote-controlled (saliva-formation, perspiration, blood-circulation, urine and foecus-discharge, hormones, semen and sperm, the process of ovulation and child-birth etc.: the list is endless). Other movements of the body are controlled by the nervous-system (brain) whose co-ordinated commands are received and implemented by the various sensory and motor organs.

---

[72] ਏਨੀ ਲੋਇਣੀ ਦੇਖਦਿਆ ਕੇਤੀ ਚਲਿ ਗਈ ॥ ਫਰੀਦਾ ਲੋਕਾਂ ਆਪੋ ਆਪਣੀ ਮੈ ਆਪਣੀ ਪਈ ॥ ੯੪ ॥ ਆਪੁ ਸਵਾਰਹਿ ਮੈ ਮਿਲਹਿ ਮੈ ਮਿਲਿਆ ਸੁਖੁ ਹੋਇ ॥ ਫਰੀਦਾ ਜੇ ਤੂੰ ਮੇਰਾ ਹੋਇ ਰਹਿ ਸਭੁ ਜਗੁ ਤੇਰਾ ਹੋਇ ॥ ੯੫ ॥ ਕੰਧੀ ਉਤੈ ਰੁਖੜਾ ਕਿਚਰਕੁ ਬੰਨੈ ਧੀਰੁ ॥ ਫਰੀਦਾ ਕਚੈ ਭਾਂਡੈ ਰਖੀਐ ਕਿਚਰ ਤਾਈ ਨੀਰੁ ॥ ੯੬ ॥ (pg. 1382 A.G.)

Words, when organized in a certain fashion, yield the effect of poetry or prose. The disciplining of instruments and vocal-chords result in music. And the co-ordinated movements of the limbs and gesticulations (involving facial expressions) produce the beautiful art-form of dance. All this is a direct consequence of the DISCIPLINE that GOD adhered to, while carving out this super-structure, comprising a brain, a heart, the senses, bones, flesh and blood, with air and water, as significant ingredients. Discipline gives peace, joy and happiness, to self and others. Otherwise, its bound to be all misery, pain and jeopardy.

To become organized and to master the Godly-Attributes (to attain them) of calm and composure, compassion and concession, contentment and compromise, one needs to perform serious meditation, and to exercise extreme control over the mind. On the contrary, no special or extra effort is required to become a crazy maniac, a cruel marauder, a sadist, a lustful rapist, or a greedy miser. Water has the natural tendency to flow downhill . But, extra pressure has to be built-up for pumping up water, to a height greater than its original source or level.

Man has succeeded in providing a disciplined-structure and shape to various aspects of life, but, ironically, life (itself) has NOT been disciplined. Intensive and laborious effort produced crops, turned raw gold into ornaments, gave clay the form of decorative artifacts, and chiseled out stone to get life-like statues. Alas, only if a fraction of this discipline would illumine the life of the modern man. This is possible with personal will and desire and effort, on the part of the creature.

In the Fear of God, the winds ever blow. In the Fear of God, thousands of rivers flow. In the Fear of God, fire engulfs all. In the Fear of God, the earth is crushed under its burden. In the Fear of God, the clouds move across the sky. In the Fear of God, the Righteous Judge of Dharma stands at His Door. In the Fear of God, the sun shines, and in the Fear of God, the moon reflects. They traverse millions of miles, endlessly. In the Fear of God, the Siddhas exist, as do the Buddhas, the demi-gods and Yogis. In the Fear of God, the Akaashic (heavenly) ethers are stretched across the sky. In the Fear of God, the warriors and the most powerful heroes exist. In the Fear of God, multitudes come and go. God has inscribed the Inscription of His Fear upon the fore-heads of all. Declares Nanak : the Fearless Lord, the Formless Lord, the True Lord, is One.[73]

---

[73] ਭੈ ਵਿਚਿ ਪਵਣੁ ਵਹੈ ਸਦਵਾਉ ॥ ਭੈ ਵਿਚਿ ਚਲਹਿ ਲਖ ਦਰੀਆਉ ॥ ਭੈ ਵਿਚਿ ਅਗਨਿ ਕਢੈ ਵੇਗਾਰਿ ॥ ਭੈ ਵਿਚਿ ਧਰਤੀ ਦਬੀ ਭਾਰਿ ॥ ਭੈ ਵਿਚਿ ਇੰਦੁ ਫਿਰੈ ਸਿਰ ਭਾਰਿ ॥ ਭੈ ਵਿਚਿ ਰਾਜਾ ਧਰਮੁ ਦੁਆਰੁ ॥ ਭੈ ਵਿਚਿ ਸੂਰਜੁ ਭੈ ਵਿਚਿ ਚੰਦੁ ॥ ਕੋਹ ਕਰੋੜੀ ਚਲਤ ਨ ਅੰਤੁ ॥ ਭੈ ਵਿਚਿ ਸਿਧ ਬੁਧ ਸੁਰ ਨਾਥ ॥ ਭੈ ਵਿਚਿ ਆਡਾਣੇ ਆਕਾਸ ॥ ਭੈ ਵਿਚਿ ਜੋਧ ਮਹਾਬਲ ਸੂਰ ॥ ਭੈ ਵਿਚਿ ਆਵਹਿ ਜਾਵਹਿ ਪੂਰ ॥ ਸਗਲਿਆ ਭਉ ਲਿਖਿਆ ਸਿਰਿ ਲੇਖੁ ॥ ਨਾਨਕ ਨਿਰਭਉ ਨਿਰੰਕਾਰੁ ਸਚੁ ਏਕੁ ॥ ੧ ॥ (Pg.464 A.G.)

To practice forgiveness is the true form of fasting, good conduct and contentment. Disease does not afflict me, nor does the pain of death. I am liberated, and absorbed into God, who has no form or feature. [74]

Searching, endlessly, I drink in the Ambrosial Nectar. I have adopted the way of tolerance, and surrendered my mind to the True Guru. [75]

Abide in truth and contentment, O humble Siblings of Destiny. Hold tight to compassion and the Sanctuary of the True Guru. Know your soul, and know the Supreme Soul; associating with the Guru, you shall be emancipated. [76]

If the soul-bride adorns herself with compassion and forgiveness, God is pleased, and her mind is illumined with the lamp of the Guru's wisdom. With happiness and ecstasy, my God enjoys her; I offer each and every bit of my soul to Him. [77]

Those who have truth as their fast, contentment as their sacred shrine of pilgrimage, spiritual wisdom and meditation as their cleansing bath, kindness as their deity, and forgiveness as their chanting beads, are the really emancipated souls. Those who adopt the Way of the Lord, as their loin-cloth, and intuitive awareness as their ritualistically purified enclosure, and good deeds as their ceremonial fore-head mark, and love their food, such souls, says Nanak, are very rare. [78]

---

[74] ਖਿਮਾ ਗਹੀ ਬ੍ਰਤੁ ਸੀਲ ਸੰਤੋਖੰ ॥ ਰੋਗੁ ਨ ਬਿਆਪੈ ਨਾ ਜਮ ਦੋਖੰ ॥ ਮੁਕਤ ਭਏ ਪ੍ਰਭ ਰੂਪ ਨ ਰੇਖੰ ॥ ੧ ॥ (pg. 223 A.G.)

[75] ਖੋਜਤ ਖੋਜਤ ਅੰਮ੍ਰਿਤੁ ਪੀਆ ॥ ਖਿਮਾ ਗਹੀ ਮਨੁ ਸਤਗੁਰਿ ਦੀਆ ॥ (Pg.932 A.G.)

[76] ਖਿਮਾ ਗਹਹੁ ਸਤਿਗੁਰ ਸਰਣਾਈ ॥ ਆਤਮੁ ਚੀਨਿ ਪਰਾਤਮੁ ਚੀਨਹੁ ਗੁਰ ਸੰਗਤਿ ਇਹੁ ਨਿਸਤਾਰਾ ਹੇ ॥ ੮ ॥ (Pg.1030 A.G.)

[77] ਖਿਮਾ ਸੀਗਾਰ ਕਰੇ ਪ੍ਰਭ ਖੁਸੀਆ ਮਨਿ ਦੀਪਕ ਗੁਰ ਗਿਆਨੁ ਬਲਈਆ ॥ ਰਸਿ ਰਸਿ ਭੋਗ ਕਰੇ ਪ੍ਰਭ ਮੇਰਾ ਹਮ ਤਿਸੁ ਆਗੈ ਜੀਉ ਕਟਿ ਕਟਿ ਪਈਆ ॥ ੫ ॥ (Pg.836 A.G.)

[78] ਸਚੁ ਵਰਤੁ ਸੰਤੋਖੁ ਤੀਰਥੁ ਗਿਆਨੁ ਧਿਆਨੁ ਇਸਨਾਨੁ ॥ ਦਇਆ ਦੇਵਤਾ ਖਿਮਾ ਜਪਮਾਲੀ ਤੇ ਮਾਣਸ ਪਰਧਾਨ ॥ ਜੁਗਤਿ ਧੋਤੀ ਸੁਰਤਿ ਚਉਕਾ ਤਿਲਕੁ ਕਰਣੀ ਹੋਇ ॥ ਭਾਉ ਭੋਜਨੁ ਨਾਨਕਾ ਵਿਰਲਾ ਤ ਕੋਈ

Without patience and forgiveness, countless hundreds of thousands have perished. Their numbers cannot be counted; how could I count them? Tormented and bewildered, an infinite number have died. One who realizes his Lord and Master is set free, and not bound. By the blessing of the Lord's Word, enter the Mansion of the Lord's Presence; you shall be blessed with patience, forgiveness, truth and peace. And you shall be unfettered. Partake of the true wealth of meditation, and the Lord Himself shall abide within your body. Chant His Glorious Virtues forever; courage and composure shall enter deep within your mind. Through egotism, one is distracted and ruined; other than the Lord, all things are corrupt. Forming His creatures, He placed Himself within them; the Creator is unattached and infinite.[79]

ਕੋਇ ॥ ੧ ॥ (Pg. 1245 A.G.)

[79] ਖਿਮਾ ਵਿਹੂਣੇ ਖਪਿ ਗਏ ਖੂਹਣਿ ਲਖ ਅਸੰਖ ॥ ਗਣਤ ਨ ਆਵੈ ਕਿਉ ਗਣੀ ਖਪਿ ਖਪਿ ਮੁਏ ਬਿਸੰਖ ॥ ਖਸਮੁ ਪਛਾਣੈ ਆਪਣਾ ਖੁਲੈ ਬੰਧੁ ਨ ਪਾਇ ॥ ਸਬਦਿ ਮਹਲੀ ਖਰਾ ਤੂ ਖਿਮਾ ਸਚੁ ਸੁਖ ਭਾਇ ॥ ਖਰਚੁ ਖਰਾ ਧਨੁ ਧਿਆਨੁ ਤੂ ਆਪੇ ਵਸਹਿ ਸਰੀਰਿ ॥ ਮਨਿ ਤਨਿ ਮੁਖਿ ਜਾਪੈ ਸਦਾ ਗੁਣ ਅੰਤਰਿ ਮਨਿ ਧੀਰ ॥ ਹਉਮੈ ਖਪੈ ਖਪਾਇਸੀ ਬੀਜਉ ਵਥੁ ਵਿਕਾਰੁ ॥ ਜੰਤ ਉਪਾਇ ਵਿਚਿ ਪਾਇਆਨੁ ਕਰਤਾ ਅਲਗੁ ਅਪਾਰੁ ॥ ੪੯ ॥ (pg. 937 A.G.)

The chosen ones, the self-elect, are accepted and approved. The chosen ones are honoured in the Court of the Lord. The chosen ones look beautiful in the courts of kings. The chosen ones meditate single-mindedly on the Guru. No matter how much anyone tries to explain and describe them, the actions of the Creator cannot be counted and narrated. The mythical bull is called Dharma (Righteousness), the son of compassion; this is what patiently holds the earth in its place. One who understands this becomes truthful. What a great load there is on the bull! So many worlds beyond this world—so very many! What power holds them, and supports their weight? The names and the colours of the assorted species of beings were all inscribed by the Ever-flowing Pen of God. Who could ever dream of keeping track of all of these. Just imagine what a huge scroll it would take require. But what power does any mortal have to perform this gigantic, Herculean Task. What fascinating beauty! And what gifts! Who can know their extent? You created the vast expanse of the Universe with One Word! Hundreds of thousands of rivers began to flow. How can Your Creative Potency be described? I cannot even once be a sacrifice to You. Whatever pleases You is the only good done, You, Eternal and Formless One! [80]

Make compassion the cotton, contentment the thread, modesty the knot and truth the twist. This is the sacred thread of the soul; if you have it, then go ahead and put it on me. It does not break, it cannot be soiled by filth, it cannot be burnt, or lost. Blessed are those mortal beings, says Nanak, who wear such a thread around their necks. You buy the

---

[80]ਪੰਚ ਪਰਵਾਣ ਪੰਚ ਪਰਧਾਨੁ ॥ ਪੰਚੇ ਪਾਵਹਿ ਦਰਗਹਿ ਮਾਨੁ ॥ ਪੰਚੇ ਸੋਹਹਿ ਦਰਿ ਰਾਜਾਨੁ ॥ ਪੰਚਾ ਕਾ ਗੁਰੁ ਏਕੁ ਧਿਆਨੁ ॥ ਜੇ ਕੋ ਕਹੈ ਕਰੈ ਵਿਚਾਰੁ ॥ ਕਰਤੇ ਕੈ ਕਰਣੈ ਨਾਹੀ ਸੁਮਾਰੁ ॥ ਧੌਲੁ ਧਰਮੁ ਦਇਆ ਕਾ ਪੂਤੁ ॥ ਸੰਤੋਖੁ ਥਾਪਿ ਰਖਿਆ ਜਿਨਿ ਸੂਤਿ ॥ ਜੇ ਕੋ ਬੁਝੈ ਹੋਵੈ ਸਚਿਆਰੁ ॥ ਧਵਲੈ ਉਪਰਿ ਕੇਤਾ ਭਾਰੁ ॥ ਧਰਤੀ ਹੋਰੁ ਪਰੈ ਹੋਰੁ ਹੋਰੁ ॥ ਤਿਸ ਤੇ ਭਾਰੁ ਤਲੈ ਕਵਣੁ ਜੋਰੁ ॥ ਜੀਅ ਜਾਤਿ ਰੰਗਾ ਕੇ ਨਾਵ ॥ ਸਭਨਾ ਲਿਖਿਆ ਵੁੜੀ ਕਲਾਮ ॥ ਏਹੁ ਲੇਖਾ ਲਿਖਿ ਜਾਣੈ ਕੋਇ ॥ ਲੇਖਾ ਲਿਖਿਆ ਕੇਤਾ ਹੋਇ ॥ ਕੇਤਾ ਤਾਣੁ ਸੁਆਲਿਹੁ ਰੂਪੁ ॥ ਕੇਤੀ ਦਾਤਿ ਜਾਣੈ ਕੌਣੁ ਕੂਤੁ ॥ ਕੀਤਾ ਪਸਾਉ ਏਕੋ ਕਵਾਉ ॥ ਤਿਸ ਤੇ ਹੋਏ ਲਖ ਦਰੀਆਉ ॥ ਕੁਦਰਤਿ ਕਵਣ ਕਹਾ ਵੀਚਾਰੁ ॥ ਵਾਰਿਆ ਨ ਜਾਵਾ ਏਕ ਵਾਰ ॥ ਜੋ ਤੁਧੁ ਭਾਵੈ ਸਾਈ ਭਲੀ ਕਾਰ ॥ ਤੂ ਸਦਾ ਸਲਾਮਤਿ ਨਿਰੰਕਾਰ ॥ ੧੬ ॥ (pg. 3 A.G.)

thread for a few shells, and seated in your enclosure, you put it on. Whispering instructions into others' ears, the Brahmin becomes a guru. But the recipient dies, and the sacred thread falls away, and the soul departs without it.[81]

If you are wise, be simple; if you are powerful, be weak; and when there is nothing to share, then share with others. How rare is such a devotee. Do not utter even a single harsh word; your True Lord and Master abides in all. Do not break anyone's heart; these are all priceless jewels.[82]

One who works for what he eats, and gives some of what he has, Says Nanak, he knows the Path.[83]

Compassion and contentment are intertwined-entities. Both lend discipline to Life. Only a compassionate person would be of service to others, and only a contented person could meditate, in tranquility and serenity. An uncontented person shall always be complaining of the lack of everything, in life (wealth, children, comforts, status), or about everything that went wrong (losses, ill-health, etc.).

God likes contented people, and answers their prayers. HE grants them certain special powers of healing others, and bestows, upon them, certain skills and talents, which even some learned and experienced persons might lack, and envy.

While performing selfless-service, a person must strive to continue meditation, thus lending a unique radiance and vibrance to the already

---

[81] ਦਇਆ ਕਪਾਹ ਸੰਤੋਖੁ ਸੂਤੁ ਜਤੁ ਗੰਢੀ ਸਤੁ ਵਟੁ ॥ ਏਹੁ ਜਨੇਊ ਜੀਅ ਕਾ ਹਈ ਤ ਪਾਡੇ ਘਤੁ ॥ ਨਾ ਏਹੁ ਤੁਟੈ ਨ ਮਲੁ ਲਗੈ ਨਾ ਏਹੁ ਜਲੈ ਨ ਜਾਇ ॥ ਧੰਨੁ ਸੁ ਮਾਣਸ ਨਾਨਕਾ ਜੋ ਗਲਿ ਚਲੇ ਪਾਇ ॥ ਚਉਕੜਿ ਮੁਲਿ ਅਣਾਇਆ ਬਹਿ ਚਉਕੈ ਪਾਇਆ ॥ ਸਿਖਾ ਕੰਨਿ ਚੜਾਈਆ ਗੁਰੁ ਬ੍ਰਾਹਮਣੁ ਥਿਆ ॥ ਓਹੁ ਮੁਆ ਓਹੁ ਝੜਿ ਪਇਆ ਵੇਤਗਾ ਗਇਆ ॥ ੧ ॥ (Pg.471 A.G.)

[82] ਮਤਿ ਹੋਦੀ ਹੋਇ ਇਆਣਾ ॥ ਤਾਣ ਹੋਦੇ ਹੋਇ ਨਿਤਾਣਾ ॥ ਅਣਹੋਦੇ ਆਪੁ ਵੰਡਾਏ ॥ ਕੋ ਐਸਾ ਭਗਤੁ ਸਦਾਏ ॥ ੧੨੮ ॥ ਇਕੁ ਫਿਕਾ ਨ ਗਾਲਾਇ ਸਭਨਾ ਮੈ ਸਚਾ ਧਣੀ ॥ ਹਿਆਉ ਨ ਕੈਹੀ ਠਾਹਿ ਮਾਣਕ ਸਭ ਅਮੋਲਵੇ ॥ ੧੨੯ ॥ (Pg.1384 A.G.)

[83] ਘਾਲਿ ਖਾਇ ਕਿਛੁ ਹਥਹੁ ਦੇਇ ॥ ਨਾਨਕ ਰਾਹੁ ਪਛਾਣਹਿ ਸੇਇ ॥ ੧ ॥ (Pg.1245 A.G.)

bejeweled Mind-with-a-religious-temper. It's then that the ornamentation of the 'Bride' becomes complete, replete with God's Name.

Religion, sans compassion and meditation and service, is like a 'corpse', rotten in substance, and releasing odours, despised by all.

The sight of a compassionate person is equivalent to bathing at the places of pilgrimage, in the holy-waters.

Without compassion, all service is a hoax. This, then, cannot be termed as an exemplary service to humankind. There would be eternal bliss in any selfless service performed with compassion.

Without contentment, meditation becomes another ordinary ritual done according to a routine schedule, and ritual gives birth to egocentrism of the worst kind. Where there is meditation, the Primal Power resides there.

Says Sheikh Fareed : become the grass on the path, if you long for the Lord of all. One will cut you down, and another will trample you underfoot; then, you shall enter the Court of the Lord (once you become a humble person).[84]

The simmal tree is straight as an arrow; it is very tall, and very thick. But those birds which visit it hopefully, depart disappointed. Its fruits are tasteless, its flowers are nauseating, and its leaves are useless. Sweetness and humility, Says Nanak, are the essence of virtue and goodness. Nobody likes to prostrate bows down to another. When something is placed on the balancing scale and weighed, the side which descends is heavier. The sinner, like the deer hunter, bows down twice as much. But what can be achieved by bowing the head, when the heart is impure?[85]

Among all persons, the supreme person is the one who gives up his egotistical pride in the Company of the Holy. One who sees himself as lowly, shall be accounted as the highest of all. One whose mind is the dust of all, recognizes the Name of the Lord,, in each and every heart. One who eradicates cruelty from within his own mind, looks upon all the world as his friend. One who looks upon pleasure and pain as one and the same, Affirms Nanak, is not affected by sin or virtue. [86]

---

[84] ਫਰੀਦਾ ਥੀਉ ਪਵਾਹੀ ਦਭੁ ॥ ਜੇ ਸਾਂਈ ਲੋੜਹਿ ਸਭੁ ॥ ਇਕੁ ਛਿਜਹਿ ਬਿਆ ਲਤਾੜੀਅਹਿ ॥ ਤਾਂ ਸਾਈ ਦੈ ਦਰਿ ਵਾੜੀਅਹਿ ॥ ੧੬ ॥ (Pg.1378 A.G.)

[85] ਸਿੰਮਲ ਰੁਖੁ ਸਰਾਇਰਾ ਅਤਿ ਦੀਰਘ ਅਤਿ ਮੁਚੁ ॥ ਓਇ ਜਿ ਆਵਹਿ ਆਸ ਕਰਿ ਜਾਹਿ ਨਿਰਾਸੇ ਕਿਤੁ ॥ ਫਲ ਫਿਕੇ ਫੁਲ ਬਕਬਕੇ ਕੰਮਿ ਨ ਆਵਹਿ ਪਤ ॥ ਮਿਠਤੁ ਨੀਵੀ ਨਾਨਕਾ ਗੁਣ ਚੰਗਿਆਈਆ ਤਤੁ ॥ ਸਭੁ ਕੋ ਨਿਵੈ ਆਪ ਕਉ ਪਰ ਕਉ ਨਿਵੈ ਨ ਕੋਇ ॥ ਹਰਿ ਤਾਰਾਜੁ ਤੋਲੀਐ ਨਿਵੈ ਸੁ ਗਉਰਾ ਹੋਇ ॥ ਅਪਰਾਧੀ ਦੂਣਾ ਨਿਵੈ ਜੋ ਹੰਤਾ ਮਿਰਗਾਹਿ ॥ ਸੀਸਿ ਨਿਵਾਇਐ ਕਿਆ ਥੀਐ ਜਾ ਰਿਦੈ ਕੁਸੁਧੇ ਜਾਹਿ ॥ ੧ ॥ (Pg.470 A.G.)

[86] ਸਗਲ ਪੁਰਖ ਮਹਿ ਪੁਰਖੁ ਪ੍ਰਧਾਨੁ ॥ ਸਾਧਸੰਗਿ ਜਾ ਕਾ ਮਿਟੈ ਅਭਿਮਾਨੁ ॥ ਆਪਸ ਕਉ ਜੋ ਜਾਣੈ ਨੀਚਾ ॥ ਸੋਊ ਗਨੀਐ ਸਭ ਤੇ ਊਚਾ ॥ ਜਾ ਕਾ ਮਨੁ ਹੋਇ ਸਗਲ ਕੀ ਰੀਨਾ ॥ ਹਰਿ ਹਰਿ ਨਾਮੁ ਤਿਨਿ ਘਟਿ ਘਟਿ ਚੀਨਾ ॥ ਮਨ ਅਪੁਨੇ ਤੇ ਬੁਰਾ ਮਿਟਾਨਾ ॥ ਪੇਖੈ ਸਗਲ ਸ੍ਰਿਸਟਿ ਸਾਜਨਾ ॥ ਸੁਖ ਦੁਖ ਜਨ ਸਮ ਦ੍ਰਿਸਟੇਤਾ ॥ ਨਾਨਕ ਪਾਪ ਪੁੰਨ ਨਹੀ ਲੇਪਾ ॥ ੬ ॥ (pg. 266 A.G.)

If one becomes the slave of the Lord's slaves, then he finds the Lord, and eradicates ego from within. The Lord of bliss is his object of devotion; night and day, he sings the Glorious Praises of the Lord. Attuned to the Word of the Holy hymns, the Lord's devotees remain ever absorbed in the Lord. Dear Lord, Your Glance of Grace is True. Be merciful to Your slave, O Beloved Lord, and preserve my honour. [87]

Humility must not be misconstrued to imply timidity and weakness. It is, on the contrary, a powerful characteristic, that speaks volumes about the humble one's personality. The humble person is bestowed fame and fortune, even without asking (praying) for it. On the other hand, someone who seeks recognition, on account of one's wealth, status or knowledge, is not a humble person. Occasionally, one needs to remind oneself, of the destructibility of the human-body (by looking downwards, towards the earth, and at the dust and ashes, unto which this body shall merge).

---

[87] ਦਾਸਨਿ ਦਾਸੁ ਹੋਵੈ ਤਾ ਹਰਿ ਪਾਏ ਵਿਚਹੁ ਆਪੁ ਗਵਾਈ ॥ ਭਗਤਾ ਕਾ ਕਾਰਜੁ ਹਰਿ ਅਨੰਦੁ ਹੈ ਅਨਦਿਨੁ ਹਰਿ ਗੁਣ ਗਾਈ ॥ ਸਬਦਿ ਰਤੇ ਸਦਾ ਇਕ ਰੰਗੀ ਹਰਿ ਸਿਉ ਰਹੇ ਸਮਾਈ ॥ ੧ ॥ ਹਰਿ ਜੀਉ ਸਾਚੀ ਨਦਰਿ ਤੁਮਾਰੀ ॥ ਆਪਣਿਆ ਦਾਸਾ ਨੋ ਕ੍ਰਿਪਾ ਕਰਿ ਪਿਆਰੇ ਰਾਖਹੁ ਪੈਜ ਹਮਾਰੀ ॥ (pg. 600 A.G.)

XX : FAITH

One who has faith in the Guru comes to dwell upon God. He is acclaimed as a devotee, a humble devotee throughout the three worlds. The Lord resides in his heart. True are his actions; true are his ways. True is his heart; Truth is what he utters. True is his vision; true is his form. He distributes Truth and he spreads Truth. One who recognizes the Supreme Lord as The True ONE, that humble being immerses himself, in meditation, and merges his identity with THE SOLE ENTITY.[88]

And, this trust prods one onto realization of the self, and one's roots, which ultimately results in God-realization.

One must try, always, to remain in a state of equilibrium and stability, and never to let dilemma invade the mind. That's possible only when one tends to have an abiding faith in the Guru's sayings (Word / Command / Advice). On that foundation is the marvellous palace, having bejewelled walls, raised. Such a devotee is entitled to be the recipient of lavish eulogies and encomiums, all over, on the surface of earth, and has a rare and unique glow and radiance, on his face.[89]

Like, faith in Water leads one to the ultimate hope of thirst being quenched on drinking it. And, like faith in Sun reassures the needy, that its warmth shall prove to be comforting, on a cold, chilly-night, in the winters, Faith in the Supreme-Reality would lead one to the fulfillment of all worldly desires. And, finally, this faith and trust would assist the bearer, to be ferried across the Ocean-of-Fire (Life), in a befitting and honourable fashion. This would be Salvation, for an aspiring Soul.

---

[88] ਜਾ ਕੈ ਮਨਿ ਗੁਰ ਕੀ ਪਰਤੀਤਿ ॥ ਤਿਸੁ ਜਨ ਆਵੈ ਹਰਿ ਪ੍ਰਭੁ ਚੀਤਿ ॥ ਭਗਤੁ ਭਗਤੁ ਸੁਨੀਐ ਤਿਹੁ ਲੋਇ ॥ ਜਾ ਕੈ ਹਿਰਦੈ ਏਕੋ ਹੋਇ ॥ ਸਚੁ ਕਰਣੀ ਸਚੁ ਤਾ ਕੀ ਰਹਤ ॥ ਸਚੁ ਹਿਰਦੈ ਸਤਿ ਮੁਖਿ ਕਹਤ ॥ ਸਾਚੀ ਦ੍ਰਿਸਟਿ ਸਾਚਾ ਆਕਾਰੁ ॥ ਸਚੁ ਵਰਤੈ ਸਾਚਾ ਪਾਸਾਰੁ ॥ ਪਾਰਬ੍ਰਹਮੁ ਜਿਨਿ ਸਚੁ ਕਰਿ ਜਾਤਾ ॥ ਨਾਨਕ ਸੋ ਜਨੁ ਸਚਿ ਸਮਾਤਾ ॥ ੮ ॥ ੧੫ ॥ (pg. 283 A.G.)

[89] ਅਸਥਿਰੁ ਰਹਹੁ ਡੋਲਹੁ ਮਤ ਕਬਹੂ ਗੁਰ ਕੈ ਬਚਨਿ ਅਧਾਰਿ ॥ ਜੈ ਜੈ ਕਾਰੁ ਸਗਲ ਭੂ ਮੰਡਲ ਮੁਖ ਊਜਲ ਦਰਬਾਰ ॥ ੩ ॥ ਜਿਨ ਕੇ ਜੀਅ ਤਿਨੈ ਹੀ ਫੇਰੇ ਆਪੇ ਭਇਆ ਸਹਾਈ ॥ ੪ ॥ ੪ ॥ ੨੮ ॥ (Pg. 678 A.G.)

64

XXI : TWIN CONCEPTS OF AN IDEAL-CITIZEN & AN IDEAL-SOCIETY

God's Kingdom is steady, stable and eternal. There is no second or third status; all are equal there. That city is populous and eternally famous. Those who live there are wealthy and contented. They stroll about freely, just as they please, and no one blocks their way. [90]

The True Guru is the Merciful Giver; He is always compassionate. The True Guru has no hatred within Him; He beholds the One God everywhere. Anyone who directs hate against the One who has no hate, shall never be satisfied within. The True Guru wishes everyone well; how can anything bad happen to Him? As one feels towards the True Guru, so are the rewards he receives. Says Nanak : the Creator knows everything; nothing can be hidden from Him. [91]

The Twin-Concepts are based on the express premise that an ideal society can thrive and survive only when the individuals, who constitute it, are contented, prosperous and happy. Only then could higher attainments be probable, in other fields like religion and spirituality.

Without the basic requirements being fulfilled, one can never have the peace-of-mind, a pre-requisite for Sincere Devotion & Meditation, which frame-of-mind would, then, prod one onto the path of expanding one's horizons, to think of the humanity, at large.

---

[90] ਕਾਇਮੁ ਦਾਇਮੁ ਸਦਾ ਪਾਤਿਸਾਹੀ ॥ ਦੋਮ ਨ ਸੇਮ ਏਕ ਸੋ ਆਹੀ ॥ ਆਬਾਦਾਨੁ ਸਦਾ ਮਸਹੂਰ ॥ ਉਹਾਂ ਗਨੀ ਬਸਹਿ ਮਾਮੂਰ ॥ ੨ ॥ ਤਿਉ ਤਿਉ ਸੈਲ ਕਰਹਿ ਜਿਉ ਭਾਵੈ ॥ਮਹਰਮ ਮਹਲ ਨ ਕੋ ਅਟਕਾਵੈ ॥ ਕਹਿ ਰਵਿਦਾਸ ਖਲਾਸ ਚਮਾਰਾ ॥ ਜੋ ਹਮ ਸਹਰੀ ਸੁ ਮੀਤੁ ਹਮਾਰਾ ॥ ੩ ॥ ੨ ॥ (Pg.345 A.G.)

[91] ਸਤਿਗੁਰੁ ਦਾਤਾ ਦਇਆਲੁ ਹੈ ਜਿਸ ਨੋ ਦਇਆ ਸਦਾ ਹੋਇ ॥ ਸਤਿਗੁਰੁ ਅੰਦਰਹੁ ਨਿਰਵੈਰੁ ਹੈ ਸਭੁ ਦੇਖੈ ਬ੍ਰਹਮੁ ਇਕੁ ਸੋਇ ॥ ਨਿਰਵੈਰਾ ਨਾਲਿ ਜਿ ਵੈਰੁ ਚਲਾਇਦੇ ਤਿਨ ਵਿਚਹੁ ਤਿਸਟਿਆ ਨ ਕੋਇ ॥ ਸਤਿਗੁਰੁ ਸਭਨਾ ਦਾ ਭਲਾ ਮਨਾਇਦਾ ਤਿਸ ਦਾ ਬੁਰਾ ਕਿਉ ਹੋਇ ॥ ਸਤਿਗੁਰ ਨੋ ਜੇਹਾ ਕੋ ਇਛਦਾ ਤੇਹਾ ਫਲੁ ਪਾਏ ਕੋਇ ॥ ਨਾਨਕ ਕਰਤਾ ਸਭੁ ਕਿਛੁ ਜਾਣਦਾ ਜਿਦੁ ਕਿਛੁ ਗੁਝਾ ਨ ਹੋਇ ॥ ੨ ॥ (Pg.302 A.G.)

The Ruler, King or the Establishment/Government should be endowed with such qualities, that the subjects could repose their trust and confidence, in that authority, without any fear or doubt, whatsoever. The Keyword, here, must be "SERVICE", and NOT "TYRANNY". Only if the reign is democratic and secular and tolerant and just shall it survive long enough.

The Four basic Postulates for a Contented Life have been thus formulated :

Piety, Wealth, Desire-Fulfillment, & Final-Emancipation.

All of these can be accomplished, and enjoyed, even while leading the regular life of a householder.

The position and relevance of womenfolk, in the body-politik and social-structure is of paramount import and significance. Being the one who bears and rears the future-leaders, in the fields of religion, politics, business, and all other important spheres of endeavor, a woman deserves the honor and esteem, that has been denied to her, for a long time, only until recently, when the winds of change brought about a "Renaissance & Revolution", for the betterment of humanity. The reverential treatment, given to women, now, is the ideal that the THIRD NANAK, Guru Amar Das had propounded and advocated, forcefully, centuries ago.

An individual must be strong, in all respects: spiritual, moral, religious, social, mental, psychological, emotional, financial. Its only then that one could discharge the obligations towards one's own soul and God, humankind and family, and to be so humble as to remain, always, accountable to the CREATOR.

Make your deals, O' traders, and take care of your merchandise. Buy that object which will go along with you. In the next world, the All-knowing Merchant will take this object and shall reward you. O Siblings of Destiny, chant the Lord's Name, and focus your consciousness on Him. Take the Merchandise of the Lord's Praises with you. Your Lord shall see this and approve. Those who do not have the Assets of Truth—how can they find peace? By dealing in falsehood, their minds and bodies become false. Like the deer caught in the trap, they suffer in terrible agony; they continually cry out in pain. The counterfeit coins are not put into the Treasury; they do not obtain the Blessed Vision of the Lord-Guru. The false ones have no social status or honor. No one succeeds through falsehood. Practicing falsehood again and again, people come and go in reincarnation, and forfeit their honor. Advises Nanak : instruct your mind through the Word of the Guru's Word, and praise the Lord. Those who are imbued with the love of the Name of the Lord are not burdened by doubt. Those who chant the Name of the Lord earn great profits; the Fearless Lord abides within their minds.[92]

Praise the Formless Lord in your mind. O my mind, make this your true occupation. Let your tongue become pure, to taste the Ambrosial Nectar. Your soul shall be, forever, peaceful. With your eyes, see the wondrous play of your Lord and Master. The Company of the Holy is the all-important one. With your feet, walk in the Way of the Lord. Sins are washed away, chanting the Lord's Name, even for a moment. Hence, perform the tasks assigned, to you, by the Lord, and listen to

---

[92] ਵਣਜੁ ਕਰਹੁ ਵਣਜਾਰਿਹੋ ਵਖਰੁ ਲੇਹੁ ਸਮਾਲਿ ॥ ਤੈਸੀ ਵਸਤੁ ਵਿਸਾਹੀਐ ਜੈਸੀ ਨਿਬਹੈ ਨਾਲਿ ॥ ਅਗੈ ਸਾਹੁ ਸੁਜਾਣੁ ਹੈ ਲੈਸੀ ਵਸਤੁ ਸਮਾਲਿ ॥ ੧ ॥ ਭਾਈ ਰੇ ਰਾਮੁ ਕਹਹੁ ਚਿਤੁ ਲਾਇ ॥ ਹਰਿ ਜਸੁ ਵਖਰੁ ਲੈ ਚਲਹੁ ਸਹੁ ਦੇਖੈ ਪਤੀਆਇ ॥ ੧ ॥ ਰਹਾਉ ॥ ਜਿਨਾ ਰਾਸਿ ਨ ਸਚੁ ਹੈ ਕਿਉ ਤਿਨਾ ਸੁਖੁ ਹੋਇ ॥ ਖੋਟੈ ਵਣਜਿ ਵਣੰਜਿਐ ਮਨੁ ਤਨੁ ਖੋਟਾ ਹੋਇ ॥ ਫਾਹੀ ਫਾਥੇ ਮਿਰਗ ਜਿਉ ਦੁਖੁ ਘਣੋ ਨਿਤ ਰੋਇ ॥ ੨ ॥ ਖੋਟੇ ਪੋਤੈ ਨਾ ਪਵਹਿ ਤਿਨ ਹਰਿ ਗੁਰ ਦਰਸੁ ਨ ਹੋਇ ॥ ਖੋਟੇ ਜਾਤਿ ਨ ਪਤਿ ਹੈ ਖੋਟਿ ਨ ਸੀਝਸਿ ਕੋਇ ॥ ਖੋਟੇ ਖੋਟੁ ਕਮਾਵਣਾ ਆਇ ਗਇਆ ਪਤਿ ਖੋਇ ॥ ੩ ॥ ਨਾਨਕ ਮਨੁ ਸਮਝਾਈਐ ਗੁਰ ਕੈ ਸਬਦਿ ਸਾਲਾਹ ॥ ਰਾਮ ਨਾਮ ਰੰਗਿ ਰਤਿਆ ਭਾਰੁ ਨ ਭਰਮੁ ਤਿਨਾਹ ॥ ਹਰਿ ਜਪਿ ਲਾਹਾ ਅਗਲਾ ਨਿਰਭਉ ਹਰਿ ਮਨ ਮਾਹ ॥ ੪ ॥ ੨੩ ॥ (Pg.22 A.G.)

the Lord's Sermon. In the Lord's Court, your face shall be radiant, so Promises Nanak. [93]

With greed within them, their minds are filthy, and they spread filth around. They indulge in filthy deeds, and suffer in pain. They deal in falsehood, and nothing but falsehood; telling lies, they suffer in pain. Rare is that person who enshrines the Immaculate Guru's Word within his mind. By Guru's Grace, his skepticism is removed. He walks in harmony with the Guru's Will, day and night; remembering the Name of the Lord, he attains peace. [94]

An ideal business is one from whose profits, society benefits. Such a businessperson is God's chosen one. His service to humanity, and his humanism shall be the cause of receiving rewards, forever, financially, and spiritually.

---

[93] ਉਸਤਤਿ ਮਨ ਮਹਿ ਕਰਿ ਨਿਰੰਕਾਰ ॥ ਕਰਿ ਮਨ ਮੇਰੇ ਸਤਿ ਬਿਉਹਾਰ ॥ ਨਿਰਮਲ ਰਸਨਾ ਅੰਮ੍ਰਿਤੁ ਪੀਉ ॥ ਸਦਾ ਸੁਹੇਲਾ ਕਰਿ ਲੇਹਿ ਜੀਉ ॥ ਨੈਨਹੁ ਪੇਖੁ ਠਾਕੁਰ ਕਾ ਰੰਗੁ ॥ ਸਾਧਸੰਗਿ ਬਿਨਸੈ ਸਭ ਸੰਗੁ ॥ ਚਰਨ ਚਲਉ ਮਾਰਗਿ ਗੋਬਿੰਦ ॥ ਮਿਟਹਿ ਪਾਪ ਜਪੀਐ ਹਰਿ ਬਿੰਦ ॥ ਕਰ ਹਰਿ ਕਰਮ ਸ੍ਰਵਨਿ ਹਰਿ ਕਥਾ ॥ ਹਰਿ ਦਰਗਹ ਨਾਨਕ ਉਜਲ ਮਥਾ ॥ ੨ ॥ (pg. 281 A.G.)

[94] ਅੰਤਰਿ ਲੋਭੁ ਮਨਿ ਮੈਲੈ ਮਲੁ ਲਾਏ ॥ ਮੈਲੇ ਕਰਮ ਕਰੇ ਦੁਖੁ ਪਾਏ ॥ ਕੂੜੋ ਕੂੜੁ ਕਰੇ ਵਾਪਾਰਾ ਕੂੜੁ ਬੋਲਿ ਦੁਖੁ ਪਾਇਦਾ ॥ ੧੨ ॥ ਨਿਰਮਲ ਬਾਣੀ ਕੋ ਮੰਨਿ ਵਸਾਏ ॥ ਗੁਰ ਪਰਸਾਦੀ ਸਹਸਾ ਜਾਏ ॥ ਗੁਰ ਕੈ ਭਾਣੈ ਚਲੈ ਦਿਨੁ ਰਾਤੀ ਨਾਮੁ ਚੇਤਿ ਸੁਖੁ ਪਾਇਦਾ ॥ ੧੩ ॥ (pg. 1062 A.G.)

From the One Light, the entire universe welled up. So who is good, and who is bad? : First, Allah created the Light; then, by His Creative Power, He made all mortal beings. O' Siblings of Destiny, do not wander deluded by doubt. The Creation is in the Creator, and the Creator is in the Creation, totally pervading and permeating all places. The clay is the same, but the Potter has fashioned it in various ways. There is nothing wrong with the pot of clay — there is nothing wrong with the Potter. The One True Lord abides in all; by His making, everything is made. Whoever realizes the Power of His Command, knows the One Lord. He alone is said to be the Lord's slave. The Lord is Invisible; The Guru has blessed me with this sweet molasses. Says Kabeer, my anxiety and fear have been taken away; I see the Immaculate Lord pervading everywhere. Do not say that the Vedas, the Bible and the Koran are false. Those who do not contemplate them are false.[95]

If a beggar cries out at the door, the Master hears it in His Mansion. Whether He receives him or pushes him away, it is Lord's decision. Recognize the Lord's Light within all, and do not consider social class or status; there are no classes or castes in the world hereafter (so why create distinctions, on earth). He Himself acts, and He Himself inspires us to act. He Himself considers our complaints. Since You, O' Creator, are the Doer, why should I submit to the world?[96]

---

[95] ਅਵਲਿ ਅਲਹ ਨੂਰੁ ਉਪਾਇਆ ਕੁਦਰਤਿ ਕੇ ਸਭ ਬੰਦੇ ॥ ਏਕ ਨੂਰ ਤੇ ਸਭੁ ਜਗੁ ਉਪਜਿਆ ਕਉਨ ਭਲੇ ਕੋ ਮੰਦੇ ॥ ੧ ॥ ਲੋਗਾ ਭਰਮਿ ਨ ਭੂਲਹੁ ਭਾਈ ॥ ਖਾਲਿਕੁ ਖਲਕ ਖਲਕ ਮਹਿ ਖਾਲਿਕੁ ਪੂਰਿ ਰਹਿਓ ਸ੍ਰਬ ਠਾਂਈ ॥ ੧ ॥ ਰਹਾਉ ॥ ਮਾਟੀ ਏਕ ਅਨੇਕ ਭਾਂਤਿ ਕਰਿ ਸਾਜੀ ਸਾਜਨਹਾਰੈ ॥ ਨਾ ਕਛੁ ਪੋਚ ਮਾਟੀ ਕੇ ਭਾਂਡੇ ਨਾ ਕਛੁ ਪੋਚ ਕੁੰਭਾਰੈ ॥ ੨ ॥ ਸਭ ਮਹਿ ਸਚਾ ਏਕੋ ਸੋਈ ਤਿਸ ਕਾ ਕੀਆ ਸਭੁ ਕਛੁ ਹੋਈ ॥ ਹੁਕਮੁ ਪਛਾਨੈ ਸੁ ਏਕੋ ਜਾਨੈ ਬੰਦਾ ਕਹੀਐ ਸੋਈ ॥ ੩ ॥ ਅਲਹੁ ਅਲਖੁ ਨ ਜਾਈ ਲਖਿਆ ਗੁਰਿ ਗੁੜੁ ਦੀਨਾ ਮੀਠਾ ॥ ਕਹਿ ਕਬੀਰ ਮੇਰੀ ਸੰਕਾ ਨਾਸੀ ਸਰਬ ਨਿਰੰਜਨੁ ਡੀਠਾ ॥ ੪ ॥ ੩ ॥ (Pg.1349-1350 A.G.)

[96] ਜੇ ਦਰਿ ਮਾਂਗਤੁ ਕੂਕ ਕਰੇ ਮਹਲੀ ਖਸਮੁ ਸੁਣੇ ॥ ਭਾਵੈ ਧੀਰਕ ਭਾਵੈ ਧਕੇ ਏਕ ਵਡਾਈ ਦੇਇ ॥ ੧ ॥ ਜਾਣਹੁ ਜੋਤਿ ਨ ਪੂਛਹੁ ਜਾਤੀ ਆਗੈ ਜਾਤਿ ਨ ਹੇ ॥ ੧ ॥ ਰਹਾਉ ॥ ਆਪਿ ਕਰਾਏ ਆਪਿ ਕਰੇਇ ॥ ਆਪਿ ਉਲਾਮੇ ਚਿਤਿ ਧਰੇਇ ॥ ਜਾ ਤੂੰ ਕਰਣਹਾਰੁ ਕਰਤਾਰੁ ॥ ਕਿਆ ਮੁਹਤਾਜੀ ਕਿਆ ਸੰਸਾਰੁ ॥ ੨ ॥ (Pg. 349 A.G.)

Tell me: who should we call good or bad? Behold the Lord ; the truth is revealed to the God-loving souls. I speak the Unspoken Speech of the Lord, adhering to the Guru's Teachings. I join the Guru's Congregation, and I find God's limits. The Shaastras, the Vedas, the Simritees and all their many secrets; bathing at the sixty-eight holy places of pilgrimage — all this is found by enshrining the sublime essence of the Lord in the heart. The ones with Godly-attributes are immaculately pure; no filth sticks to them. Says Nanak : the Name of the Lord, abides in the heart, by the greatest pre-ordained destiny.[97]

In the dwelling of the womb, there is no ancestry or social status. All have originated from the Seed of God. Tell me, O' religious scholar: since when have you been a preacher? Don't waste your life by continually claiming to be a preacher. If you are indeed a Brahmin (considered to be one of the highest castes in Hindu society), born of a Brahmin mother, then why didn't you come by some other way? How is it that you are a Brahmin, and I am of a low social status? How is it that I am formed of blood, and you are made of milk? Says Kabeer : one who contemplates God, is said to be a Brahmin (the learned and the wise, on account of merit, and not due to caste or class) among us.[98]

The foolish demon, who does evil deeds, does not know his Lord and Master. Call him insane, if he does not understand himself. The strife of this world is evil; these struggles are consuming it. Without the Lord's Name, life is worthless. Through doubt, the people are being destroyed. One who recognizes that all spiritual paths lead to the One

---

[97] ਬੁਰਾ ਭਲਾ ਕਹੁ ਕਿਸ ਨੋ ਕਹੀਐ ॥ ਦੀਸੈ ਬ੍ਰਹਮੁ ਗੁਰਮੁਖਿ ਸਚੁ ਲਹੀਐ ॥ ਅਕਥੁ ਕਥਉ ਗੁਰਮਤਿ ਵੀਚਾਰੁ ॥ ਮਿਲਿ ਗੁਰ ਸੰਗਤਿ ਪਾਵਉ ਪਾਰੁ ॥ ੩ ॥ ਸਾਸਤ ਬੇਦ ਸਿੰਮ੍ਰਿਤਿ ਬਹੁ ਭੇਦ ॥ ਅਠਸਠਿ ਮਜਨੁ ਹਰਿ ਰਸੁ ਰੇਦ ॥ ਗੁਰਮੁਖਿ ਨਿਰਮਲੁ ਮੈਲੁ ਨ ਲਾਗੈ ॥ ਨਾਨਕ ਹਿਰਦੈ ਨਾਮੁ ਵਡੇ ਧੁਰਿ ਭਾਗੈ ॥ ੪ ॥ ੧੫ ॥ (Pg.353 A.G.)

[98] ਗਰਭ ਵਾਸ ਮਹਿ ਕੁਲੁ ਨਹੀ ਜਾਤੀ ॥ ਬ੍ਰਹਮ ਬਿੰਦੁ ਤੇ ਸਭ ਉਤਪਾਤੀ ॥ ੧ ॥ ਕਹੁ ਰੇ ਪੰਡਿਤ ਬਾਮਨ ਕਬ ਕੇ ਹੋਏ ॥ ਬਾਮਨ ਕਹਿ ਕਹਿ ਜਨਮੁ ਮਤ ਖੋਏ ॥ ੧ ॥ ਰਹਾਉ ॥ ਜੌ ਤੂੰ ਬ੍ਰਾਹਮਣੁ ਬ੍ਰਹਮਣੀ ਜਾਇਆ ॥ ਤਉ ਆਨ ਬਾਟ ਕਾਹੇ ਨਹੀ ਆਇਆ ॥ ੨ ॥ ਤੁਮ ਕਤ ਬ੍ਰਾਹਮਣ ਹਮ ਕਤ ਸੂਦ ॥ ਹਮ ਕਤ ਲੋਹੁ ਤੁਮ ਕਤ ਦੂਧ ॥ ੩ ॥ ਕਹੁ ਕਬੀਰ ਜੋ ਬ੍ਰਹਮੁ ਬੀਚਾਰੈ ॥ ਸੋ ਬ੍ਰਾਹਮਣੁ ਕਹੀਅਤੁ ਹੈ ਹਮਾਰੈ ॥ ੪ ॥ ੭ ॥ (Pg.324 A.G.)

shall be emancipated. One who speaks lies shall fall into hell and be reduced to ashes. The most blessed and sanctified are those who remain absorbed in Truth. One who eliminates selfishness and conceit is redeemed in the Court of the Lord. [99]

The Sri Guru Granth Sahib emphasizes, categorically, that ALL religions and faiths propagate the exemplary virtues and guidelines, so very essential for leading a purposeful and fulfilled life. And the various Prophets and Seers, belonging to diverse schools-of-thought, were unanimous in their spiritual-beliefs. It is the devilish tendency of the human mind that 'conceives and delivers the deformed baby' of rift and conflict, of mistrust and discord.

---

[99] ਬਦਫੈਲੀ ਗੈਬਾਨਾ ਖਸਮੁ ਨ ਜਾਣਈ ॥ ਸੋ ਕਹੀਐ ਦੇਵਾਨਾ ਆਪੁ ਨ ਪਛਾਣਈ ॥ ਕਲਹਿ ਬੁਰੀ ਸੰਸਾਰਿ ਵਾਦੇ ਖਪੀਐ ॥ ਵਿਣੁ ਨਾਵੈ ਵੇਕਾਰਿ ਭਰਮੇ ਪਚੀਐ ॥ ਰਾਹ ਦੋਵੈ ਇਕੁ ਜਾਣੈ ਸੋਈ ਸਿਝਸੀ ॥ ਕੁਫਰ ਗੋਅ ਕੁਫਰਾਣੈ ਪਇਆ ਦਝਸੀ ॥ ਸਭ ਦੁਨੀਆ ਸੁਬਹਾਨੁ ਸਚਿ ਸਮਾਈਐ ॥ ਸਿਝੈ ਦਰਿ ਦੀਵਾਨਿ ਆਪੁ ਗਵਾਈਐ ॥ ੯ ॥ (pg. 142 A.G.)

She should make the Lord, the Slayer of demons, her ring, and take the Transcendent Lord as her silken clothes. The soul-bride should weave patience into the braids of her hair, and apply the lotion of the Lord, the Great Lover. If she lights the lamp in the mansion of her mind, and makes her body the nuptial-bed of the Lord, then, when the King of spiritual wisdom comes to her bed, He shall accept her, and she shall experience an ecstatic bliss.[100]

Patience, glory and honor are bestowed upon those who listen to the Name of the Lord. That yearning soul, whose heart remains merged with the Lord, says Nanak, obtains glorious greatness.[101]

Says Sheikh Fareed : work for your Lord and Master; dispel the doubts of your heart. The humble devotees, have the strength and endurance of trees.[102]

The God-conscious being has a steady patience, like the earth, which bears the ignominy and cruelty of being dug up by one, but is later anointed with sandal paste by another (the soil is worshipped in some cultures and religions).[103]

---

[100] ਮਧੁਸੂਦਨ ਕਰ ਮੁੰਦਰੀ ਪਹਿਰੈ ਪਰਮੇਸਰੁ ਪਟੁ ਲੇਈ ॥ ਧੀਰਜੁ ਧੜੀ ਬੰਧਾਵੈ ਕਾਮਣਿ ਸ੍ਰੀਰੰਗੁ ਸੁਰਮਾ ਦੇਈ ॥ ੩ ॥ ਮਨ ਮੰਦਰਿ ਜੇ ਦੀਪਕੁ ਜਾਲੇ ਕਾਇਆ ਸੇਜ ਕਰੇਈ ॥ ਗਿਆਨ ਰਾਉ ਜਬ ਸੇਜੈ ਆਵੈ ਤ ਨਾਨਕ ਭੋਗੁ ਕਰੇਈ ॥ ੪ ॥ ੧ ॥ ੩੫ ॥ (Pg.359 A.G.)

[101] ਧੀਰਜੁ ਜਸੁ ਸੋਭਾ ਤਿਹ ਬਨਿਆ ॥ ਹਰਿ ਹਰਿ ਨਾਮੁ ਸ੍ਰਵਨ ਜਿਹ ਸੁਨਿਆ ॥ ਗੁਰਮੁਖਿ ਜਿਹ ਘਟਿ ਰਹੇ ਸਮਾਈ ॥ ਨਾਨਕ ਤਿਹ ਜਨ ਮਿਲੀ ਵਡਾਈ ॥ ੩੫ ॥ (Pg.257 A.G.)

[102] ਫਰੀਦਾ ਸਾਹਿਬ ਕੀ ਕਰਿ ਚਾਕਰੀ ਦਿਲ ਹੀ ਲਾਹਿ ਭਰਾਂਦਿ ॥ ਦਰਵੇਸਾਂ ਨੋ ਲੋੜੀਐ ਰੁਖਾਂ ਦੀ ਜੀਰਾਂਦਿ ॥ ੬੦ ॥ (Pg.1381 A.G.)

[103] ਬ੍ਰਹਮ ਗਿਆਨੀ ਕੈ ਧੀਰਜੁ ਏਕ ॥ ਜਿਉ ਬਸੁਧਾ ਕੋਉ ਖੋਦੈ ਕੋਉ ਚੰਦਨ ਲੇਪ ॥ ਬ੍ਰਹਮ ਗਿਆਨੀ ਕਾ ਇਹੈ ਗੁਨਾਉ ॥ ਨਾਨਕ ਜਿਉ ਪਾਵਕ ਕਾ ਸਹਜ ਸੁਭਾਉ ॥ ੧ ॥ (Pg.272 A.G.)

NOTES

HAVE MERCY ON CHILDREN

Lack of parental-guidance, and the absence of a spiritual-temper, could lead the children to becoming vulnerable to perils of the worst kind: addictions, criminal-tendencies, sexual-indulgence, et al.

Obsession of the parents, with materialistic-comforts, and the prevalence of divorce, in some cases, are the major causes, responsible for the worsening scenario.

SECTION : 3

THE TUG OF WAR

As per Sikh Marriage-Rites, the bride and the groom go round the Holy Scripture (Sri Guru Granth Sahib) four times, while the relevent Hymns are being recited by the Priest , and the appointed minstrels. The four rounds represent the Progression of Love, between spouses, and, also, the Spiritual Attachment, between God and Human-Soul.

In the first round of the marriage ceremony, the Lord sets out His Instructions for performing the daily duties of married life. Embrace the Conduct of Righteousness, and renounce sinful actions. Enshrine the contemplative remembrance of the Lord, in your hearts. The significance of the Institution of Marriage is the key-word, because Celibacy has been repudiated and denounced, in the strongest terms.

In the second round of the marriage ceremony, the Lord leads you to meet the True Guru, the Primal Being. With the Fear of the Fearless Lord in the mind, the filth of egotism is eradicated, and one is blessed with the Gracious Audience with the Immaculate Lord. The bride prepares to start a new life, in a new home, on leaving her parental abode.

In the third round of the marriage ceremony, the mind is filled with Divine Love. The stress, here, is on the soul-bride's detachment from external influences, thereby immersing and merging it's Entity unto the Eternal-Power. Likewise, the spouses, too, must follow the adage : "two bodies, one soul".

In the fourth and final round, the emphasis is on Unison, between the spouses, as also Communion between God and Human-Soul. I lovingly focus my consciousness on the Lord. I have obtained my Lord and Master, the cherished fruit of my mind's desires. God, my Lord and Master, blends with His bride, and her heart blossoms forth in His Devotion. Servant Nanak so proclaims, in this, the fourth round.[104]

---

[104] ਹਰਿ ਪਹਿਲੜੀ ਲਾਵ ਪਰਵਿਰਤੀ ਕਰਮ ਦ੍ਰਿੜਾਇਆ ਬਲਿ ਰਾਮ ਜੀਉ ॥ ਬਾਣੀ ਬ੍ਰਹਮਾ ਵੇਦੁ ਧਰਮੁ ਦ੍ਰਿੜਹੁ ਪਾਪ ਤਜਾਇਆ ਬਲਿ ਰਾਮ ਜੀਉ ॥ ਧਰਮੁ ਦ੍ਰਿੜਹੁ ਹਰਿ ਨਾਮੁ ਧਿਆਵਹੁ ਸਿਮ੍ਰਿਤਿ ਨਾਮੁ

As per Sikh customs and traditions (and as governed by the religious-spiritual Diktat of the Gurus) woman and man undertake to tie the nuptial-knot, in accordance with the prescribed code-of-conduct. The institution of wedlock rests on a very high pedestal, in Sikh Theology. The ideal couple must reciprocate mutual love and understanding, while taking due care of recognizing each other's individuality and uniqueness, thereby ensuring equality (as a human-being, and as a life-partner). This shall eliminate any occurrence of conflict on the basis of a perceived threat to either's identity.

Harmony shall prevail, and all crisis situations shall be dealt with, in a spirit of compromise and adjustment, coupled with commitment shall keep divorce at bay. The ascending divorce-rate, in the Western Society & Culture, is attributable to the fact that the institution of marriage is considered to be no more than a Legal-Contract, that can be nullified, with the stroke of the pens of the two parties and a Judge. When a minor irritant develops in a marital relationship, the weapon-of-divorce is readily, and easily, available. And it is resorted to, at the slightest pretext. Marriage is a social, moral, religious and spiritual contract that is sacred, and is not, merely, a legal-instrument, nor only a means of fulfilling the carnal-instincts. The two must strive to achieve a state of unison and camaraderie, at all planes: emotional, physical, financial, intellectual, and spiritual.

ਦ੍ਰਿੜਾਇਆ ॥ ਸਤਿਗੁਰੁ ਗੁਰੁ ਪੂਰਾ ਆਰਾਧਹੁ ਸਭਿ ਕਿਲਵਿਖ ਪਾਪ ਗਵਾਇਆ ॥ ਸਹਜ ਅਨੰਦੁ ਹੋਆ ਵਡਭਾਗੀ ਮਨਿ ਹਰਿ ਹਰਿ ਮੀਠਾ ਲਾਇਆ ॥ ਜਨੁ ਕਹੈ ਨਾਨਕੁ ਲਾਵ ਪਹਿਲੀ ਆਰੰਭੁ ਕਾਜੁ ਰਚਾਇਆ ॥ ੧ ॥ ਹਰਿ ਦੂਜੜੀ ਲਾਵ ਸਤਿਗੁਰੁ ਪੁਰਖੁ ਮਿਲਾਇਆ ਬਲਿ ਰਾਮ ਜੀਉ ॥ ਨਿਰਭਉ ਭੈ ਮਨੁ ਹੋਇ ਹਉਮੈ ਮੈਲੁ ਗਵਾਇਆ ਬਲਿ ਰਾਮ ਜੀਉ ॥ ਨਿਰਮਲੁ ਭਉ ਪਾਇਆ ਹਰਿ ਗੁਣ ਗਾਇਆ ਹਰਿ ਵੇਖੈ ਰਾਮੁ ਹਦੂਰੇ ॥ ਹਰਿ ਆਤਮ ਰਾਮੁ ਪਸਾਰਿਆ ਸੁਆਮੀ ਸਰਬ ਰਹਿਆ ਭਰਪੂਰੇ ॥ ਅੰਤਰਿ ਬਾਹਰਿ ਹਰਿ ਪ੍ਰਭੁ ਏਕੋ ਮਿਲਿ ਹਰਿ ਜਨ ਮੰਗਲ ਗਾਏ ॥ ਜਨ ਨਾਨਕ ਦੂਜੀ ਲਾਵ ਚਲਾਈ ਅਨਹਦ ਸਬਦ ਵਜਾਏ ॥ ੨ ॥ ਹਰਿ ਤੀਜੜੀ ਲਾਵ ਮਨਿ ਚਾਉ ਭਇਆ ਬੈਰਾਗਿਆ ਬਲਿ ਰਾਮ ਜੀਉ ॥ ਸੰਤ ਜਨਾ ਹਰਿ ਮੇਲੁ ਹਰਿ ਪਾਇਆ ਵਡਭਾਗੀਆ ਬਲਿ ਰਾਮ ਜੀਉ ॥ ਨਿਰਮਲੁ ਹਰਿ ਪਾਇਆ ਹਰਿ ਗੁਣ ਗਾਇਆ ਮੁਖਿ ਬੋਲੀ ਹਰਿ ਬਾਣੀ ॥ ਸੰਤ ਜਨਾ ਵਡਭਾਗੀ ਪਾਇਆ ਹਰਿ ਕਥੀਐ ਅਕਥ ਕਹਾਣੀ ॥ ਹਿਰਦੈ ਹਰਿ ਹਰਿ ਹਰਿ ਧੁਨਿ ਉਪਜੀ ਹਰਿ ਜਪੀਐ ਮਸਤਕਿ ਭਾਗੁ ਜੀਉ ॥ ਜਨੁ ਨਾਨਕ ਬੋਲੇ ਤੀਜੀ ਲਾਵੈ ਹਰਿ ਉਪਜੈ ਮਨਿ ਬੈਰਾਗੁ ਜੀਉ ॥ ੩ ॥ ਹਰਿ ਚਉਥੜੀ ਲਾਵ ਮਨਿ ਸਹਜੁ ਭਇਆ ਹਰਿ ਪਾਇਆ ਬਲਿ ਰਾਮ ਜੀਉ ॥ ਗੁਰਮੁਖਿ ਮਿਲਿਆ ਸੁਭਾਇ ਹਰਿ ਮਨਿ ਤਨਿ ਮੀਠਾ ਲਾਇਆ ਬਲਿ ਰਾਮ ਜੀਉ ॥ ਹਰਿ ਮੀਠਾ ਲਾਇਆ ਮੇਰੇ ਪ੍ਰਭ ਭਾਇਆ ਅਨਦਿਨੁ ਹਰਿ ਲਿਵ ਲਾਈ ॥ ਮਨ ਚਿੰਦਿਆ ਫਲੁ ਪਾਇਆ ਸੁਆਮੀ ਹਰਿ ਨਾਮਿ ਵਜੀ ਵਾਧਾਈ ॥ ਹਰਿ ਪ੍ਰਭਿ ਠਾਕੁਰਿ ਕਾਜੁ ਰਚਾਇਆ ਧਨ ਹਿਰਦੈ ਨਾਮਿ ਵਿਗਾਸੀ ॥ ਜਨੁ ਨਾਨਕੁ ਬੋਲੇ ਚਉਥੀ ਲਾਵੈ ਹਰਿ ਪਾਇਆ ਪ੍ਰਭੁ ਅਵਿਨਾਸੀ ॥ ੪ ॥ ੨ ॥ (pg. 773 A.G.)

76

Only this is your chance, a golden one at that. Just ponder, and analyze, hypothetically, this very moment, for later you might lose this opportunity, and then, nothing more than a sordid feeling of remorse and repentance shall remain, in your heart.[105]

(This 'CHANCE' pertains to the optimum and best utilization of this lifetime, for meditation, and for doing good to others. One's own welfare would be a natural consequence, and a foregone conclusion).

First conquer the fear of death, learn to accept/embrace death; only then would you become worthy of living a pristinely sublime and selfless life. Humility and faith in God would result in fortitude.

First, accept death, and give up any hope of life. Become the dust of the feet of all, and then, you may come to ME (GOD). Accept that only one who has died, truly lives, and one who is alive, consider him dead. Those who are in love with the One Lord, are the blessed ones. Pain does not even approach that person, within whose mind God resides. Hunger and thirst do not affect him, and the Messenger of Death does not terrorize him.[106]

The amalgamation of the elements, the flow of blood, and the rhythm of the heart-beat, all together, constitute a living person. And all such life-forms live in constant and perennial fear of death, like the proverbial "Damocles' Sword" dangling over one's head.

Whomsoever discovered this treasure-chest of Noumenon, his treasury shall, always, be overflowing with piety, humility, prosperity and service.

---

[105] ਇਹੀ ਤੇਰਾ ਅਉਸਰੁ ਇਹ ਤੇਰੀ ਬਾਰ ॥ ਘਟ ਭੀਤਰਿ ਤੂ ਦੇਖੁ ਬਿਚਾਰਿ ॥ ਕਹਤ ਕਬੀਰੁ ਜੀਤਿ ਕੈ ਹਾਰਿ ॥ ਬਹੁ ਬਿਧਿ ਕਹਿਓ ਪੁਕਾਰਿ ਪੁਕਾਰਿ ॥ ੫ ॥ ੧ ॥ ੮ ॥ (pg. 1159 A.G.)

[106] ਪਹਿਲਾ ਮਰਣੁ ਕਬੂਲਿ ਜੀਵਣ ਕੀ ਛਡਿ ਆਸ ॥ ਹੋਹੁ ਸਭਨਾ ਕੀ ਰੇਣੁਕਾ ਤਉ ਆਉ ਹਮਾਰੈ ਪਾਸਿ ॥ ੧ ॥ ਮਃ ੫ ॥ ਮੁਆ ਜੀਵੰਦਾ ਪੇਖੁ ਜੀਵੰਦੇ ਮਰਿ ਜਾਨਿ ॥ ਜਿਨ੍ਹਾ ਮੁਹਬਤਿ ਇਕ ਸਿਉ ਤੇ ਮਾਣਸ ਪਰਧਾਨ ॥ ੨ ॥ ਮਃ ੫ ॥ ਜਿਸੁ ਮਨਿ ਵਸੈ ਪਾਰਬ੍ਰਹਮੁ ਨਿਕਟਿ ਨ ਆਵੈ ਪੀਰ ॥ ਭੁਖ ਤਿਖ ਤਿਸੁ ਨ ਵਿਆਪਈ ਜਮੁ ਨਹੀ ਆਵੈ ਨੀਰ ॥ ੩ ॥ (pg. 1102 A.G.)

During one's lifetime, one remains attached to blood-relations, friends, material-wealth and power, food and clothing, for enjoyment and satisfaction. When one experiences and realizes God, one finds solace and serenity and joy, in lieu of all the aforementioned, so-called 'facets and commodities yielding happiness'. Now, one's fear of death is vanquished, instantaneously.

Sleep and death have been the subjects of comparison. Just as a proverb goes: " A sleeping person is no better than a dead one", thereby implying that, most often, one is unaware of the 'goings-on' around oneself, during one's sleep. So much so that, one, no longer, remains entangled with the bonds of relationships and materials. But, prior to dosing off, one reassures oneself, that the "contact" shall be re-established, upon waking up.

Man has, always, been desirous of longevity, least bothering about the quality of life, and about the contributions to mankind, that one could make. Instead, one is busy accumulating material, so painstakingly. Even Seers and Sages have been in search of ways and means of enhancing their ages, but to what avail. All time and energy was spent in the futile pursuit of a 'dream', because death is inevitable.

All the extra-effort could have been gainfully and constructively utilized, for generating peace and happiness, in one's own life, as well as that of others. This is only possible by dwelling upon God's Name, and by forgetting about one's Ego.

Death is the pre-ordained Reality. And, it is so destined that the Bride of Life shall merge unto the identity of its beloved 'death', and that they would elope together, on a given day, at a given time. The sickle of death does not discriminate between young and old, rich and poor, man and woman.

As the soul enjoys eternal life, it merges into the source and essence of its existence (GOD). When the noose of death captures the body, nothing is destroyed . The elements reunite with their original forms : air mixing with air, water with water, light merging unto light, and earth returning to the soil. This is the wonder of wonders, a miracle, so to say.

Modern science, now, has concluded with authority, the indestructibility of mass or matter. But, the ancient GURUS, SEERS & PROPHETS could, long ago, declare this TRUTH, with assertive authority, gained intuitively. Soul is consciousness. Without the soul, the body is only a skeleton. After death, the subtle body rises out of the gross body.

The emphasis is on the Theory of Karma and Transmigration. The path that the Soul Traverses, after death, is dark and hazardous. But, if one has the requisite knowledge of the technique to illumine it, with the Light of the Lord's Name, all perils and obstacles shall disintegrate and vanish, as if they were a whiff of air or a bubble of water.

Wherever the saints reside, such a place reverberates with the ambience of heaven. They enshrine the Lotus Feet of God within their hearts. Listen, O my mind and body, and let me show you the way to find peace, so that you may eat and enjoy the various delicacies of the Lord. Taste the Ambrosial Nectar of the Naam, the Name of the Lord, within your mind. Its taste is wondrous — it cannot be described. Your greed shall die, and your thirst shall be quenched. The humble beings seek the Sanctuary of the Supreme Lord God. The Lord dispels the fears and attachments of countless incarnations. God has showered His Mercy and Grace upon slave Nanak. [107]

Creating the Universe, God remains diffused throughout it. In the wind, water and fire, the Supreme is all-pervasive. The waving mind seeks indulgence in evil passions and vices, forgetting its primal obligation towards the Creator. Forgetting God, one must be prepared to bear innumerable miseries. Consequently, such a misguided one suffers the ignominy of having to undergo 8.4 million reincarnations. This viscious cycle of death and rebirth has been termed as hell. Due to the present life misdeeds, one may be reborn as a four-legged animal, as a crawling serpent, as a flying bird, as a small insect or as a creature in water. In such dire straits, none from one's kith and kin shall be the savior; only God is empowered to rescue and redeem. Discard falsehood and attain the truth, and thus become the recipient of the rewards you desire. This, then, is the ideal and profitable bartering practice. [108]

---

[107] ਬੈਕੁੰਠ ਨਗਰੁ ਜਹਾ ਸੰਤ ਵਾਸਾ ॥ ਪ੍ਰਭ ਚਰਣ ਕਮਲ ਰਿਦ ਮਾਹਿ ਨਿਵਾਸਾ ॥ ੧ ॥ ਸੁਣਿ ਮਨ ਤਨ ਤੁਝੁ ਸੁਖੁ ਦਿਖਲਾਵਉ ॥ ਹਰਿ ਅਨਿਕ ਬਿੰਜਨ ਤੁਝੁ ਭੋਗ ਭੁੰਚਾਵਉ ॥ ੧ ॥ ਰਹਾਉ ॥ ਅੰਮ੍ਰਿਤ ਨਾਮੁ ਭੁੰਚੁ ਮਨ ਮਾਹੀ ॥ ਅਚਰਜ ਸਾਦ ਤਾ ਕੇ ਬਰਨੇ ਨ ਜਾਹੀ ॥ ੨ ॥ ਲੋਭੁ ਮੂਆ ਤ੍ਰਿਸਨਾ ਬੁਝਿ ਥਾਕੀ ॥ ਪਾਰਬ੍ਰਹਮ ਕੀ ਸਰਣਿ ਜਨ ਤਾਕੀ ॥ ੩ ॥ ਜਨਮ ਜਨਮ ਕੇ ਭੈ ਮੋਹ ਨਿਵਾਰੇ ॥ ਨਾਨਕ ਦਾਸ ਪ੍ਰਭ ਕਿਰਪਾ ਧਾਰੇ ॥ ੪ ॥ ੨੧ ॥ ੨੨ ॥ (pg. 742 A.G.)

[108] ਸ੍ਰਿਸਟਿ ਉਪਾਇ ਰਹੇ ਪ੍ਰਭ ਛਾਜੈ ॥ ਪਉਣ ਪਾਣੀ ਬੈਸੰਤਰੁ ਗਾਜੈ ॥ ਮਨੂਆ ਡੋਲੈ ਦੂਤ ਸੰਗਤਿ ਮਿਲਿ ਸੋ ਪਾਏ ਜੋ ਕਿਛੁ ਕੀਨਾ ਹੇ ॥ ੭ ॥ ਨਾਮੁ ਵਿਸਾਰਿ ਦੋਖ ਦੁਖ ਸਹੀਐ ॥ ਹੁਕਮੁ ਭਇਆ ਚਲਣਾ ਕਿਉ ਰਹੀਐ ॥ ਨਰਕ ਕੂਪ ਮਹਿ ਗੋਤੇ ਖਾਵੈ ਜਿਉ ਜਲ ਤੇ ਬਾਹਰਿ ਮੀਨਾ ਹੇ ॥ ੮ ॥ ਚਉਰਾਸੀਹ ਨਰਕ

ਸਾਕਤੁ ਭੋਗਾਈਐ ॥ ਜੈਸਾ ਕੀਚੈ ਤੈਸੋ ਪਾਈਐ ॥ ਸਤਿਗੁਰ ਬਾਝਹੁ ਮੁਕਤਿ ਨ ਹੋਈ ਕਿਰਤਿ ਬਾਧਾ ਗ੍ਰਸਿ ਦੀਨਾ ਹੇ ॥ ੯ ॥ ਖੰਡੇ ਧਾਰ ਗਲੀ ਅਤਿ ਭੀੜੀ ॥ ਲੇਖਾ ਲੀਜੈ ਤਿਲ ਜਿਉ ਪੀੜੀ ॥ ਮਾਤ ਪਿਤਾ ਕਲਤ੍ਰ ਸੁਤ ਬੇਲੀ ਨਾਹੀ ਬਿਨੁ ਹਰਿ ਰਸ ਮੁਕਤਿ ਨ ਕੀਨਾ ਹੇ ॥ ੧੦ ॥ ਮੀਤ ਸਖੇ ਕੇਤੇ ਜਗ ਮਾਹੀ ॥ ਬਿਨੁ ਗੁਰ ਪਰਮੇਸਰ ਕੋਈ ਨਾਹੀ ॥ ਗੁਰ ਕੀ ਸੇਵਾ ਮੁਕਤਿ ਪਰਾਇਣਿ ਅਨਦਿਨੁ ਕੀਰਤਨੁ ਕੀਨਾ ਹੇ ॥ ੧੧ ॥ ਕੂੜੁ ਛੋਡਿ ਸਾਚੇ ਕਉ ਧਾਵਹੁ ॥ ਜੋ ਇਛਹੁ ਸੋਈ ਫਲੁ ਪਾਵਹੁ ॥ ਸਾਚ ਵਖਰ ਕੇ ਵਾਪਾਰੀ ਵਿਰਲੇ ਲੈ ਲਾਹਾ ਸਉਦਾ ਕੀਨਾ ਹੇ ॥ ੧੨ ॥ (pg. 1028 A.G.)

81

One who forgets the Primal Lord, the Architect of karma, wanders around, tormented by the raging fires of desires. No one can save such an ungrateful person; he must suffer the terrors of the horrendous chambers of hell. He blessed you with your soul, the breath of life, your body and wealth; He preserved and nurtured you in your mother's womb. Forsaking His Love, you are entangled with another; you shall never achieve your goals (of being happy).[109]

Forgetting Him, one's body turns to dust, and everyone calls him a ghost. And those, with whom he was deeply attached— they do not let him stay in their home, even for an instant. Practicing exploitation, he gathers wealth, but to what avail? As one sows, so does one reap; the body is the field of actions (karma). The ungrateful wretches forget the Lord, and wander in reincarnation.[110]

They wear and eat the gifts from the Lord; how can they be so lazy and complacent, as to forget Him, O' mother? Forgetting her Husband Lord, and attaching herself to other affairs, the soul-bride foolishly discards the precious jewel in exchange for a mere shell. Forsaking God, she is attached to other desires. They consume food and drink, delicious and sublime as ambrosial nectar. But the dog does not know the One who has bestowed these. Says Nanak : I have been unfaithful to my own nature. Please forgive me, O God, O Searcher of hearts. You are aware of my sincere desire of being pardoned.[111]

---

[109] ਜਿਸ ਨੋ ਬਿਸਰੈ ਪੁਰਖੁ ਬਿਧਾਤਾ ॥ ਜਲਤਾ ਫਿਰੈ ਰਹੈ ਨਿਤ ਤਾਤਾ ॥ ਅਕਿਰਤਘਣੈ ਕਉ ਰਖੈ ਨ ਕੋਈ ਨਰਕ ਘੋਰ ਮਹਿ ਪਾਵਣਾ ॥ ੭ ॥ ਜੀਉ ਪ੍ਰਾਣ ਤਨੁ ਧਨੁ ਜਿਨਿ ਸਾਜਿਆ ॥ ਮਾਤ ਗਰਭ ਮਹਿ ਰਾਖਿ ਨਿਵਾਜਿਆ ॥ ਤਿਸ ਸਿਉ ਪ੍ਰੀਤਿ ਛਾਡਿ ਅਨ ਰਾਤਾ ਕਾਹੂ ਸਿਰੈ ਨ ਲਾਵਣਾ ॥ ੮ ॥ (Pg.1086 A.G.)

[110] ਜਿਸੁ ਬਿਸਰਤ ਤਨੁ ਭਸਮ ਹੋਇ ਕਹਤੇ ਸਭਿ ਪ੍ਰੇਤੁ ॥ ਖਿਨੁ ਗ੍ਰਿਹ ਮਹਿ ਬਸਨ ਨ ਦੇਵਹੀ ਜਿਨ ਸਿਉ ਸੋਈ ਹੇਤੁ ॥ ਕਰਿ ਅਨਰਥ ਦਰਬੁ ਸੰਚਿਆ ਸੋ ਕਾਰਜਿ ਕੇਤੁ ॥ ਜੈਸਾ ਬੀਜੈ ਸੋ ਲੁਣੈ ਕਰਮ ਇਹੁ ਖੇਤੁ ॥ ਅਕਿਰਤਘਣਾ ਹਰਿ ਵਿਸਰਿਆ ਜੋਨੀ ਭਰਮੇਤੁ ॥ ੪ ॥ (Pg.706 A.G.)

[111] ਜਿਸ ਕਾ ਦੀਆ ਪੈਨੈ ਖਾਇ ॥ ਤਿਸੁ ਸਿਉ ਆਲਸੁ ਕਿਉ ਬਨੈ ਮਾਇ ॥ ੧ ॥ ਖਸਮੁ ਬਿਸਾਰਿ ਆਨ ਕੰਮਿ ਲਗਹਿ ॥ ਕਉਡੀ ਬਦਲੇ ਰਤਨੁ ਤਿਆਗਹਿ ॥ ੧ ॥ ਰਹਾਉ ॥ ਪ੍ਰਭੁ ਤਿਆਗਿ ਲਾਗਤ ਅਨ ਲੋਭਾ

The sinner is unfaithful to himself; he is ignorant, with shallow understanding. He does not know the essence of all, the One who gave him body, soul and peace. In the illusionary lure of temptation, he goes out, searching in the ten directions. He does not enshrine the Generous Lord, the Great Giver, in his mind, even for an instant. Greed, falsehood, corruption and emotional attachment — these are what he stores, within his mind. The worst perverts, thieves and slanderers are his constant companions. But if it pleases You, Lord, then You forgive the counterfeit along with the genuine. Prays Nanak: if it pleases the Supreme, then even a stone (a person burdened with Sins) will float on water.[112]

|| ਦਾਸਿ ਸਲਾਮੁ ਕਰਤ ਕਤ ਸੋਭਾ || ੨ || ਅੰਮ੍ਰਿਤ ਰਸੁ ਖਾਵਹਿ ਖਾਨ ਪਾਨ || ਜਿਨਿ ਦੀਏ ਤਿਸਹਿ ਨ ਜਾਨਹਿ ਸੁਆਨ || ੩ || ਕਹੁ ਨਾਨਕ ਹਮ ਲੂਣ ਹਰਾਮੀ || ਬਖਸਿ ਲੇਹੁ ਪ੍ਰਭ ਅੰਤਰਜਾਮੀ ੪ || ੨੬ || ੧੪੫ || (Pg.195 A.G.)

[112] ਲੂਣ ਹਰਾਮੀ ਗੁਨਹਗਾਰ ਬੇਗਾਨਾ ਅਲਪ ਮਤਿ || ਜੀਉ ਪਿੰਡੁ ਜਿਨਿ ਸੁਖ ਦੀਏ ਤਾਹਿ ਨ ਜਾਨਤ ਤਤ || ਲਾਹਾ ਮਾਇਆ ਕਾਰਨੇ ਦਹ ਦਿਸਿ ਢੁਢਨ ਜਾਇ || ਦੇਵਨਹਾਰ ਦਾਤਾਰ ਪ੍ਰਭ ਨਿਮਖ ਨ ਮਨਹਿ ਬਸਾਇ || ਲਾਲਚ ਝੂਠ ਬਿਕਾਰ ਮੋਹ ਇਆ ਸੰਪੈ ਮਨ ਮਾਹਿ || ਲੰਪਟ ਚੋਰ ਨਿੰਦਕ ਮਹਾ ਤਿਨਹੂ ਸੰਗਿ ਬਿਹਾਇ || ਤੁਧੁ ਭਾਵੈ ਤਾ ਬਖਸਿ ਲੈਹਿ ਖੋਟੇ ਸੰਗਿ ਖਰੇ ਨਾਨਕ ਭਾਵੈ ਪਾਰਬ੍ਰਹਮ ਪਾਹਨ ਨੀਰਿ ਤਰੇ || ੫੨ || (Pg.261 A.G.)

83

You have avoided the slumber of attachment and impurity — by whose favour has this happened? The greatest of enticers and seducers do not affect you. Where has your laziness gone? How have you escaped from the treachery of sexual desire, anger and egotism? The holy beings, angels and demons of the three worlds have been deceived by these temptresses. The forest fire has burnt down so much of the grass; how rare are the plants which have remained green. He is so All-powerful, that I cannot even describe Him; no one can chant His Praises. The Guru has implanted the Great Mantra, within my heart, and I have heard the wondrous Name of the Lord. Displaying His Mercy, God has looked upon me with favour, and He has permitted me to rest at His Lotus-feet. Through loving devotional worship, Nanak hath obtained peace; in the Company of the Holy, I am absorbed into the Lord. [113]

Burning and burning, writhing in pain, I wring my hands. I have gone insane, seeking my Husband Lord. O my Husband Lord, You are angry. The fault is with me, and not with my Husband Lord. O my Lord and Master, I do not know Your excellence and worth. Having wasted my youth, now I come to regret and repent. [114]

When the people of the world are suffering in pain, they call upon the Lord in loving prayer. The True Lord naturally listens and hears and gives comfort. He commands the God of rain, and the rain pours down

---

[113] ਮੋਹ ਮਲਨ ਨੀਦ ਤੇ ਛੁਟਕੀ ਕਉਨੁ ਅਨੁਗ੍ਰਹੁ ਭਇਓ ਰੀ ॥ ਮਹਾ ਮੋਹਨੀ ਤੁਧੁ ਨ ਵਿਆਪੈ ਤੇਰਾ ਆਲਸੁ ਕਹਾ ਗਇਓ ਰੀ ॥ ੧ ॥ ਰਹਾਉ ॥ ਕਾਮੁ ਕ੍ਰੋਧੁ ਅਹੰਕਾਰੁ ਗਾਖਰੋ ਸੰਜਮਿ ਕਉਨ ਛੁਟਿਓ ਰੀ ॥ ਸੁਰਿ ਨਰ ਦੇਵ ਅਸੁਰ ਤ੍ਰੈ ਗੁਨੀਆ ਸਗਲੋ ਭਵਨ ਲੁਟਿਓ ਰੀ ॥ ੧ ॥ ਦਾਵਾ ਅਗਨਿ ਬਹੁਤੁ ਤ੍ਰਿਣ ਜਾਲੇ ਕੋਈ ਹਰਿਆ ਬੂਟੁ ਰਹਿਓ ਰੀ ॥ ਐਸੋ ਸਮਰਥੁ ਵਰਨਿ ਨ ਸਾਕਉ ਤਾ ਕੀ ਉਪਮਾ ਜਾਤ ਨ ਕਹਿਓ ਰੀ ॥ ੨ ॥ ਕਾਜਰ ਕੋਠ ਮਹਿ ਭਈ ਨ ਕਾਰੀ ਨਿਰਮਲ ਬਰਨ ਬਨਿਓ ਰੀ ॥ ਮਹਾ ਮੰਤੁ ਗੁਰ ਹਿਰਦੈ ਬਸਿਓ ਅਚਰਜ ਨਾਮੁ ਸੁਨਿਓ ਰੀ ॥ ੩ ॥ ਕਰਿ ਕਿਰਪਾ ਪ੍ਰਭ ਨਦਰਿ ਅਵਲੋਕਨ ਅਪੁਨੈ ਚਰਨਿ ਲਗਾਈ ॥ ਪ੍ਰੇਮ ਭਗਤਿ ਨਾਨਕ ਸੁਖੁ ਪਾਇਆ ਸਾਧੂ ਸੰਗਿ ਸਮਾਈ ॥ ੪ ॥ ੧੨ ॥ ੫੧ ॥ (pg. 384 A.G.)

[114] ਤਪਿ ਤਪਿ ਲੁਹਿ ਲੁਹਿ ਹਾਥ ਮਰੋਰਉ ॥ ਬਾਵਲਿ ਹੋਈ ਸੋ ਸਹੁ ਲੋਰਉ ॥ ਤੈ ਸਹਿ ਮਨ ਮਹਿ ਕੀਆ ਰੋਸੁ ॥ ਮੁਝੁ ਅਵਗਨ ਸਹ ਨਾਹੀ ਦੋਸੁ ॥ ੧ ॥ ਤੈ ਸਾਹਿਬ ਕੀ ਮੈ ਸਾਰ ਨ ਜਾਨੀ ॥ ਜੋਬਨੁ ਖੋਇ ਪਾਛੈ ਪਛੁਤਾਨੀ ॥ ੧ ॥ (pg. 794 A.G.)

in torrents. Corn and wealth are produced in great abundance and prosperity; their value cannot be estimated. Sayeth Nanak : praise the Name of the Lord; He reaches out and gives sustains all beings. The mortal, never again, suffers in pain. [115]

In scientific-parlance, the 'Rotations & Revolutions', pertaining to the Earth and the Sun, bring about the change-of-seasons. It is a routine that is pre-programmed (in computer-jargon) in the characteristics of 'NATURE'.

During scorching summers, the flow of rivers gets bogged down, while the same rivers get inundated, during rainy season. They dry out in summers, and submerge the entire region, when they are flooded. Vegetation cries out and birds and animals wail for a dew-drop and a rain-drop, to quench their thirst.

On hearing the pleas of the tormented souls, rains pour down, and flowers blossom, once again, and earth is rejuvenated.

Similarly, 'HEAT' is generated on the plane of the Mind & Soul, when desire, lust, anger, greed, attachment and other vices take their toll by vibrations and reverberations, attacking the human psyche.

All the 'POSITIVES' have a cooling-effect on the human mind and body. Compassion and contentment, forgiveness and morality, alongwith other qualities of the head and the heart, forge a powerful alliance to counter the armies of aggressive elements (vices). Soothing signals emanate from such calm souls, and both, the sender and the receiver, experience 'BLISS'.

---

[115] ਕਲਮਲਿ ਹੋਈ ਮੇਦਨੀ ਅਰਦਾਸਿ ਕਰੇ ਲਿਵ ਲਾਇ ॥ ਸਚੈ ਸੁਣਿਆ ਕੰਨੁ ਦੇ ਧੀਰਕ ਦੇਵੈ ਸਹਜਿ ਸੁਭਾਇ ॥ ਇੰਦ੍ਰੈ ਨੋ ਫੁਰਮਾਇਆ ਵੁਠਾ ਛਹਬਰ ਲਾਇ ॥ ਅਨੁ ਧਨੁ ਉਪਜੈ ਬਹੁ ਘਣਾ ਕੀਮਤਿ ਕਹਣੁ ਨ ਜਾਇ ॥ ਨਾਨਕ ਨਾਮੁ ਸਲਾਹਿ ਤੂ ਸਭਨਾ ਜੀਆ ਦੇਦਾ ਰਿਜਕੁ ਸੰਬਾਹਿ ॥ ਜਿਤੁ ਖਾਧੈ ਸੁਖੁ ਉਪਜੈ ਫਿਰਿ ਦੂਖੁ ਨ ਲਾਗੈ ਆਇ ॥ ੨ ॥ (pg. 1281 A.G.)

85

Renounce both praise and criticism; seek, instead, the state of Nirvaana (Salvation). Says Nanak: this is such a difficult game; only those with faith in God understand it! [116]

I have been burnt by the fires of the world. Some speak well of me, and some speak ill of me, but I have surrendered my body to You. Whoever comes to Your Sanctuary, O God, Lord and Master, You save by Your Merciful Grace. Humble Nanak has entered Your Sanctuary, Dear Lord, please protect his honour! [117]

Even if you could live throughout the four ages, or even ten times more, and even if you were known throughout the nine continents and followed by all, with a good name and reputation, with praise and fame throughout the world—still, if the Lord does not bless you with His Glance of Grace, then who cares? What is the use? Among worms, you would be considered a lowly worm, and even contemptible sinners would hold you in contempt.. [118]

It is not good to slander anyone, but the foolish, self-willed still do it. The faces of the slanderers are blackened, and they fall into the most horrible hell. [119]

Praise is an intoxicant, but self-aggrandisement is a Vice. When one is praised, by another, the former is, naturally, on cloud-nine. Ironically,

---

[116] ਉਸਤਤਿ ਨਿੰਦਾ ਦੋਊ ਤਿਆਗੈ ਖੋਜੈ ਪਦੁ ਨਿਰਬਾਨਾ ॥ ਜਨ ਨਾਨਕ ਇਹੁ ਖੇਲੁ ਕਠਨੁ ਹੈ ਕਿਨਹੂੰ ਗੁਰਮੁਖਿ ਜਾਨਾ ॥ ੨ ॥ ੧ ॥ (pg. 219 A.G.)

[117] ਲੋਕਨ ਕੀ ਚਤੁਰਾਈ ਉਪਮਾ ਤੇ ਬੈਸੰਤਰਿ ਜਾਰਿ ॥ ਕੋਈ ਭਲਾ ਕਹਉ ਭਾਵੈ ਬੁਰਾ ਕਹਉ ਹਮ ਤਨੁ ਦੀਓ ਹੈ ਢਾਰਿ ॥ ੧ ॥ ਜੋ ਆਵਤ ਸਰਣਿ ਠਾਕੁਰ ਪ੍ਰਭੁ ਤੁਮਰੀ ਤਿਸੁ ਰਾਖਹੁ ਕਿਰਪਾ ਧਾਰਿ ॥ ਜਨ ਨਾਨਕ ਸਰਣਿ ਤੁਮਾਰੀ ਹਰਿ ਜੀਉ ਰਾਖਹੁ ਲਾਜ ਮੁਰਾਰਿ ॥ ੨ ॥ ੪ ॥ (pg. 528 A.G.)

[118] ਜੇ ਜੁਗ ਚਾਰੇ ਆਰਜਾ ਹੋਰ ਦਸੂਣੀ ਹੋਇ ॥ ਨਵਾ ਖੰਡਾ ਵਿਚਿ ਜਾਣੀਐ ਨਾਲਿ ਚਲੈ ਸਭੁ ਕੋਇ ॥ ਚੰਗਾ ਨਾਉ ਰਖਾਇ ਕੈ ਜਸੁ ਕੀਰਤਿ ਜਗਿ ਲੇਇ ॥ ਜੇ ਤਿਸੁ ਨਦਰਿ ਨ ਆਵਈ ਤ ਵਾਤ ਨ ਪੁਛੈ ਕੇ ॥ ਕੀਟਾ ਅੰਦਰਿ ਕੀਟੁ ਕਰਿ ਦੋਸੀ ਦੋਸੁ ਧਰੇ (pg. 2 A.G.)

[119] ਨਿੰਦਾ ਭਲੀ ਕਿਸੈ ਕੀ ਨਾਹੀ ਮਨਮੁਖ ਮੁਗਧ ਕਰੰਨਿ ॥ ਮੁਹ ਕਾਲੇ ਤਿਨ ਨਿੰਦਕਾ ਨਰਕੇ ਘੋਰਿ ਪਵੰਨਿ ॥ ੬ ॥ (Pg.755 A.G.)

one does not like some one else being praised. This is the characteristic of a jealous mind. Criticism hurts, and it hurts all the more when someone, having the ulterior motive of defaming another, criticises a noble and praise-worthy person. On the contrary, a sycophant (again, someone with a vested interest) would leave no stone unturned, to heap accolades and eulogies, on an undeserving person.

I bow down, and fall to the ground in humble prostration and adoration, countless times, before the All-powerful Lord. Please protect me, and save me from wandering, God. Reach out and give Nanak Your Hand. [120]

By Guru's Grace, one understands himself; know that, then, his negative desires are mollified/pacified (and his spiritual and wordly aspirations are fulfilled). In the Company of the Holy, one chants the Praises of the Lord. Such a devotee of the Lord is free of all disease. Night and day, sing the Holy hymns, the Praises of the One Lord. In the midst of your household, remain balanced and unattached. One who places his hopes in the One Lord — the noose of Death is cut away from his neck. One whose mind hungers for the Supreme Lord, Says Nanak, shall not suffer pain. One who focuses his conscious mind on the Lord — that Saint is at peace; he does not waver. Those unto whom God has granted His Grace — who do those servants need to fear? As God is, so does He appear; in His Own creation, He Himself is pervading. Searching, tirelessly, the devotee achieves success, finally. By Guru's Grace, the essence of all reality is understood. Wherever I look, there I see Him, at the root of all things. Observes Nanak : He is the subtle, and He is also the manifest. [121]

---

[120] ਡੰਡਉਤਿ ਬੰਦਨ ਅਨਿਕ ਬਾਰ ਸਰਬ ਕਲਾ ਸਮਰਬ ॥ ਡੋਲਨ ਤੇ ਰਾਖਹੁ ਪ੍ਰਭੁ ਨਾਨਕ ਦੇ ਕਰਿ ਹਥ ॥ ੧ ॥ (Pg.256 A.G.)

[121] ਗੁਰ ਪ੍ਰਸਾਦਿ ਆਪਨ ਆਪੁ ਸੁਝੈ ॥ ਤਿਸ ਕੀ ਜਾਨਹੁ ਤ੍ਰਿਸਨਾ ਬੁਝੈ ॥ ਸਾਧਸੰਗਿ ਹਰਿ ਹਰਿ ਜਸੁ ਕਹਤ ॥ ਸਰਬ ਰੋਗ ਤੇ ਓਹੁ ਹਰਿ ਜਨੁ ਰਹਤ ॥ ਅਨਦਿਨੁ ਕੀਰਤਨੁ ਕੇਵਲ ਬਖ੍ਯਾਨੁ ॥ ਗ੍ਰਿਹਸਤ ਮਹਿ ਸੋਈ ਨਿਰਬਾਨੁ ॥ ਏਕ ਉਪਰਿ ਜਿਸੁ ਜਨ ਕੀ ਆਸਾ ॥ ਤਿਸ ਕੀ ਕਟੀਐ ਜਮ ਕੀ ਫਾਸਾ ॥ ਪਾਰਬ੍ਰਹਮ ਕੀ ਜਿਸੁ ਮਨਿ ਭੂਖ ॥ ਨਾਨਕ ਤਿਸਹਿ ਨ ਲਾਗਹਿ ਦੂਖ ॥ ੪ ॥ ਜਿਸ ਕਉ ਹਰਿ ਪ੍ਰਭੁ ਮਨਿ ਚਿਤਿ ਆਵੈ ॥ ਸੋ ਸੰਤੁ ਸੁਹੇਲਾ ਨਹੀ ਡੁਲਾਵੈ ॥ ਜਿਸੁ ਪ੍ਰਭੁ ਅਪਨਾ ਕਿਰਪਾ ਕਰੈ ॥ ਸੋ ਸੇਵਕੁ ਕਹੁ ਕਿਸ ਤੇ ਡਰੈ ॥ ਜੈਸਾ ਸਾ ਤੈਸਾ ਦ੍ਰਿਸਟਾਇਆ ॥ ਅਪੁਨੇ ਕਾਰਜ ਮਹਿ ਆਪਿ ਸਮਾਇਆ ॥ ਸੋਧਤ ਸੋਧਤ ਸੋਧਤ ਸੀਝਿਆ ॥ ਗੁਰ ਪ੍ਰਸਾਦਿ ਤਤੁ ਸਭੁ ਬੁਝਿਆ ॥ ਜਬ ਦੇਖਉ ਤਬ ਸਭੁ ਕਿਛੁ ਮੂਲੁ ॥ ਨਾਨਕ ਸੋ ਸੂਖਮੁ ਸੋਈ ਅਸਥੂਲੁ ॥ ੫ ॥ (pg. 281 A.G.)

O my soul, grasp the Support of the One Lord; give up your hopes in others, meditating on the Name of the Lord, your affairs shall be resolved. The mind's wanderings cease, when one comes to dwell in the Society of the Saints. If the Lord is Merciful from the very beginning, then one's mind is enlightened. Those who have the true wealth are the true bankers. The Lord, is their wealth, and they trade in His Name. Patience, glory and honour come to those who listen to the Name of the Lord. That God-loving person whose heart remains merged with the Lord, obtains glorious greatness. [122]

---

[122] ਧਰ ਜੀਅਰੇ ਇਕ ਟੇਕ ਤੂ ਲਾਹਿ ਬਿਡਾਨੀ ਆਸ ॥ ਨਾਨਕ ਨਾਮੁ ਧਿਆਈਐ ਕਾਰਜੁ ਆਵੈ ਰਾਸਿ ॥ ੧ ॥ ਪਉੜੀ ॥ ਧਧਾ ਧਾਵਤ ਤਉ ਮਿਟੈ ਸੰਤਸੰਗਿ ਹੋਇ ਬਾਸੁ ॥ ਧੁਰ ਤੇ ਕਿਰਪਾ ਕਰਹੁ ਆਪਿ ਤਉ ਹੋਇ ਮਨਹਿ ਪਰਗਾਸੁ ॥ ਧਨੁ ਸਾਚਾ ਤੇਊ ਸਚ ਸਾਹਾ ॥ ਹਰਿ ਹਰਿ ਪੂੰਜੀ ਨਾਮ ਬਿਸਾਹਾ ॥ ਧੀਰਜੁ ਜਸੁ ਸੋਭਾ ਤਿਹ ਬਨਿਆ ॥ ਹਰਿ ਹਰਿ ਨਾਮੁ ਸ੍ਰਵਨ ਜਿਹ ਸੁਨਿਆ ॥ ਗੁਰਮੁਖਿ ਜਿਹ ਘਟਿ ਰਹੇ ਸਮਾਈ ॥ ਨਾਨਕ ਤਿਹ ਜਨ ਮਿਲੀ ਵਡਾਈ ॥ ੩੫ ॥ (pg. 257 A.G.)

89

They alone are beautiful and attractive, who abide in the Company of the Holy. Those who have accumulated the wealth of the Lord's Name—they alone are wise and serious investors, and are praised by all and sundry. [123]

Power is fraudulent, beauty is fraudulent, and wealth is fraudulent, as is pride of ancestry. One may gather poison through deception and fraud, Says Nanak, but without the Lord, nothing shall go along with him in the end. Beholding the bitter melon, he is deceived, since it appears so pretty. But it is not worth even a shell ; the illusionary riches will not go along with anyone. [124]

Without the Name of the Lord, the beautiful are just like the noseless ones. Like the son, born into the house of a prostitute, his name is cursed, and he bears the ignominy of being prefixed and suffixed with a low reputation of his mother. Those who do not have the Name of their Lord and Master within their hearts, are the most wretched, deformed lepers. Like the person who has no Guru, they may know many things, but they are cursed in the Court of the Lord. Those, to whom my Lord Master becomes Merciful, long for the feet of the Holy. Says Nanak, the sinners become pure, joining the Company of the Holy; following the True Guru, they are emancipated. [125]

---

[123] ਸੇਈ ਸੁੰਦਰ ਸੋਹਣੇ ॥ ਸਾਧਸੰਗਿ ਜਿਨ ਬੈਹਣੇ ॥ ਹਰਿ ਧਨੁ ਜਿਨੀ ਸੰਜਿਆ ਸੇਈ ਗੰਭੀਰ ਅਪਾਰ ਜੀਉ ॥ ੩ ॥(Pg. 132 A.G.)

[124] ਰਾਜ ਕਪਟੰ ਰੂਪ ਕਪਟੰ ਧਨ ਕਪਟੰ ਕੁਲ ਗਰਬਤਹ ॥ ਸੰਚੰਤਿ ਬਿਖਿਆ ਛਲੰ ਛਿਦ੍ਰੰ ਨਾਨਕ ਬਿਨੁ ਹਰਿ ਸੰਗਿ ਨ ਚਾਲਤੇ ॥ ੧ ॥ ਪੇਖੰਦੜੋ ਕੀ ਭੁਲੁ ਤੁੰਮਾ ਦਿਸਮੁ ਸੋਹਣਾ ॥ ਅਢੁ ਨ ਲਹੰਦੜੋ ਮੂਲੁ ਨਾਨਕ ਸਾਥਿ ਨ ਜੁਲਈ ਮਾਇਆ ॥ ੨ ॥ (pg. 708 A.G.)

[125] ਹਰਿ ਕੇ ਨਾਮ ਬਿਨਾ ਸੁੰਦਰਿ ਹੈ ਨਕਟੀ ॥ ਜਿਉ ਬੇਸੁਆ ਕੇ ਘਰਿ ਪੂਤੁ ਜਮਤੁ ਹੈ ਤਿਸੁ ਨਾਮੁ ਪਰਿਓ ਹੈ ਪ੍ਰਕਟੀ ॥ ੧ ॥ ਰਹਾਉ ॥ ਜਿਨ ਕੈ ਹਿਰਦੈ ਨਾਹਿ ਹਰਿ ਸੁਆਮੀ ਤੇ ਬਿਗੜ ਰੂਪ ਬੇਰਕਟੀ ॥ ਜਿਉ ਨਿਗੁਰਾ ਬਹੁ ਬਾਤਾ ਜਾਣੈ ਓਹੁ ਹਰਿ ਦਰਗਹ ਹੈ ਭ੍ਰਸਟੀ ॥ ੧ ॥ ਜਿਨ ਕਉ ਦਇਆਲੁ ਹੋਆ ਮੇਰਾ ਸੁਆਮੀ ਤਿਨਾ ਸਾਧ ਜਨਾ ਪਗ ਚਕਟੀ ॥ ਨਾਨਕ ਪਤਿਤ ਪਵਿਤ ਮਿਲਿ ਸੰਗਤਿ ਗੁਰ ਸਤਿਗੁਰ ਪਾਛੈ ਛੁਕਟੀ ॥ ੨ ॥ ੬ ॥ ਛਕਾ ੧ (pg. 528 A.G.)

Those who do not meditate on the Lord — I do not even want to see them. Those whose inner beings are not in harmony with the Lord, are nothing more than beasts. Prays Naam Dev : a human without a nose does not look handsome, even if he has the thirty-two beauty marks. [126]

"Beauty lies in the eyes of the beholder" is a realistically pertinent statement. And, equally true is the fact that Beauty, besides being external and physical, is, also, internal and intellectual and spiritual. For the admiration of the latter, the observor must be endowed with the 'THIRD EYE' that would have the potential of penetrating through bone and flesh, to have the heavenly-view of the inner-beauty of someone's heart and soul.

Beauty is widespread all over the Universe. Vegetation, oceans, rivulets, snow-clad mountain-summits, the sun, the moon and the stars, birds and animals, flowers and fruits, are the innumerable manifestations of Beauty. Human faces are beautiful, too, and very much lovable. But LUST vitiates the environment.

A living personification of this statement is the CRANE, exquisitely adorable, but so deceitful, inside. The antonym is the ugly-looking Nightingale, which has been blessed with the most meluflous voice, churning out soothing music (even while it may be the regular language of the species). Similarly, some beautiful people are treacherous and wicked and cunning, while the so-described ugly ones could be pious, learned and compassionate.

A child is showered with love and affection by all and sundry, owing to its qualities of beauty and innocence. It is free of the vices of greed, lust, malice, anger and ego. It is more carefree than the birds that fly in gay-abandon.

The child-like traits are visible in God's chosen few, who continue to retain the charm and innocence, in word and spirit, until their last day.

---

[126] ਜੋ ਨ ਭਜੰਤੇ ਨਾਰਾਇਣਾ ॥ ਤਿਨ ਕਾ ਮੈ ਨ ਕਰਉ ਦਰਸਨਾ ॥ ੧ ॥ ਰਹਾਉ ॥ ਜਿਨ ਕੈ ਭੀਤਰਿ ਹੈ ਅੰਤਰਾ ॥ ਜੈਸੇ ਪਸੁ ਤੈਸੇ ਓਇ ਨਰਾ ॥ ੨ ॥ ਪ੍ਰਣਵਤਿ ਨਾਮਦੇਉ ਨਾਕਹਿ ਬਿਨਾ ॥ ਨਾ ਸੋਹੈ ਬਤੀਸ ਲਖਨਾ ॥ ੩ ॥ ੨ ॥ (pg. 1163 A.G.)

This Godly-attribute cannot be replenished and substituted by donning expensive ornaments and using cosmetics, to look beautiful.

Saints, Seers, Saviours and Prophets, have a radiant gleam and glow on their faces, and a magnetic field and halo, around them, that would, instataneously captivate anyone in range. Such vibrant personalities owe their charismatic-influence to the great meditation performed by them. They surrender, unconditionally, before GOD, and, in lieu, are granted the everlasting Peace. Their word is honoured as God's OWN Command. None has the tenacity to challenge them.

The Guru has given the healing ointment of spiritual wisdom, and dispelled the darkness of ignorance. By the Lord's Grace, I have met the Saint; Says Nanak : my mind is enlightened.[127]

If a hundred moons were to rise, and a thousand suns appeared, even with such light, there would still be terrifying darkness (in the mind), without the Guru's guidance. Says Nanak : those who do not think of the Guru, and who think of themselves as clever, shall be left abandoned in the field, like the scattered sesame.[128]

Worshipping their idols, some die; others perish bowing their heads. Some cremate their dead, while the others bury theirs; neither finds Your true state, Lord, if one just indulges in the ritualistic prayer and meditation, sans the FAITH & DEVOTION, within. O mind, the world is a deep, dark pit. On all four sides, Death has spread his net. Reciting their poems, the poets die; the mystical ascetics die while journeying to Kaydaar Naath (a pilgrimage-site on a high mountain, in India). The Yogis die, with their matted hair, but even they do not find Your state, Lord. The kings die, gathering and hoarding their money, burying great quantities of gold. The Pundits die, reading and reciting the Scriptures; women die, praising their own beauty. Without the Lord's Name, all come to ruin; behold, and know this, O body. Without the Name of the Lord, who can find salvation? Saint Kabeer speaks the Truth.[129]

---

[127] ਗਿਆਨ ਅੰਜਨੁ ਗੁਰਿ ਦੀਆ ਅਗਿਆਨ ਅੰਧੇਰ ਬਿਨਾਸੁ ॥ ਹਰਿ ਕਿਰਪਾ ਤੇ ਸੰਤ ਭੇਟਿਆ ਨਾਨਕ ਮਨਿ ਪਰਗਾਸੁ ॥ ੧ ॥ (Pg. 293 A.G.)

[128] ਜੇ ਸਉ ਚੰਦਾ ਉਗਵਹਿ ਸੂਰਜ ਚੜਹਿ ਹਜਾਰ ॥ ਏਤੇ ਚਾਨਣ ਹੋਦਿਆਂ ਗੁਰ ਬਿਨੁ ਘੋਰ ਅੰਧਾਰ ॥ ੨ ॥ ਮਃ ੧ ॥ ਨਾਨਕ ਗੁਰੂ ਨ ਚੇਤਨੀ ਮਨਿ ਆਪਣੈ ਸੁਚੇਤ ॥ ਛੁਟੇ ਤਿਲ ਬੂਆੜ ਜਿਉ ਸੁੰਞੇ ਅੰਦਰਿ ਖੇਤ ॥ (Pg.463 A.G.)

[129] ਭੂਤ ਪੂਜਿ ਪੂਜਿ ਹਿੰਦੂ ਮੂਏ ਤੁਰਕ ਮੂਏ ਸਿਰੁ ਨਾਈ ॥ ਓਇ ਲੇ ਜਾਰੇ ਓਇ ਲੇ ਗਾਡੇ ਤੇਰੀ ਗਤਿ ਦੁਹੂ ਨ ਪਾਈ ॥ ੧ ॥ ਮਨ ਰੇ ਸੰਸਾਰੁ ਅੰਧ ਗਹੇਰਾ ॥ ਚਹੁ ਦਿਸ ਪਸਰਿਓ ਹੈ ਜਮ ਜੇਵਰਾ ॥ ੧ ॥ ਰਹਾਉ ॥ ਕਬਿਤ ਪੜੇ ਪੜਿ ਕਬਿਤਾ ਮੂਏ ਕਪੜ ਕੇਦਾਰੈ ਜਾਈ ॥ ਜਟਾ ਧਾਰਿ ਧਾਰਿ ਜੋਗੀ ਮੂਏ ਤੇਰੀ ਗਤਿ ਇਨਹਿ ਨ ਪਾਈ ॥ ੨ ॥ ਦਰਬੁ ਸੰਚਿ ਸੰਚਿ ਰਾਜੇ ਮੂਏ ਗਾਡਿ ਲੇ ਕੰਚਨ ਭਾਰੀ ॥ ਬੇਦ ਪੜੇ ਪੜਿ

I seek my Friend the Lord. In each and every home, sing the sublime songs of rejoicing; He abides in each and every heart. In good times, worship and adore Him; in bad times, worship and adore Him; do not ever forget Him. Chanting the Name of the Lord, the light of millions of suns shines forth, and the terrifying darkness of doubt is dispelled, forever, from the mind of a devotee. In all the spaces and interspaces, everywhere, whatever we see is Yours. One who joins the Society of the Saints, says Nanak, is not consigned to reincarnation again.[130]

Darkness is to be found all over, and in great measure, within man's mind, and without. The earth's crust is dark, towards the interior. The deeper levels of the oceans are dark, the sun's light being unable to permeate, beyond a specified range (fathoms).

Due to the increased effect of the vices of Lust, Greed, Egocentricism, Hatred, Jealosy, Violence and Addictions, even more darkness can be found within the hearts and minds and souls of the modern human.

The germs of disease originate in dark regions. Snakes and scorpions are often found in dark areas. Dacoits and marauders wait for their preys, in dark and nether confines. AND, so do the LOWLY VICES wait for the opportune moment to launch a vicious attack targeted towards persons with a weak power of resilience.

'Darkness' is a synonym for 'sorrow', 'grief' and 'penury'. And ostentatious illuminations and fireworks are on display, during festivities and rejoicing. Due to the darkness of ignorance, coupled with a lack of will and interest, to search and pray for the True Light, today's man is lost and frightened. Finding oneself in deep peril, there seems to be no happiness, notwithstanding the rapid strides towards the destinations of acquiring material-wealth and accruing knowledge.

ਪੰਡਿਤ ਮੁਏ ਰੂਪੁ ਦੇਖਿ ਦੇਖਿ ਨਾਰੀ ॥ ੩ ॥ ਰਾਮ ਨਾਮ ਬਿਨੁ ਸਭੈ ਬਿਗੂਤੇ ਦੇਖਹੁ ਨਿਰਖਿ ਸਰੀਰਾ ॥ ਹਰਿ ਕੇ ਨਾਮ ਬਿਨੁ ਕਿਨਿ ਗਤਿ ਪਾਈ ਕਹਿ ਉਪਦੇਸੁ ਕਬੀਰਾ ॥ ੪ ॥ ੧ ॥ (pg. 654 A.G.)
[130] ਲੋੜੀਦੜਾ ਸਾਜਨੁ ਮੇਰਾ ॥ ਘਰਿ ਘਰਿ ਮੰਗਲ ਗਾਵਹੁ ਨੀਕੇ ਘਟਿ ਘਟਿ ਤਿਸਹਿ ਬਸੇਰਾ ॥ ੧ ॥ ਰਹਾਉ ॥ ਸੁਖਿ ਅਰਾਧਨੁ ਦੁਖਿ ਅਰਾਧਨੁ ਬਿਸਰੈ ਨ ਕਾਹੂ ਬੇਰਾ ॥ ਨਾਮੁ ਜਪਤ ਕੋਟਿ ਸੂਰ ਉਜਾਰਾ ਬਿਨਸੈ ਭਰਮੁ ਅੰਧੇਰਾ ॥ ੧ ॥ ਥਾਨਿ ਥਨੰਤਰਿ ਸਭਨੀ ਜਾਈ ਜੋ ਦੀਸੈ ਸੋ ਤੇਰਾ ॥ ਸੰਤਸੰਗਿ ਪਾਵੈ ਜੋ ਨਾਨਕ ਤਿਸੁ ਬਹੁਰਿ ਨ ਹੋਈ ਹੈ ਫੇਰਾ ॥ ੨ ॥ ੩ ॥ ੪ ॥ (pg. 700 A.G.)

Says Saint Kabir Das: A person performing a misdeed, fully well aware and conscious of the repercussions, thereof, and realizing the fallout, is deemed to be the greatest fool. Instead of feeling guilt or remorse, he becomes arrogant and egocentric, and takes pride in his actions, is like one who falls into a well, despite carrying a glowing lamp, with him[131]

The same person is foolish and wise; the same light within has two names. Utterly foolish are those who do not believe in the Name. Through the Guru's Gate, the Gurdwara, the Name is obtained. Without the True Guru, it is not received. Through the Pleasure of the True Guru's Will, the Name comes to dwell in the mind, and then, night and day, one remains lovingly absorbed in the Lord. In power, pleasures, beauty, wealth and youth, one gambles his life away. Bound by the Command of God, the dice is cast; he is just a piece on the chess-board. The world is clever and wise, but it is deluded by doubt, and forgets the Name; the religious scholar, studies the scriptures, but he is still a fool. Forgetting the Name, he dwells upon the Scriptures; he writes, but he is confused by his vitriolic-corruption, of his ego-centric mind.[132]

Nobody has attained You by clever calculations, O True, Unseen and Infinite Lord. That scholar who is full of greed, arrogant pride and egotism, is known to be a fool. So read the Name, and realize the Name, and contemplate the Guru's Teachings.[133]

---

[131] ਕਬੀਰ ਮਨੁ ਜਾਨੈ ਸਭ ਬਾਤ ਜਾਨਤ ਹੀ ਅਉਗਨੁ ਕਰੈ ॥ ਕਾਹੇ ਕੀ ਕੁਸਲਾਤ ਹਾਥਿ ਦੀਪੁ ਕੂਏ ਪਰੈ ॥ ੨੧੬ ॥ (pg. 1376 A.G.)

[132] ਮੂਰਖੁ ਸਿਆਣਾ ਏਕੁ ਹੈ ਏਕ ਜੋਤਿ ਦੁਇ ਨਾਉ ॥ ਮੂਰਖਾ ਸਿਰਿ ਮੂਰਖੁ ਹੈ ਜਿ ਮੰਨੇ ਨਾਹੀ ਨਾਉ ॥ ੨ ॥ ਗੁਰ ਦੁਆਰੈ ਨਾਉ ਪਾਈਐ ਬਿਨੁ ਸਤਿਗੁਰ ਪਲੈ ਨ ਪਾਇ ॥ ਸਤਿਗੁਰ ਕੈ ਭਾਣੈ ਮਨਿ ਵਸੈ ਤਾ ਅਹਿਨਿਸਿ ਰਹੈ ਲਿਵ ਲਾਇ ॥ ੩ ॥ ਰਾਜੰ ਰੰਗੰ ਰੂਪੰ ਮਾਲੰ ਜੋਬਨੁ ਤੇ ਜੂਆਰੀ ॥ ਹੁਕਮੀ ਬਾਧੇ ਪਾਸੈ ਖੇਲਹਿ ਚਉਪੜਿ ਏਕਾ ਸਾਰੀ ॥ ੪ ॥ ਜਗਿ ਚਤੁਰੁ ਸਿਆਣਾ ਭਰਮਿ ਭੁਲਾਣਾ ਨਾਉ ਪੰਡਿਤ ਪੜਹਿ ਗਾਵਾਰੀ ॥ ਨਾਉ ਵਿਸਾਰਹਿ ਬੇਦੁ ਸਮਾਲਹਿ ਬਿਖੁ ਭੂਲੇ ਲੇਖਾਰੀ ॥ ੫ ॥ (pg. 1015 A.G.)

[133] ਤੂੰ ਗਣਤੈ ਕਿਨੈ ਨ ਪਾਇਓ ਸਚੇ ਅਲਖ ਅਪਾਰਾ ॥ ਪੜਿਆ ਮੂਰਖੁ ਆਖੀਐ ਜਿਸੁ ਲਬੁ ਲੋਭੁ

Even if the self-willed person is instructed, he stills goes into the wilderness. Without the Lord's Name, he shall not be emancipated; he shall die, and sink into the deepest and darkest dungeons of Hell (misery of being reborn, and not the 'Imaginary' Hell). He wanders through birth and death, and never chants the Lord's Name. He is worthless, without serving the Guru.[134]

GOD gave man the unique gift of the power of analysis and hypothesis, and by the optimum utilization of the nervous system (the brain), one could achieve wonders. But, rarely, does that happen. A child's thinking faculties are not fully developed, hence it cannot be called a fool. But, such an adult is a fool, who does not think and act rationally. A person lacking in wisdom, does not act in consonance with certain universally acclaimed and socially acceptable norms.

A literate or educated person may not, necessarily, be a wise one, too. But, God may gift an illiterate person with the blessing of wisdom. And, there's no guarantee that an educated person would realize God, while there have been great devotees, who never learnt the Three "Rs" in school, but mastered the highest techniques of Communion with God.

Another MYTH and ill-conceived notion pertains to the prevalent practice of linking intelligence and wisdom with wealth and prestige. A person who is sucessful in a given vocation/profession might not, necessarily, be considered wise, in other spheres, too. But, generally, there is a tendency to become dependant, upon such people, in various matters, including Spiritual-Religious and Socio-economic, even though the concerned person might not be, remotely, having an affinity with the said issues.

ਅਹੰਕਾਰਾ ॥ ਨਾਉ ਪੜੀਐ ਨਾਉ ਬੁਝੀਐ ਗੁਰਮਤੀ ਵੀਚਾਰਾ ॥   (pg. 140 A.G.)

[134] ਮਨਮੁਖ ਜੋ ਸਮਝਾਈਐ ਭੀ ਉਝੜਿ ਜਾਏ ॥ ਬਿਨੁ ਹਰਿ ਨਾਮ ਨ ਛੂਟਸੀ ਮਰਿ ਨਰਕ ਸਮਾਏ ॥ ੫ ॥ ਜਨਮਿ ਮਰੈ ਭਰਮਾਈਐ ਹਰਿ ਨਾਮੁ ਨ ਲੇਵੈ ॥ ਤਾ ਕੀ ਕੀਮਤਿ ਨਾ ਪਵੈ ਬਿਨੁ ਗੁਰ ਕੀ ਸੇਵੈ ॥ ੬ ॥   (pg. 420 A.G.)

96

Many speak and talk about God. But one who understands the essence of a 'Life-Divine', such a humble one (ever in God's servitude) is very rare. He has, not even, an iota of pain, and is, totally, at peace. With his eyes, he sees only the One Lord. No one seems evil to him — all are good. There is no defeat — he is totally victorious. He is never in sorrow — he is happy, always. Says Nanak: the humble servant of the Lord is himself the Lord (becomes identical; resembles Godly-Attributes); he does not come and go in reincarnation.[135]

Sorrow and pain is like an epidemic, the only cure for it being the regular administering of dosages of Noumenon of God. None has escaped the octopus-like tentacles of sorrow.

Since the desires are innumerable, the causes of sorrow are countless, too. When desires are not fulfilled, pain is born, therefrom. A perennial river of sorrow is constantly flowing in the lifetime of a human-being, because of the desires increasing, rapidly and rampantly, in volume and content.

In hope, there is very great pain; the self-willed focuses his consciousness on it. The God-loving become desireless, and attain supreme peace. In the midst of their household, they remain detached; they are lovingly attuned to the Detached Lord. Sorrow and separation do not cling to them at all. They are pleased with the Lord's Will. Says Nanak, they remain forever immersed in the Primal Lord, who blends them with Himself.[136]

---

[135] ਕਹਨ ਕਹਾਵਨ ਕਉ ਕਈ ਕੇਤੇ ॥ ਐਸੋ ਜਨੁ ਬਿਰਲੋ ਹੈ ਸੇਵਕੁ ਜੋ ਤਤ ਜੋਗ ਕਉ ਬੇਤੈ ॥ ੧ ॥ ਰਹਾਉ ॥ ਦੁਖੁ ਨਾਹੀ ਸਭੁ ਸੁਖੁ ਹੀ ਹੈ ਰੇ ਏਕੈ ਏਕੀ ਨੇਤੈ ॥ ਬੁਰਾ ਨਹੀ ਸਭੁ ਭਲਾ ਹੀ ਹੈ ਰੇ ਹਾਰ ਨਹੀ ਸਭ ਜੇਤੈ ॥ ੧ ॥ ਸੋਗੁ ਨਾਹੀ ਸਦਾ ਹਰਖੀ ਹੈ ਰੇ ਛੋਡਿ ਨਾਹੀ ਕਿਛੁ ਲੇਤੈ ॥ ਕਹੁ ਨਾਨਕ ਜਨੁ ਹਰਿ ਹਰਿ ਹਰਿ ਹੈ ਕਤ ਆਵੈ ਕਤ ਰਮਤੈ ॥ ੨ ॥ ੩ ॥ ੨੨ ॥ (pg. 1302 A.G)

[136] ਆਸਾ ਵਿਚਿ ਅਤਿ ਦੁਖੁ ਘਣਾ ਮਨਮੁਖਿ ਚਿਤੁ ਲਾਇਆ ॥ ਗੁਰਮੁਖਿ ਭਏ ਨਿਰਾਸ ਪਰਮ ਸੁਖੁ ਪਾਇਆ ॥ ਵਿਚੇ ਗਿਰਹ ਉਦਾਸ ਅਲਿਪਤ ਲਿਵ ਲਾਇਆ ॥ ਓਨਾ ਸੋਗੁ ਵਿਜੋਗੁ ਨ ਵਿਆਪਈ ਹਰਿ ਭਾਣਾ ਭਾਇਆ ॥ ਨਾਨਕ ਹਰਿ ਸੇਤੀ ਸਦਾ ਰਵਿ ਰਹੇ ਧੁਰਿ ਲਏ ਮਿਲਾਇਆ ॥ ੩੧ ॥ (pg. 1249 A.G.)

Its human-nature to be jealous of another's happiness, and to cry hoarse at one's own sorrow. But, in reality, NONE is actually happy, in this world. The nodal-point and focus of all happiness (the reservoir of Joy and Bliss) is GOD and meditation on His Name.

First, I gave up slandering others. All the anxiety of my mind was dispelled. Greed and attachment were totally banished. I see God ever-present, close at hand; I have become a great devotee. Such a renunciate is very rare. Such a humble servant chants the Name of the Lord. [137]

Perform good deeds, always. Do not try to blame anyone else. Forgetting the Transcendent Lord, all sorts of illnesses are contracted. Those who turn their backs on the Lord shall be separated from Him and consigned to reincarnation, over and over again. In an instant, all illusionary sensual pleasures turn bitter. No one can then serve as your intermediary. Unto whom can we turn and cry? By one's own actions, nothing can be done; destiny was pre-ordained. [138]

Every laughter is attached with the apprehension of a wail looming large. And behind the curtain of all praise and accolades, lurks the dangerous snake of exposure, insult and defamation. Profits are, naturally, made, at great stakes and risks.

All life-forms must culminate in death. Hence, all efforts should be made to decorate this life with all worthy attributes and ornamentation, so as to be received by God, in His Magnificent Kingdom, with Honor and Praise. At that moment, disgrace and rebuke can be avoided, if one had the wisdom, of doing so, during the time that was available, for meditation, during the life-time.

---

[137] ਸੁਖੁ ਨਾਹੀ ਬਹੁਤੈ ਧਨਿ ਖਾਟੇ ॥ ਸੁਖੁ ਨਾਹੀ ਪੇਖੇ ਨਿਰਤਿ ਨਾਟੇ ॥ ਸੁਖ ਨਾਹੀ ਬਹੁ ਦੇਸ ਕਮਾਏ ॥ ਸਰਬ ਸੁਖਾ ਹਰਿ ਹਰਿ ਗੁਣ ਗਾਏ ॥ ੧ ॥ ਸੁਖ ਸਹਜ ਆਨੰਦ ਲਹਹੁ ॥ ਸਾਧਸੰਗਤਿ ਪਾਈਐ ਵਡਭਾਗੀ ਗੁਰਮੁਖਿ ਹਰਿ ਹਰਿ ਨਾਮੁ ਕਹਹੁ ॥ ੧ ॥ (pg. 1147 A.G.)

[138] ਕਤਿਕਿ ਕਰਮ ਕਮਾਵਣੇ ਦੋਸੁ ਨ ਕਾਹੂ ਜੋਗੁ ॥ ਪਰਮੇਸਰ ਤੇ ਭੁਲਿਆਂ ਵਿਆਪਨਿ ਸਭੇ ਰੋਗ ॥ ਵੇਮੁਖ ਹੋਏ ਰਾਮ ਤੇ ਲਗਨਿ ਜਨਮ ਵਿਜੋਗ ॥ ਖਿਨ ਮਹਿ ਕਉੜੇ ਹੋਇ ਗਏ ਜਿਤੜੇ ਮਾਇਆ ਭੋਗ ॥ ਵਿਚ ਨ ਕੋਈ ਕਰਿ ਸਕੈ ਕਿਸ ਥੈ ਰੋਵਹਿ ਰੋਜ ॥ ਕੀਤਾ ਕਿਛੁ ਨ ਹੋਵਈ ਲਿਖਿਆ ਧੁਰਿ ਸੰਜੋਗ ॥ (pg. 135 A.G.)

What good is food, and what good are attires & adornments, if the True Lord does not abide within the mind? What good are fruits, what good is butter, what good is sweet molasses, and what good is flour? What good are clothes, and what good is a soft bed, to enjoy pleasures and sensual delights? What good is an army, and what good are soldiers, servants and mansions to live in? Says Nanak : without the True Name, all this paraphernalia is perishable.[139]

Nanak wonders : what has happened to the world? There is no guide or friend. There is no love, even among brothers and relatives. For the sake of worldly riches, people have lost their faith. They weep and wail. They slap their faces and pull their hair out. But if they chant the Name of the Lord, they shall be absorbed into it.[140]

People eat what they believe to be sweet, but it turns out to be bitter in taste. They attach their affections to brothers and friends, uselessly engrossed in corruption and attachment. They vanish without a moment's delay; without God's Name, they are stunned and amazed. O my mind, attach yourself to the service of the True Guru. Whatever is seen, shall pass away. Abandon the intellectual vibrations of your mind. Like the mad dog running around in all directions, the greedy person, unaware, consumes everything, edible and non-edible alike. Engrossed in the intoxication of sexual desire and anger, people wander through reincarnation over and over again, aimlessly.[141]

---

[139] ਕਿਆ ਖਾਧੈ ਕਿਆ ਪੈਧੈ ਹੋਇ ॥ ਜਾ ਮਨਿ ਨਾਹੀ ਸਚਾ ਸੋਇ ॥ ਕਿਆ ਮੇਵਾ ਕਿਆ ਘਿਓ ਗੁੜੁ ਮਿਠਾ ਕਿਆ ਮੈਦਾ ਕਿਆ ਮਾਸੁ ॥ ਕਿਆ ਕਪੜੁ ਕਿਆ ਸੇਜ ਸੁਖਾਲੀ ਕੀਜਹਿ ਭੋਗ ਬਿਲਾਸ ॥ ਕਿਆ ਲਸਕਰ ਕਿਆ ਨੇਬ ਖਵਾਸੀ ਆਵੈ ਮਹਲੀ ਵਾਸੁ ॥ ਨਾਨਕ ਸਚੇ ਨਾਮ ਵਿਣੁ ਸਭੇ ਟੋਲ ਵਿਣਾਸੁ ॥ ੨ ॥(Pg.142 A.G.)
[140] ਨਾਨਕ ਦੁਨੀਆ ਕੈਸੀ ਹੋਈ ॥ ਸਾਲਕੁ ਮਿਤੁ ਨ ਰਹਿਓ ਕੋਈ ॥ ਭਾਈ ਬੰਧੀ ਹੇਤੁ ਚੁਕਾਇਆ ॥ ਦੁਨੀਆ ਕਾਰਣਿ ਦੀਨੁ ਗਵਾਇਆ ॥ ੫ ॥ ਹੈ ਹੈ ਕਰਿ ਕੈ ਓਹਿ ਕਰੇਨਿ ॥ ਗਲਾ ਪਿਟਨਿ ਸਿਰੁ ਖੋਹੇਨਿ ॥ ਨਾਉ ਲੈਨਿ ਅਰੁ ਕਰਨਿ ਸਮਾਇ ॥ ਨਾਨਕ ਤਿਨ ਬਲਿਹਾਰੈ ਜਾਇ ॥ ੬ ॥ (Pg.1410 A.G.)
[141] ਮਿਠਾ ਕਰਿ ਕੈ ਖਾਇਆ ਕਉੜਾ ਉਪਜਿਆ ਸਾਦੁ ॥ ਭਾਈ ਮੀਤ ਸੁਰਿਦ ਕੀਏ ਬਿਖਿਆ ਰਚਿਆ ਬਾਦੁ ॥ ਜਾਂਦੇ ਬਿਲਮ ਨ ਹੋਵਈ ਵਿਣੁ ਨਾਵੈ ਬਿਸਮਾਦੁ ॥ ੧ ॥ ਮੇਰੇ ਮਨ ਸਤਗੁਰ ਕੀ ਸੇਵਾ ਲਾਗੁ ॥ ਜੋ ਦੀਸੈ ਸੋ ਵਿਣਸਣਾ ਮਨ ਕੀ ਮਤਿ ਤਿਆਗੁ ॥ ੧ ॥ ਰਹਾਉ ॥ ਜਿਉ ਕੂਕਰੁ ਹਰਕਾਇਆ ਧਾਵੈ ਦਹ

The boat is old, and it has thousands of holes. Those who are light get across, while those who carry the weight of their sins on their heads are drowned. The bones burn like wood, and the hair burns like straw. Seeing the world burning thus, Kabeer has become sad. Do not be so proud of your bones wrapped up in flesh. Those who were on their horses and under their canopies, were eventually buried under the ground. Do not be so proud of your high mansions. Today or tomorrow, you shall lie beneath the ground, and the grass shall grow above you. Do not be so proud, and do not ridicule the poor. Your boat is still out at sea; who knows what will happen?[142]

Earning a thousand, he runs after a hundred thousand. Satisfaction is not obtained by chasing Illusionary thoughts and pursuing such objectives. He may enjoy all sorts of corrupt pleasures, but he is still not satisfied; he indulges again and again, wearing himself out, until he dies. Without contentment, no one is satisfied. Like the objects in a dream, all his efforts are in vain. Through the love of the Lord's Name, all peace is obtained. Only a few obtain this, by great good fortune. He Himself is Himself, the Root-Cause of ALL Known and Unknown Causes. Forever and ever, Says Nanak, chant the Lord's Name.[143]

GREED is considered to be a major vice that leads one onto other dangerous vices like violence and deceit. It assumes the proportions of a mental disease, when in reaches the saturation point.

ਦਿਸ ਜਾਇ ॥ ਲੋਭੀ ਜੰਤੁ ਨ ਜਾਣਈ ਭਖੁ ਅਭਖੁ ਸਭ ਖਾਇ ॥ ਕਾਮ ਕ੍ਰੋਧ ਮਦਿ ਬਿਆਪਿਆ ਫਿਰਿ ਫਿਰਿ ਜੋਨੀ ਪਾਇ ॥ ੨ ॥ (pg. 50 A.G.)

[142] ਕਬੀਰ ਬੇੜਾ ਜਰਜਰਾ ਫੂਟੇ ਛੇਂਕ ਹਜਾਰ ॥ ਹਰੂਏ ਹਰੂਏ ਤਿਰਿ ਗਏ ਡੂਬੇ ਜਿਨ ਸਿਰ ਭਾਰ ॥ ੩੫ ॥ ਕਬੀਰ ਹਾਡ ਜਰੇ ਜਿਉ ਲਾਕਰੀ ਕੇਸ ਜਰੇ ਜਿਉ ਘਾਸੁ ॥ ਇਹੁ ਜਗੁ ਜਰਤਾ ਦੇਖਿ ਕੈ ਭਇਓ ਕਬੀਰੁ ਉਦਾਸੁ ॥ ੩੬ ॥ ਕਬੀਰ ਗਰਬੁ ਨ ਕੀਜੀਐ ਚਾਮ ਲਪੇਟੇ ਹਾਡ ॥ ਹੈਵਰ ਊਪਰਿ ਛਤ੍ਰ ਤਰ ਤੇ ਫੁਨਿ ਧਰਨੀ ਗਾਡ ॥ ੩੭ ॥ ਕਬੀਰ ਗਰਬੁ ਨ ਕੀਜੀਐ ਊਚਾ ਦੇਖਿ ਅਵਾਸੁ ॥ ਆਜੁ ਕਾਲ੍ਹਿ ਭੁਇ ਲੇਟਣਾ ਊਪਰਿ ਜਾਮੈ ਘਾਸੁ ॥ ੩੮ ॥ ਕਬੀਰ ਗਰਬੁ ਨ ਕੀਜੀਐ ਰੰਕੁ ਨ ਹਸੀਐ ਕੋਇ ॥ ਅਜਹੁ ਸੁ ਨਾਉ ਸਮੁੰਦ੍ਰ ਮਹਿ ਕਿਆ ਜਾਨਉ ਕਿਆ ਹੋਇ ॥ ੩੯ ॥ (pg. 1366 A.G.)

[143] ਸਹਸ ਖਟੇ ਲਖ ਕਉ ਉਠਿ ਧਾਵੈ ॥ ਤ੍ਰਿਪਤਿ ਨ ਆਵੈ ਮਾਇਆ ਪਾਛੈ ਪਾਵੈ ॥ ਅਨਿਕ ਭੋਗ ਬਿਖਿਆ ਕੇ ਕਰੈ ॥ ਨਹ ਤ੍ਰਿਪਤਾਵੈ ਖਪਿ ਖਪਿ ਮਰੈ ॥ ਬਿਨਾ ਸੰਤੋਖ ਨਹੀ ਕੋਊ ਰਾਜੈ ॥ ਸੁਪਨ ਮਨੋਰਥ ਬ੍ਰਿਥੇ ਸਭ ਕਾਜੈ ॥ ਨਾਮ ਰੰਗਿ ਸਰਬ ਸੁਖੁ ਹੋਇ ॥ ਬਡਭਾਗੀ ਕਿਸੈ ਪਰਾਪਤਿ ਹੋਇ ॥ ਕਰਨ ਕਰਾਵਨ ਆਪੇ ਆਪਿ ਸਦਾ ਸਦਾ ਨਾਨਕ ਹਰਿ ਜਾਪਿ ॥ ੫ ॥ (pg. 278-79 A.G.)

The natural equilibrium is disturbed, when a greedy person accumulates immense wealth, while another person has to shiver in the cold, shelterless, sans clothing.

To remain happy with whatsoever one has, is True Contentment. This should not be misconstrued to imply that being ambitious is negative, provided the rapid strides towards success DO NOT, in any way, impinge upon another's interests.

Abundance of wealth and materials does not guarantee happiness. Peace is the direct consequence of Contentment. Being progressive is welcome, without usurping another's rights and privileges.

Where is that door, where You live, O Lord? What is that door called? Among all doors, who can find that door? For the sake of that door, I wander around sadly, detached from the world; if only someone would come and tell me about that door. How can I cross over the world-ocean? While I am living, I cannot be dead.[144]

The True Devotee is the one with whom God is thoroughly pleased. He dwells apart from Illusion. Performing good deeds, he does not seek rewards. Spotlessly pure is the religious-belief, and life, of such a devotee; he has no desire for the fruits of his efforts. He is absorbed in devotional worship and the recitation of the Holy Hymns that are laudatory of the Lord's Glory. Within his mind and body, he meditates upon the Lord of the Universe. He is kind to all creatures.[145]

I have no anxiety about dying, and no hope of living. You are the Cherisher of all beings; You keep the account of our breaths and morsels of food. You abide within the God-loving souls. As it pleases You, You decide our allotment. Chant the Name of the Lord ; the mind will be pleased and appeased. The raging fires within are extinguished; the aspirant obtains spiritual wisdom.[146]

One observes no difference between Optimism & Pessimism, in a state of Real Detachment. The literal meaning (of detachment) would be, being in a state of utter despair, sadness, even to the extreme of becoming a recluse. But, the deeper, philosophic implication, in the

---

[144] ਜਿਤੁ ਦਰਿ ਵਸਹਿ ਕਵਨੁ ਦਰੁ ਕਹੀਐ ਦਰਾ ਭੀਤਰਿ ਦਰੁ ਕਵਨੁ ਲਹੈ ॥ ਜਿਸੁ ਦਰ ਕਾਰਣਿ ਫਿਰਾ ਉਦਾਸੀ ਸੋ ਦਰੁ ਕੋਈ ਆਇ ਕਹੈ ॥ ੧ ॥ ਕਿਨ ਬਿਧਿ ਸਾਗਰੁ ਤਰੀਐ ॥ ਜੀਵਤਿਆ ਨਹ ਮਰੀਐ ॥ ੧ ॥ (pg. 877 A.G.)

[145] ਬੈਸਨੋ ਸੋ ਜਿਸੁ ਉਪਰਿ ਸੁਪ੍ਰਸੰਨ ॥ ਬਿਸਨ ਕੀ ਮਾਇਆ ਤੇ ਹੋਇ ਭਿੰਨ ॥ ਕਰਮ ਕਰਤ ਹੋਵੈ ਨਿਹਕਰਮ ॥ ਤਿਸੁ ਬੈਸਨੋ ਕਾ ਨਿਰਮਲ ਧਰਮ ॥ ਕਾਹੂ ਫਲ ਕੀ ਇਛਾ ਨਹੀ ਬਾਛੈ ॥ ਕੇਵਲ ਭਗਤਿ ਕੀਰਤਨ ਸੰਗਿ ਰਾਚੈ ॥ ਮਨ ਤਨ ਅੰਤਰਿ ਸਿਮਰਨ ਗੋਪਾਲ ॥ ਸਭ ਊਪਰਿ ਹੋਵਤ ਕਿਰਪਾਲ ॥ (pg. 274 A.G.)

[146] ਮਰਣੈ ਕੀ ਚਿੰਤਾ ਨਹੀ ਜੀਵਣ ਕੀ ਨਹੀ ਆਸ ॥ ਤੂ ਸਰਬ ਜੀਆ ਪ੍ਰਤਿਪਾਲਹੀ ਲੇਖੈ ਸਾਸ ਗਿਰਾਸ ॥ ਅੰਤਰਿ ਗੁਰਮੁਖਿ ਤੂ ਵਸਹਿ ਜਿਉ ਭਾਵੈ ਤਿਉ ਨਿਰਜਾਸਿ ॥ ੧ ॥ ਜੀਅਰੇ ਰਾਮ ਜਪਤ ਮਨੁ ਮਾਨੁ ॥ ਅੰਤਰਿ ਲਾਗੀ ਜਲਿ ਬੁਝੀ ਪਾਇਆ ਗੁਰਮੁਖਿ ਗਿਆਨੁ ॥ ੧ ॥ (pg. 20 A.G.)

context of spiritual -realms, would be : Being with oneself, in solitude, with courage-of-conviction, and fortitude, in a contemplative and meditative state . Now, this frame-of- mind, and unique level could be attained even while one is sitting in a vast multitude of people, and yet calm and composed, within.. Talking, working, eating or whatever, but the thought is concentrated on the "ONLY ONE".

Under varying circumstances, the individual would, obviously react differently. In the event of the loss of a dear one, the bereaved relations of the deceased are naturally saddened. Similarly, a person afflicted with physical-ailments, financial-losses, emotional/psychological traumas, might, even, start thinking in terms of committing self-immolation/suicide. This, then, could be described as a FATAL - DETACHMENT, born out of disenchantment/disillusionment with life. This would be the direct consequence of a lack or absence of spiritual temper, and faith in God. It is developed, gradually, depending upon the intensity of the distinctly varied experiences one has had.

On the contrary, on attaining pristine knowledge, one becomes desirous of detachment, even while not foregoing worldly -existence and life. Life, now, seems as if it were a bubble of air, on the surface of water, waiting to burst any moment. All pleasures, of the senses, seem momentary. This is REJUVENATING DETACHMENT.

Treading, further ahead, on the sunlit path of detachment, one begins to be encouraged and tempted to seek "Communion with God". Now, one does not look for, or expect, rewards. There is no fear of death, now, and there exists (remains) no magnetic charm and attraction, for life, and the pleasures it has to offer (because the momentary-nature of these joys has been comprehended, with God's Divine Grace, and the Final Truth has dawned upon the devoted Soul).

A condition where one prefers to remain in solitude, with a positive attitude, and with a positive aim, of meditating upon God's Name, and not to be in a pensive and regretful frame-of-mind.

Now, the Merciful Lord hath decreed that nobody shall persecute and torture another, and that all may reside in peace and harmony, under His Benevolent Rule. [147]

Fareed implores the Lord, not to let him live on alms, and on another's mercy. Instead, he would prefer death, to slavery. [148]

The battle-drums and conch-shells signal the commencement of the battle. The spiritual warriors enter the battle-field, in all their paraphernilia and regalia. He alone is known as a spiritual hero, who fights in defense of religion (NOT the religions or faiths that we have founded, BUT the religion of the Lord : that wants us to sacrifice our lives for peace and justice, and to never let cowardice devour us). He may be cut apart, piece by piece, but he never withdraw from the war-zone. [149]

The God-loving and the God-fearing warriors would never subjugate another, but would use their power to protect the weak and the downtrodden, the oppressed and the suppressed. Freedom is the birth-right of every human, while slavery is a curse.

---

[147] ਹੁਣਿ ਹੁਕਮੁ ਹੋਆ ਮਿਹਰਵਾਣ ਦਾ ॥ ਪੈ ਕੋਇ ਨ ਕਿਸੈ ਰਞਾਣਦਾ ॥ ਸਭ ਸੁਖਾਲੀ ਵੁਠੀਆ ਇਹੁ ਹੋਆ ਹਲੇਮੀ ਰਾਜੁ ਜੀਉ ॥ ੧੩ ॥ (Pg.74 A.G.)

[148] ਫਰੀਦਾ ਬਾਰਿ ਪਰਾਇਐ ਬੈਸਣਾ ਸਾਂਈ ਮੁਝੈ ਨ ਦੇਹਿ ॥ ਜੇ ਤੂ ਏਵੈ ਰਖਸੀ ਜੀਉ ਸਰੀਰਹੁ ਲੇਹਿ ॥ ੪੨ ॥ (Pg.1380 A.G.)

[149] ਗਗਨ ਦਮਾਮਾ ਬਾਜਿਓ ਪਰਿਓ ਨੀਸਾਨੈ ਘਾਉ ॥ ਖੇਤੁ ਜੁ ਮਾਂਡਿਓ ਸੂਰਮਾ ਅਬ ਜੂਝਨ ਕੋ ਦਾਉ ॥ ੧ ॥ ਸੂਰਾ ਸੋ ਪਹਿਚਾਨੀਐ ਜੁ ਲਰੈ ਦੀਨ ਕੇ ਹੇਤ ॥ ਪੁਰਜਾ ਪੁਰਜਾ ਕਟਿ ਮਰੈ ਕਬਹੂ ਨ ਛਾਡੈ ਖੇਤੁ ॥ ੨ ॥ ੨ ॥(P.G. 1105 A.G.)

SECTION : 4

BEWARE

The egg of doubt has burst; my mind has been enlightened. The Guru has shattered the shackles on my feet, and has set me free. I have been released from the bondage, and from the vicious cycle of reincarnation. The boiling cauldron has cooled down; the Guru has blessed me with the cooling, soothing Naam, the Name of the Lord. Since I joined the Company of the Holy, those who were eyeing me have left. The one who tied me up, has released me; what can the Watchman of Death do to me now? The burdensome load of my Karma has been removed, and I am now free. I have crossed the world-ocean, and reached the other shore; the Guru has blessed me with this Dharma. True is my place, and True is my seat; I have made Truth my life's purpose. True is my capital, and True is the merchandise, which Nanak has placed into the home of the heart. The Pandit, the Hindu scholar-priest, proclaims the Vedas, but he is slow to act on them. Another person on silence sits alone, but his heart is tied in knots of desire. Another becomes an Udaasi, a renunciate; he abandons his home and walks out on his family, but his wandering impulses do not leave him. Who can I tell about the state of my soul? Where can I find such a person who is liberated, and who can unite me with my God? Someone may practice intensive meditation, and discipline his body, but his mind still runs around in ten directions. The celibate practices celibacy, but his heart is filled with pride. The renunciate wanders around at sacred shrines of pilgrimage, but his mindless anger is still within him. The temple dancers tie bells around their ankles to earn their living. Others go on fasts, take vows, perform the six rituals and wear religious robes, to brag about. Some sing songs and melodies and hymns, but their minds do not sing the praise of the Lord. The Lord's Saints are immaculately pure; they are beyond pleasure and pain, beyond greed and attachment. My mind obtains the dust of their feet, when the Lord shows mercy. Says Nanak, I met the Perfect Guru, and then the anxiety of my mind was removed. My Sovereign Lord knows my inner-most secrets. The Beloved of my soul knows everything; all trivial talk is forgotten. [150]

---

[150] ਛੁਟੋ ਆਂਡਾ ਭਰਮ ਕਾ ਮਨਹਿ ਭਇਓ ਪਰਗਾਸੁ ॥ ਕਾਟੀ ਬੇਰੀ ਪਗਹ ਤੇ ਗੁਰਿ ਕੀਨੀ ਬੰਦਿ ਖਲਾਸੁ

People are entangled in the enjoyment of fine clothes, but gold and silver are only dust. They acquire beautiful horses and elephants, and ornate carriages of many kinds. They think of nothing else, and they forget all their kith and kin, under the influence of ego, they ignore their Creator; without the Name, they are impure. Gathering wealth, you earn an evil reputation, when you harm the interests of others, employing fraudulent means. Those whom you work to please shall pass away along with you. The egotistical are engrossed in egotism, ensnared by the devious intellect of the mind. One who is deceived by God Himself, has no position and no honor.[151]

This world is an illusion; people pass their lives sleeping. By the Pleasure of His Will, He elevates some, to merge unto Him. He Himself abides in the mind, and drives out attachment to illusion. He Himself bestows glorious greatness; He inspires the God-loving to understand the distinction between reality and illusion. The One Lord

---

॥ ੧ ॥ ਆਵਣ ਜਾਣੁ ਰਹਿਓ ॥ ਤਪਤ ਕੜਾਹ ਬੁਝਿ ਗਇਆ ਗੁਰਿ ਸੀਤਲ ਨਾਮੁ ਦੀਓ ॥ ੧ ॥ ਰਹਾਉ ॥ ਜਬ ਤੇ ਸਾਧੂ ਸੰਗੁ ਭਇਆ ਤਉ ਛੋਡਿ ਗਏ ਨਿਗਹਾਰ ॥ ਜਿਸ ਕੀ ਅਟਕ ਤਿਸ ਤੇ ਛੁਟੀ ਤਉ ਕਹਾ ਕਰੈ ਕੋਟਵਾਰ ॥ ੨ ॥ ਚੂਕਾ ਭਾਰਾ ਕਰਮ ਕਾ ਹੋਏ ਨਿਹਕਰਮਾ ॥ ਸਾਗਰ ਤੇ ਕੰਢੈ ਚੜੇ ਗੁਰਿ ਕੀਨੇ ਧਰਮਾ ॥ ੩ ॥ ਸਚੁ ਥਾਨੁ ਸਚੁ ਬੈਠਕਾ ਸਚੁ ਸੁਆਉ ਬਣਾਇਆ ॥ ਸਚੁ ਪੂੰਜੀ ਸਚੁ ਵਖਰੋ ਨਾਨਕ ਘਰਿ ਪਾਇਆ ॥ ੪ ॥ ੫ ॥ ੧੪ ॥ ਮਾਰੂ ਮਹਲਾ ੫ ॥ ਬੇਦੁ ਪੁਕਾਰੈ ਮੁਖ ਤੇ ਪੰਡਿਤ ਕਾਮਾਮਨ ਕਾ ਮਾਤਾ ॥ ਮੋਨੀ ਹੋਇ ਬੈਠਾ ਇਕਾਂਤੀ ਹਿਰਦੈ ਕਲਪਨ ਗਾਤਾ ॥ ਹੋਇ ਉਦਾਸੀ ਗ੍ਰਿਹੁ ਤਜਿ ਚਲਿਓ ਛੁਟਕੈ ਨਾਹੀ ਨਾਤਾ ॥ ੧ ॥ ਜੀਅ ਕੀ ਕੈ ਪਹਿ ਬਾਤ ਕਹਾ ॥ ਆਪਿ ਮੁਕਤੁ ਮੋ ਕਉ ਪ੍ਰਭੁ ਮੇਲੇ ਐਸੋ ਕਹਾ ਲਹਾ ॥ ੧ ॥ ਰਹਾਉ ॥ ਤਪਸੀ ਕਰਿ ਕੈ ਦੇਹੀ ਸਾਧੀ ਮਨੂਆ ਦਹ ਦਿਸ ਧਾਨਾ ॥ ਬ੍ਰਹਮਚਾਰਿ ਬ੍ਰਹਮਚਜੁ ਕੀਨਾ ਹਿਰਦੈ ਭਇਆ ਗੁਮਾਨਾ ॥ ਸੰਨਿਆਸੀ ਹੋਇ ਕੈ ਤੀਰਥਿ ਭੂਮਿਓ ਉਸੁ ਮਹਿ ਕ੍ਰੋਧੁ ਬਿਗਾਨਾ ॥ ੨ ॥ ਘੁੰਘਰ ਬਾਧਿ ਭਏ ਰਾਮਦਾਸਾ ਰੋਟੀਅਨ ਕੇ ਓਪਾਵਾ ॥ ਬਰਤ ਨੇਮ ਕਰਮ ਖਟ ਕੀਨੇ ਬਾਹਰਿ ਭੇਖ ਦਿਖਾਵਾ ॥ ਗੀਤ ਨਾਦ ਮੁਖਿ ਰਾਗਾ ਅਲਾਪੇ ਮਨਿ ਨਹੀ ਹਰਿ ਹਰਿ ਗਾਵਾ ॥ ੩ ॥ ਹਰਖ ਸੋਗ ਲੋਭ ਮੋਹ ਰਹਤ ਹਹਿ ਨਿਰਮਲ ਹਰਿ ਕੇ ਸੰਤਾ ॥ ਤਿਨ ਕੀ ਧੂੜਿ ਪਾਏ ਮਨੁ ਮੇਰਾ ਜਾ ਦਇਆ ਕਰੇ ਭਗਵੰਤਾ ॥ ਕਹੁ ਨਾਨਕ ਗੁਰੁ ਪੂਰਾ ਮਿਲਿਆ ਤਾਂ ਉਤਰੀ ਮਨ ਕੀ ਚਿੰਤਾ ॥ ੪ ॥ ਮੇਰਾ ਅੰਤਰਜਾਮੀ ਹਰਿ ਰਾਇਆ ॥ ਸਭੁ ਕਿਛੁ ਜਾਣੈ ਮੇਰੇ ਜੀਅ ਕਾ ਪ੍ਰੀਤਮੁ ਬਿਸਰਿ ਗਏ ਬਕਬਾਇਆ ॥ ੧ ॥ ਰਹਾਉ ਦੂਜਾ ॥

॥ ੬ ॥ ੧੫ ॥ (Pg. 1002 A.G.)

[151] ਕਪੜਿ ਭੋਗਿ ਲਪਟਾਇਆ ਸੁਇਨਾ ਰੁਪਾ ਖਾਕੁ ॥ ਹੈਵਰ ਗੈਵਰ ਬਹੁ ਰੰਗੇ ਕੀਏ ਰਥ ਅਥਾਕ ॥ ਕਿਸ ਹੀ ਚਿਤਿ ਨ ਪਾਵਹੀ ਬਿਸਰਿਆ ਸਭ ਸਾਕ ॥ ਸਿਰਜਣਹਾਰਿ ਭੁਲਾਇਆ ਵਿਣੁ ਨਾਵੈ ਨਾਪਾਕ ॥ ੨ ॥ ਲੈਦਾ ਬਦ ਦੁਆਇ ਤੂੰ ਮਾਇਆ ਕਰਹਿ ਇਕਤ ॥ ਜਿਸ ਨੋ ਤੂੰ ਪਤੀਆਇਦਾ ਸੋ ਸਣੁ ਤੁਝੈ ਅਨਿਤ ॥ ਅਹੰਕਾਰੁ ਕਰਹਿ ਅਹੰਕਾਰੀਆ ਵਿਆਪਿਆ ਮਨ ਕੀ ਮਤਿ ॥ ਤਿਨਿ ਪ੍ਰਭਿ ਆਪਿ ਭੁਲਾਇਆ ਨਾ ਤਿਸੁ ਜਾਤਿ ਨ ਪਤਿ ॥ ੩ ॥ (pg. 42 A.G.)

is the Giver of all. He corrects those who make mistakes. He Himself has deceived some, and attached them to duality. Through the Guru's Teachings, the Lord is found, and one's light merges into the Light. [152]

The many forms of attachment to Illusionary-Hallucinations shall surely pass away — know that they are transitory. People fall in love with the shade of the tree, and when it passes away, they feel the pain of remorse and regret. Whatever is seen, shall pass away; and yet, the blindest of the blind cling to it. O mind, the love of the Name of the Lord bestows peace. Says Nanak, the Lord, in His Mercy, unites us with Himself. False are body, wealth, and all relations. False are ego, possessiveness and Illusion. False are power, youth, wealth and property. False are sexual desire and wild anger. False are chariots, elephants, horses and expensive clothes. False are deception, emotional attachment and egotistical pride. False are pride and self-conceit. Only devotional worship is permanent, and the Sanctuary of the Holy. Nanak lives by meditating, on the Lotus Feet of the Lord. [153]

---

[152] ਸੰਸਾ ਇਹੁ ਸੰਸਾਰੁ ਹੈ ਸੁਤਿਆ ਰੈਨਿ ਵਿਹਾਇ ॥ ਇਕਿ ਆਪਣੈ ਭਾਣੈ ਕਢਿ ਲਇਅਨੁ ਆਪੇ ਲਇਓਨੁ ਮਿਲਾਇ ॥ ਆਪੇ ਹੀ ਆਪਿ ਮਨਿ ਵਸਿਆ ਮਾਇਆ ਮੋਹੁ ਚੁਕਾਇ ॥ ਆਪਿ ਵਡਾਈ ਦਿਤੀਅਨੁ ਗੁਰਮੁਖਿ ਦੇਇ ਬੁਝਾਇ ॥ ੩ ॥ ਸਭਨਾ ਕਾ ਦਾਤਾ ਏਕੁ ਹੈ ਭੁਲਿਆ ਲਏ ਸਮਝਾਇ ॥ ਇਕਿ ਆਪੇ ਆਪਿ ਆਇਅਨੁ ਦੂਜੈ ਛਡਿਅਨੁ ਲਾਇ ॥ ਗੁਰਮਤੀ ਹਰਿ ਪਾਈਐ ਜੋਤੀ ਜੋਤਿ ਮਿਲਾਇ ॥ ੪ ॥ ੨੫ ॥੫੮॥ (pg. 36 A.G.)

[153] ਅਨਿਕ ਭਾਤਿ ਮਾਇਆ ਕੇ ਹੇਤ ॥ ਸਰਪਰ ਹੋਵਤ ਜਾਨੁ ਅਨੇਤ ॥ ਬਿਰਖ ਕੀ ਛਾਇਆ ਸਿਉ ਰੰਗੁ ਲਾਵੈ ॥ ਓਹ ਬਿਨਸੈ ਉਹੁ ਮਨਿ ਪਛੁਤਾਵੈ ॥ ਜੋ ਦੀਸੈ ਸੋ ਚਾਲਨਹਾਰੁ ॥ ਲਪਟਿ ਰਹਿਓ ਤਹ ਅੰਧ ਅੰਧਾਰੁ ॥ ਬਟਾਊ ਸਿਉ ਜੋ ਲਾਵੈ ਨੇਹ ॥ ਤਾ ਕਉ ਹਾਥਿ ਨ ਆਵੈ ਕੇਹ ॥ ਮਨ ਹਰਿ ਕੇ ਨਾਮ ਕੀ ਪ੍ਰੀਤਿ ਸੁਖਦਾਈ ॥ ਕਰਿ ਕਿਰਪਾ ਨਾਨਕ ਆਪਿ ਲਏ ਲਾਈ ॥ ੩ ॥ ਮਿਥਿਆ ਤਨੁ ਧਨੁ ਕੁਟੰਬੁ ਸਬਾਇਆ ॥ ਮਿਥਿਆ ਹਉਮੈ ਮਮਤਾ ਮਾਇਆ ॥ ਮਿਥਿਆ ਰਾਜ ਜੋਬਨ ਧਨ ਮਾਲ ॥ ਮਿਥਿਆ ਕਾਮ ਕ੍ਰੋਧ ਬਿਕਰਾਲ ॥ ਮਿਥਿਆ ਰਥ ਹਸਤੀ ਅਸੁ ਬਸਤ੍ਰਾ ॥ ਮਿਥਿਆ ਰੰਗ ਸੰਗਿ ਮਾਇਆ ਪੇਖਿ ਹਸਤਾ ॥ ਮਿਥਿਆ ਧ੍ਰੋਹ ਮੋਹ ਅਭਿਮਾਨੁ ॥ ਮਿਥਿਆ ਆਪਸ ਊਪਰਿ ਕਰਤ ਗੁਮਾਨੁ ॥ ਅਸਥਿਰੁ ਭਗਤਿ ਸਾਧ ਕੀ ਸਰਨ ॥ ਨਾਨਕ ਜਪਿ ਜਪਿ ਜੀਵੈ ਹਰਿ ਕੇ ਚਰਨ ॥ ੪ ॥ (pg. 268 A.G.)

The self-willed egoistic persons read and study, but they do not know the way. They do not understand the Name of the Lord; they wander, deluded and deluged by doubt. They take bribes, and give false testimony; the noose of evil-mindedness is around their necks, and they shall hang themselves. They read the Scriptures; they argue and debate, but do not know the essence of reality; they indulge in rituals and ceremonial practices. Without the Perfect Guru, the essence of reality is not obtained. The true and pure beings walk the Path of Truth. He Himself is wise, and He Himself judges the Truth. Those whom God blesses with His Glance of Grace become God-loving, and praise the Word of the Holy hymns. [154]

Such behaviour is severely deplorable, and tantamount to a grave SIN. Feeding one's children, from the money gotten through corrupt means, is just like poisoning their food, with the venom of a snake. A person whose intake is such, shall have vitriolic speech and a foul tongue, never pleasant in conversation and in his dealings with others.

Such misdemeanors of the corrupt do not go unpunished. They shall be penalized, on earth, and in God's Supreme Court.

---

[154]ਪੜਹਿ ਮਨਮੁਖ ਪਰੁ ਬਿਧਿ ਨਹੀ ਜਾਨਾ ॥ ਨਾਮੁ ਨ ਬੂਝਹਿ ਭਰਮਿ ਭੁਲਾਨਾ ॥ ਲੈ ਕੈ ਵਢੀ ਦੇਨਿ ਉਗਾਹੀ ਦੁਰਮਤਿ ਕਾ ਗਲਿ ਫਾਹਾ ਹੇ ॥ ੩ ॥ ਸਿਮ੍ਰਿਤਿ ਸਾਸਤੁ ਪੜਹਿ ਪੁਰਾਣਾ ॥ ਵਾਦੁ ਵਖਾਣਹਿ ਤਤੁ ਨ ਜਾਣਾ ॥ ਵਿਣੁ ਗੁਰ ਪੂਰੇ ਤਤੁ ਨ ਪਾਈਐ ਸਚ ਸੂਚੇ ਸਚੁ ਰਾਹਾ ਹੇ ॥ ੪ ॥ ਸਭ ਸਾਲਾਹੇ ਸੁਣਿ ਸੁਣਿ ਆਚੈ ॥ ਆਪੇ ਦਾਨਾ ਸਚੁ ਪਰਾਖੈ ॥ ਜਿਨ ਕਉ ਨਦਰਿ ਕਰੇ ਪ੍ਰਭੁ ਅਪਨੀ ਗੁਰਮੁਖਿ ਸਬਦੁ ਸਲਾਹਾ ਹੇ ॥ ੫ ॥ (pg. 1032 A.G.)

You have not forsaken sexual desire, and you have not forgotten anger; greed has not left you either. You have not stopped slandering and gossiping about others. Your service is useless and fruitless. By breaking into the houses of others and robbing them, you fill your belly, you sinner. But when you go to the world beyond, you shall be notorious, for your acts of ommission and commission, that you hath committed, due to your ignorance. Cruelty has not left your mind; you have not cherished kindness for other living beings.[155]

When oppression and tyranny are on the ascendant, a myriad array of vices controls the human-frame (body and mind). The bondage of self-aggrandizement can be gotten rid of by meditating upon God's Name. That's the only remedy for the tormented oppressor as well as the weak and cowardly oppressed.[156]

The emperor who struck down the poor, has been burnt in the fire by the Supreme Lord God. The Creator administers true justice. He is the Saving Grace of His slaves.[157]

Sayeth Saint Kabir: It is tyranny to use force; the Lord shall call you to account. And then yo shall be tortured and humiliated, in the Lord's Court. Keep the slate of your conscience clean and clear, to become the recipient of

---

[155] ਲਲ ਕਾਮੁ ਨ ਬਿਸਰਿਓ ਕ੍ਰੋਧੁ ਨ ਬਿਸਰਿਓ ਲੋਭੁ ਨ ਛੂਟਿਓ ਦੇਵਾ ॥ ਪਰ ਨਿੰਦਾ ਮੁਖ ਤੇ ਨਹੀ ਛੂਟੀ ਨਿਫਲਭਈ ਸਭ ਸੇਵਾ ॥ ੧ ॥ ਬਾਟ ਪਾਰਿ ਘਰੁ ਮੂਸਿ ਬਿਰਾਨੋ ਪੇਟੁ ਭਰੈ ਅਪ੍ਰਾਧੀ ॥ ਜਿਹਿ ਪਰਲੋਕ ਜਾਇ ਅਪਕੀਰਤਿ ਸੋਈ ਅਬਿਦਿਆ ਸਾਧੀ ॥ ੨ ॥ ਹਿੰਸਾ ਤਉ ਮਨ ਤੇ ਨਹੀ ਛੂਟੀ ਜੀਅ ਦਇਆ ਨਹੀ ਪਾਲੀ ॥ (Pg.1253 A.G.)

[156] ਜੋਰ ਜੁਲਮ ਫੂਲਹਿ ਘਨੋ ਕਾਚੀ ਦੇਹ ਬਿਕਾਰ ॥ ਅਹੰਬੁਧਿ ਬੰਧਨ ਪਰੇ ਨਾਨਕ ਨਾਮ ਛੁਟਾਰ ॥ ੧ ॥ (pg. 255 A.G.)

[157] ਗਰੀਬਾ ਉਪਰਿ ਜਿ ਖਿੰਜੈ ਦਾੜੀ ॥ ਪਾਰਬ੍ਰਹਮਿ ਸਾ ਅਗਨਿ ਮਹਿ ਸਾੜੀ ॥ ੧ ॥ ਪੂਰਾ ਨਿਆਉ ਕਰੇ ਕਰਤਾਰੁ ॥ ਅਪੁਨੇ ਦਾਸ ਕਉ ਰਾਖਨਹਾਰੁ ॥ ੧ ॥ (pg. 199 A.G.)

God's Grace. In the True Court of the Lord, you shall not be captured or put in shackles. [158]

---

[158] ਕਬੀਰ ਜੋਰੁ ਕੀਆ ਸੋ ਜੁਲਮੁ ਹੈ ਲੇਇ ਜਬਾਬੁ ਖੁਦਾਇ ॥ ਦਫਤਰਿ ਲੇਖਾ ਨੀਕਸੈ ਮਾਰ ਮੁਹੈ ਮੁਹਿ ਖਾਇ ॥ ੨੦੦ ॥ ਕਬੀਰ ਲੇਖਾ ਦੇਨਾ ਸੁਹੇਲਾ ਜਉ ਦਿਲ ਸੂਚੀ ਹੋਇ ॥ ਉਸੁ ਸਾਚੇ ਦੀਬਾਨ ਮਹਿ ਪਲਾ ਨ ਪਕਰੈ ਕੋਇ ॥ ੨੦੧ ॥ (pg. 1375 A.G.)

The man of false mind practices falsehood. He runs after illusion, and yet pretends to be a man of disciplined meditation. Deluded by doubt, he visits all the sacred shrines of pilgrimage. How can such a man of disciplined meditation attain the supreme status? By Guru's Grace, one lives the Truth. Nanak declares that such a man of disciplined meditation attains liberation. He alone is a man of disciplined meditation, who practices this self-discipline. Meeting with the True Guru, he contemplates the Word of the Holy hymns. Such a man of disciplined meditation is honoured in the Court of the Lord. [159]

Service to the Guru is the greatest sublime penance. The Dear Lord dwells in the mind, and all suffering departs. Then, at the Gate of the True Lord, one appears truthful. Serving the Guru, one comes to know the three worlds. Understanding his own self, he obtains the Lord. Through His True Word, we enter the Mansion of His Presence. Serving the Guru, all of one's generations are saved. Keep the Immaculate Name of the Lord enshrined within your heart. In the Court of the True Lord, you shall be adorned with True Glory. How very fortunate are they, who are committed to the Guru's service. Night and day, they are engaged in devotional worship; the True Name is implanted within them. Nanak chants the true thought. Keep the Name of the Lord enshrined within your heart. Imbued with devotion to the Lord, the gate of salvation is found. [160]

---

[159] ਮਨ ਕਾ ਝੂਠਾ ਝੂਠੁ ਕਮਾਵੈ ॥ ਮਾਇਆ ਨੋ ਫਿਰੈ ਤਪਾ ਸਦਾਵੈ ॥ ਭਰਮੇ ਭੂਲਾ ਸਭਿ ਤੀਰਥ ਗਹੈ ॥ ਓਹੁ ਤਪਾ ਕੈਸੇ ਪਰਮ ਗਤਿ ਲਹੈ ॥ ਗੁਰ ਪਰਸਾਦੀ ਕੋ ਸਚੁ ਕਮਾਵੈ ॥ ਨਾਨਕ ਸੋ ਤਪਾ ਮੋਖੰਤਰੁ ਪਾਵੈ ॥ ੧ ॥ ਮਃ ੩ ॥ ਸੋ ਤਪਾ ਜਿ ਇਹੁ ਤਪੁ ਘਾਲੇ ॥ ਸਤਿਗੁਰ ਨੋ ਮਿਲੈ ਸਬਦੁ ਸਮਾਲੇ ॥ ਸਤਿਗੁਰ ਕੀ ਸੇਵਾ ਇਹੁ ਤਪੁ ਪਰਵਾਣੁ ॥ ਨਾਨਕ ਸੋ ਤਪਾ ਦਰਗਹਿ ਪਾਵੈ ਮਾਣੁ ॥ ੨ ॥ (pg. 948 A.G.)
[160] ਗੁਰ ਸੇਵਾ ਤਪਾਂ ਸਿਰਿ ਤਪੁ ਸਾਰੁ ॥ ਹਰਿ ਜੀਉ ਮਨਿ ਵਸੈ ਸਭ ਦੁਖ ਵਿਸਾਰਣਹਾਰੁ ॥ ਦਰਿ ਸਾਚੈ ਦੀਸੈ ਸਚਿਆਰੁ ॥ ੪ ॥ ਗੁਰ ਸੇਵਾ ਤੇ ਤ੍ਰਿਭਵਣ ਸੋਝੀ ਹੋਇ ॥ ਆਪੁ ਪਛਾਣਿ ਹਰਿ ਪਾਵੈ ਸੋਇ ॥ ਸਾਚੀ ਬਾਣੀ ਮਹਲੁ ਪਰਾਪਤਿ ਹੋਇ ॥ ੫ ॥ ਗੁਰ ਸੇਵਾ ਤੇ ਸਭ ਕੁਲ ਉਧਾਰੇ ॥ ਨਿਰਮਲ ਨਾਮੁ ਰਖੈ ਉਰਿ ਧਾਰੇ ॥ ਸਾਚੀ ਸੋਭਾ ਸਾਚਿ ਦੁਆਰੇ ॥ ੬ ॥ ਸੇ ਵਡਭਾਗੀ ਜਿ ਗੁਰਿ ਸੇਵਾ ਲਾਏ ॥ ਅਨਦਿਨੁ ਭਗਤਿ ਸਚੁ ਨਾਮੁ ਦ੍ਰਿੜਾਏ ॥ ਨਾਮੇ ਉਧਰੇ ਕੁਲ ਸਬਾਏ ॥ ੭ ॥ ਨਾਨਕ ਸਾਚੁ ਕਹੈ ਵੀਚਾਰੁ ॥ ਹਰਿ ਕਾ ਨਾਮੁ ਰਖਹੁ ਉਰਿ ਧਾਰਿ ॥ ਹਰਿ ਭਗਤੀ ਰਾਤੇ ਮੋਖ ਦੁਆਰੁ ॥ ੮ ॥ ੨ ॥ ੨੪ ॥ (pg. 423 A.G.)

Do not heat your body like a furnace, or burn your bones like firewood. What wrong have your head and feet done to deserve such a punitive action? See your Husband Lord within yourself. God, the Cosmic Husband dwells within all hearts; without Him, there is no heart at all. Says Nanak : Such Devotees are the happy, virtuous soul-brides; the Lord is close to them.[161]

'PENANCE' & 'REPENTANCE' have been listed under the NEGATIVE-INFLUENCES, because they arise out of another negative feeling : GUILT.

---

[161] ਤਨੁ ਨ ਤਪਾਇ ਤਨੂਰ ਜਿਉ ਬਾਲਣੁ ਹਡ ਨ ਬਾਲਿ ॥ ਸਿਰਿ ਪੈਰੀ ਕਿਆ ਫੇੜਿਆ ਅੰਦਰਿ ਪਿਰੀ ਸਮਾਲਿ ॥ ੧੮ ॥ ਸਭਨੀ ਘਟੀ ਸਹੁ ਵਸੈ ਸਹ ਬਿਨੁ ਘਟੁ ਨ ਕੋਇ ॥ ਨਾਨਕ ਤੇ ਸੋਹਾਗਣੀ ਜਿਨ੍ਹਾ ਗੁਰਮੁਖਿ ਪਰਗਟੁ ਹੋਇ ॥ ੧੯ ॥ (pg. 1411 A.G.)

Twelve years pass in childhood, and for another twenty years, he does not practice self-discipline and austerity. For another thirty years, he does not worship God in any way, and then, when he is old, he repents and regrets. His life is wasted, in greed and egoistic pride. He is powerless. He makes a dam around the dried-up pool (of his power), and he makes a fence around the harvested field, but when the thief of Death comes, he quickly carries away what the fool had tried to preserve as his own. His feet and head and hands begin to tremble, and the tears flow copiously from his eyes. His tongue has not spoken the correct words, but now, he hopes to practice religion! If the Dear Lord shows His Mercy, even a sinner would earn the Profit of the Lord's Name. By Guru's Grace, he receives the wealth of the Lord's Name, which alone shall go with him, when he departs. Says Kabeer : listen, O Saints — he shall not take any other wealth with him. When the summons comes from the King, the Lord of the Universe, the mortal departs, leaving behind his wealth and mansions.[162]

Now, how do I tackle this situation and find appropriate remedies? What efforts should I make? How can I dispel the anxieties of my mind? How can I be ferried across these turbulent seas? Obtaining this human incarnation, I have done no good deeds; this makes me very afraid! In thought, word and deed, I have not sung the Lord's Praises; this thought worries my mind. I listened to the Guru's Teachings, but spiritual wisdom did not well up within me; like a

---

[162] ਬਾਰਹ ਬਰਸ ਬਾਲਪਨ ਬੀਤੇ ਬੀਸ ਬਰਸ ਕਛੁ ਤਪੁ ਨ ਕੀਓ ॥ ਤੀਸ ਬਰਸ ਕਛੁ ਦੇਵ ਨ ਪੂਜਾ ਫਿਰਿ ਪਛੁਤਾਨਾ ਬਿਰਧਿ ਭਇਓ ॥ ੧ ॥ ਮੇਰੀ ਮੇਰੀ ਕਰਤੇ ਜਨਮੁ ਗਇਓ ॥ ਸਾਇਰੁ ਸੋਖਿ ਭੁਜੰ ਬਲਇਓ ॥ ੧ ॥ ਰਹਾਉ ॥ ਸੂਕੇ ਸਰਵਰਿ ਪਾਲਿ ਬੰਧਾਵੈ ਲੂਣੈ ਖੇਤਿ ਹਥ ਵਾਰਿ ਕਰੈ ॥ ਆਇਓ ਚੋਰੁ ਤੁਰੰਤਹ ਲੇ ਗਇਓ ਮੇਰੀ ਰਾਖਤ ਮੁਗਧੁ ਫਿਰੈ ॥ ੨ ॥ ਚਰਨ ਸੀਸ ਕਰ ਕੰਪਨ ਲਾਗੇ ਨੈਨੀ ਨੀਰੁ ਅਸਾਰ ਬਹੈ ॥ ਜਿਹਵਾ ਬਚਨ ਸੁਧੁ ਨਹੀ ਨਿਕਸੈ ਤਬ ਰੇ ਧਰਮ ਕੀ ਆਸ ਕਰੈ ॥ ੩ ॥ ਹਰਿ ਜੀਉ ਕ੍ਰਿਪਾ ਕਰੈ ਲਿਵ ਲਾਵੈ ਲਾਹਾ ਹਰਿ ਹਰਿ ਨਾਮੁ ਲੀਓ ॥ ਗੁਰ ਪਰਸਾਦੀ ਹਰਿ ਧਨੁ ਪਾਇਓ ਅੰਤੇ ਚਲਦਿਆ ਨਾਲਿ ਚਲਿਓ ॥ ੪ ॥ ਕਹਤ ਕਬੀਰ ਸੁਨਹੁ ਰੇ ਸੰਤਹੁ ਅਨੁ ਧਨੁ ਕਛੂਐ ਲੈ ਨ ਗਇਓ ॥ ਆਈ ਤਲਬ ਗੋਪਾਲ ਰਾਇ ਕੀ ਮਾਇਆ ਮੰਦਰ ਛੋਡਿ ਚਲਿਓ ॥ ੫ ॥ ੨ ॥ ੧੫ ॥ (Pg.479 A.G.)

beast, I fill my belly. Says Nanak : O God, please confirm Your Law of Grace; for only then can I, the sinner, be saved. [163]

---

[163] ਅਬ ਮੈ ਕਉਨੁ ਉਪਾਉ ਕਰਉ ॥ ਜਿਹ ਬਿਧਿ ਮਨ ਕੋ ਸੰਸਾ ਚੂਕੈ ਭਉ ਨਿਧਿ ਪਾਰਿ ਪਰਉ ॥ ੧ ॥
ਰਹਾਉ ॥ ਜਨਮੁ ਪਾਇ ਕਛੁ ਭਲੋ ਨ ਕੀਨੋ ਤਾ ਤੇ ਅਧਿਕ ਡਰਉ ॥ ਮਨ ਬਚ ਕ੍ਰਮ ਹਰਿ ਗੁਨ ਨਹੀ ਗਾਏ
ਯਹ ਜੀਅ ਸੋਚ ਧਰਉ ॥ ੧ ॥ ਗੁਰਮਤਿ ਸੁਨਿ ਕਛੁ ਗਿਆਨੁ ਨ ਉਪਜਿਓ ਪਸੁ ਜਿਉ ਉਦਰੁ ਭਰਉ ॥
ਕਹੁ ਨਾਨਕ ਪ੍ਰਭ ਬਿਰਦੁ ਪਛਾਨਉ ਤਬ ਹਉ ਪਤਿਤ ਤਰਉ ॥
੨ ॥ ੪ ॥ ੯ ॥ ੯ ॥ ੧੩ ॥ ੫੮ ॥ ੪ ॥ ੯੩ ॥ (pg. 685 A.G.)

Do not harbour hatred against anyone. In each and every heart, God is contained. The All-pervading Lord is permeating and pervading the oceans and the land. How rare are those who, by Guru's Grace, sing of Him. Hatred and alienation depart from those who, as devotees, listen to the Hymns of the Lord's Praises. Says Nanak : one who becomes a devotee chants the Name of the Lord, and rises above all social classes and status symbols. Acting in egotism, selfishness and conceit, the foolish, ignorant, faithless cynic wastes his life. He dies in agony, like one dying of thirst.[164]

To some, the Lord has given silks and satins, and to some, beds decorated with cotton ribbons. Some do not even have a poor patched coat, and some live in thatched huts. Do not indulge in envy and bickering, O my mind. By continually performing good deeds, O my mind, you may have the luxuries, but not through jealousy. The potter works with the same clay, and colours the pots in different ways. Into some, he sets pearls (of contentment and compassion), while to others, he attaches filth (of hatred, and an envious nature).[165]

Harbouring animosity towards our fellow human beings is tantamount to perpetrating violence on our own soul. It's like raising a banner of revolt against God and his offspring. And, as all of us are HIS children, it is inferred that its equivalent to fighting with our own siblings, rebelling against our own kith and kin.

---

[164] ਵਵਾ ਵੈਰੁ ਨ ਕਰੀਐ ਕਾਹੂ ॥ ਘਟ ਘਟ ਅੰਤਰਿ ਬ੍ਰਹਮ ਸਮਾਹੂ ॥ ਵਾਸੁਦੇਵ ਜਲ ਥਲ ਮਹਿ ਰਵਿਆ ॥ ਗੁਰ ਪ੍ਰਸਾਦਿ ਵਿਰਲੈ ਹੀ ਗਵਿਆ ॥ ਵੈਰ ਵਿਰੋਧ ਮਿਟੇ ਤਿਹ ਮਨ ਤੇ ॥ ਹਰਿ ਕੀਰਤਨ ਗੁਰਮੁਖਿ ਜੋ ਸੁਨਤੇ ॥ ਵਰਨ ਚਿਹਨ ਸਗਲਹ ਤੇ ਰਹਤਾ ॥ ਨਾਨਕ ਹਰਿ ਹਰਿ ਗੁਰਮੁਖਿ ਜੋ ਕਹਤਾ ॥ ੪੬ ॥ ਸਲੋਕੁ ॥ ਹਉ ਹਉ ਕਰਤ ਬਿਹਾਨੀਆ ਸਾਕਤ ਮੁਗਧ ਅਜਾਨ ॥ ੧ ॥ (pg. 259 A.G.)
[165] ਕਾਹੂ ਦੀਨੇ ਪਾਟ ਪਟੰਬਰ ਕਾਹੂ ਪਲਘ ਨਿਵਾਰਾ ॥ ਕਾਹੂ ਗਰੀ ਗੋਦਰੀ ਨਾਹੀ ਕਾਹੂ ਖਾਨ ਪਰਾਰਾ ॥ ੧ ॥ ਅਹਿਰਖ ਵਾਦੁ ਨ ਕੀਜੈ ਰੇ ਮਨ ॥ ਸੁਕ੍ਰਿਤੁ ਕਰਿ ਕਰਿ ਲੀਜੈ ਰੇ ਮਨ ॥ ੧ ॥ ਰਹਾਉ ॥ ਕੁਮਰੈ ਏਕ ਜੁ ਮਾਟੀ ਗੁੰਧੀ ਬਹੁ ਬਿਧਿ ਬਾਨੀ ਲਾਈ ॥ ਕਾਹੂ ਮਹਿ ਮੋਤੀ ਮੁਕਤਾਹਲ ਕਾਹੂ ਬਿਆਧਿ ਲਗਾਈ ॥ ੨ ॥ (Pg. 479 A.G.)

The mortal does not remember the Lord; he wanders around, engrossed in greed. Committing sins, he dies, and his life ends in an instant. His body is like a clay vessel or a brittle metal pot. If you wish to keep it safe and sound, then meditate on the Lord; Chant the Name of the Lord. Chanting His Name night and day, the Lord will eventually hear your call. Says Kabeer : the body is a banana forest, and the mind is an intoxicated elephant. The jewel of spiritual wisdom is the prod, and the rare Saint is the rider.[166]

He commits innumerable robberies, countless acts of adultery, millions of falsehoods and thousands of abuses. He practices infinite number of deceptions and secret deeds, night and day, against his fellow beings.[167]

When man tries to, or thinks of fooling others, by being a master-trickster, he, too, shall, someday, become an unsuspecting victim of his own game plan, developed so very painstakingly, by him. He is sure to have a taste of his own bitter medicine/potion.

---

[166] ਕਬੀਰ ਰਾਮੁ ਨ ਚੇਤਿਓ ਫਿਰਿਆ ਲਾਲਚ ਮਾਹਿ ॥ ਪਾਪ ਕਰੰਤਾ ਮਰਿ ਗਇਆ ਅਉਧ ਪੁਨੀ ਖਿਨ ਮਾਹਿ ॥ ੨੨੧ ॥ ਕਬੀਰ ਕਾਇਆ ਕਾਚੀ ਕਾਰਵੀ ਕੇਵਲ ਕਾਚੀ ਧਾਤੁ ॥ ਸਾਬਤੁ ਰਖਹਿ ਤ ਰਾਮ ਭਜੁ ਨਾਹਿ ਤ ਬਿਨਠੀ ਬਾਤ ॥ ੨੨੨ ॥ ਕਬੀਰ ਕੇਸੋ ਕੇਸੋ ਕੂਕੀਐ ਨ ਸੋਈਐ ਅਸਾਰ ॥ ਰਾਤਿ ਦਿਵਸ ਕੇ ਕੂਕਨੇ ਕਬਹੂ ਕੇ ਸੁਨੈ ਪੁਕਾਰ ॥ ੨੨੩ ॥ ਕਬੀਰ ਕਾਇਆ ਕਜਲੀ ਬਨੁ ਭਇਆ ਮਨੁ ਕੁੰਚਰੁ ਮਯ ਮੰਤੁ ॥ ਅੰਕਸੁ ਗ੍ਯਾਨੁ ਰਤਨੁ ਹੈ ਖੇਵਟੁ ਬਿਰਲਾ ਸੰਤੁ ॥ ੨੨੪ ॥ (Pg.1376 A.G.)

[167] ਲਖ ਚੋਰੀਆ ਲਖ ਜਾਰੀਆ ਲਖ ਕੂੜੀਆ ਲਖ ਗਾਲਿ ॥ ਲਖ ਠਗੀਆ ਪਹਿਨਾਮੀਆ ਰਾਤਿ ਦਿਨਸੁ ਜੀਅ ਨਾਲਿ ॥ (Pg.471 A.G.)

Sayeth Sheikh Farid:

Answer evil with goodness; do not fill your mind with anger, thus your body shall not suffer from any disease, and you shall obtain everything. Says Fareed, the bird (human-being) is a guest in this beautiful world-garden. The morning drums are beating, indicating it is, now, time for departure (moment of death). Musk is distributed during the night ; those in deep slumber shall never become the recipients of their share of this Blessed commodity (hence do not harbour any ill-will towards another, during this short span of a 'night', that is this lifetime).[168]

Says Sheikh Fareed : do not turn around and strike those who strike you with their fists. Kiss their feet, and return to your own home (DO NOT GENERATE A FEELING OF REMORSEFUL REVENGE, as it is harmful for your progress). When there was time for you to earn name and fame, by performing worthy deeds, you were in love with the world, instead.[169]

Do not harbor evil intentions against others in your mind, and you shall not be troubled, my friends. The Name of the Lord, as preached by the True Guru, is the effective mendicant, and not the Tantric-rituals or the Mantra-recitations or the Yogic-postures. Nanak experiences this peace night and day.[170]

---

[168] ਫਰੀਦਾ ਬੁਰੇ ਦਾ ਭਲਾ ਕਰਿ ਗੁਸਾ ਮਨਿ ਨ ਹਢਾਇ ॥ ਦੇਹੀ ਰੋਗੁ ਨ ਲਗਈ ਪਲੈ ਸਭੁ ਕਿਛੁ ਪਾਇ ॥ ੭੮ ॥ ਫਰੀਦਾ ਪੰਖ ਪਰਾਹੁਣੀ ਦੁਨੀ ਸੁਹਾਵਾ ਬਾਗੁ ॥ ਨਉਬਤਿ ਵਜੀ ਸੁਬਹ ਸਿਉ ਚਲਣ ਕਾ ਕਰਿ ਸਾਜੁ ॥ ੭੯ ॥ ਫਰੀਦਾ ਰਾਤਿ ਕਥੂਰੀ ਵੰਡੀਐ ਸੁਤਿਆ ਮਿਲੈ ਨ ਭਾਉ ॥ ਜਿੰਨਾ ਨੈਣ ਨੀਦਾਵਲੇ ਤਿੰਨਾ ਮਿਲਣੁ ਕੁਆਉ ॥ ੮੦ ॥ (pg. 1381-82 A.G.)

[169] ਫਰੀਦਾ ਜੋ ਤੈ ਮਾਰਨਿ ਮੁਕੀਆਂ ਤਿਨਾ ਨ ਮਾਰੇ ਘੁੰਮਿ ॥ ਆਪਨੜੈ ਘਰਿ ਜਾਈਐ ਪੈਰ ਤਿਨਾ ਦੇ ਚੁੰਮਿ ॥ ੭ ॥ ਫਰੀਦਾ ਜਾਂ ਤਉ ਖਟਣ ਵੇਲ ਤਾਂ ਤੂ ਰਤਾ ਦੁਨੀ ਸਿਉ ॥ (Pg.1378 A.G.)

[170] ਪਰ ਕਾ ਬੁਰਾ ਨ ਰਾਖਹੁ ਚੀਤ ॥ ਤੁਮ ਕਉ ਦੁਖੁ ਨਹੀ ਭਾਈ ਮੀਤ ॥ ੩ ॥ ਹਰਿ ਹਰਿ ਤੰਤੁ ਮੰਤੁ ਗੁਰਿ ਦੀਨਾ ॥ ਇਹੁ ਸੁਖੁ ਨਾਨਕ ਅਨਦਿਨੁ ਚੀਨਾ ॥ ੪ ॥ ੧੧ ॥ ੬੨ ॥ (Pg.386 A.G.)

The sinners act, and perform nefarious acts (misdeeds), and then they weep and wail, when such acts misfire and backfire. Says Nanak: just as the churning stick churns the butter, so does the Judge of Righteousness torture them. Meditating on the NAME, O friend, the Treasure-Chest of a Life of Divinity. Says Nanak : speaking in Righteousness, one's world (home) becomes sanctified.[171]

I am a sacrifice to that one who binds in bondage his evil and corrupted gaze. One who does not know the difference between vice and virtue wanders around uselessly, and aimlessly. Speak the True Name of the Creator Lord. Then, you shall, never again, have to revisit this world, by suffering, for the umpteenth time, the fearful zones of a mother's womb. The Creator transforms the high into the low, and makes the lowly into kings. Those who know the All-knowing Lord are approved and certified as perfect in this world.[172]

Due to ignorance, egotism, and lust for power, sex and wealth, man has sacrificed man, at the altar, of his multifarious cravings. The height of inhumanism was when man did not think twice, before sacrificing fellow-beings, to appease "GOD" (A very common ritual prevelent in India and some other nations, until as late as the last century). NOW, this is an absurd and ridiculous level, to which man stooped. How could GOD, the FATHER & MOTHER, be asking for the sacrifice of one child, to be perpetrated by another. The same feeble argument (Appeasement of God) has been, repeatedly, advanced, regarding man enslaving man, over the centuries, and for retaining extra-judicial control over others' land, life and family-members. Bonded labor

---

[171] ਪਾਪੀ ਕਰਮ ਕਮਾਵਦੇ ਕਰਦੇ ਹਾਏ ਹਾਇ ॥ ਨਾਨਕ ਜਿਉ ਮਥਨਿ ਮਾਧਾਣੀਆ ਤਿਉ ਮਥੇ ਧ੍ਰਮ ਰਾਇ ॥ ੯ ॥ ਨਾਮੁ ਧਿਆਇਨਿ ਸਾਜਨਾ ਜਨਮ ਪਦਾਰਥੁ ਜੀਤਿ ॥ ਨਾਨਕ ਧਰਮ ਐਸੇ ਚਵਹਿ ਕੀਤੋ ਭਵਨ ਪੁਨੀਤ ॥ ੧੦ ॥ (pg. 1425 A.G.)

[172] ਦਿਸਟਿ ਬਿਕਾਰੀ ਬੰਧਨਿ ਬਾਂਧੈ ਹਉ ਤਿਸ ਕੈ ਬਲਿ ਜਾਈ ॥ ਪਾਪ ਪੁੰਨ ਕੀ ਸਾਰ ਨ ਜਾਣੈ ਭੂਲਾ ਫਿਰੈ ਅਜਾਈ ॥ ੧ ॥ ਬੋਲਹੁ ਸਚੁ ਨਾਮੁ ਕਰਤਾਰ ॥ ਫੁਨਿ ਬਹੁੜਿ ਨ ਆਵਣ ਵਾਰ ॥ ੧ ॥ ਰਹਾਉ ॥ ਊਚਾ ਤੇ ਫੁਨਿ ਨੀਚੁ ਕਰਤੁ ਹੈ ਨੀਚ ਕਰੈ ਸੁਲਤਾਨੁ ॥ ਜਿਨੀ ਜਾਣੁ ਸੁਜਾਣਿਆ ਜਗਿ ਤੇ ਪੂਰੇ ਪਰਵਾਣੁ ॥ ੨ ॥ (pg. 1329 A.G.)

meant that children of slaves would, automatically, taken to be slaves. Inhuman and undignified behavior was evident when man forced women to marry several husbands, at any given point in time, and when man had a 'Harem' comprising of hundreds of ladies, for the satisfaction of his carnal-instincts. And the irony of the whole scenario is that he was eulogized and respected as : KING IS GOD. Religious intolerance was at its pinnacle, but the fanatic was considered to be the most pious one. Untouchability, and discrimination, on account of race, sex, color, creed, status, caste, religion have been the other indelible black-spots, on the canvas.

All such thoughts, words and deeds, that are detrimental or prejudicial, to the interests of another, are tantamount to being a "SIN". Quite often, a SIN may be an act of omission, rather than that of commission, and might not, even, be deliberate, but a SIN is a SIN is a SIN, planned or otherwise, intended or unintentional.

All comfort and luxury, achieved at the expense of hurting or defrauding another, shall never be long-lasting. And all the treachery and injustice, perpetrated on another, shall return, manifold, in diverse forms, hues and colors, sooner or later.

Cruelty may be committed by an individual, or by a society, on a section of people, or even by nations against other nations. The history of human-civilization is replete with tales of horror and misery inflicted upon people, by an autocratic, power-hungry oppressor. Hitler, Napoleon, Mussolini, Taimur, Chenghiz, Alexander, Czar, all fall into this classification. In fact, they are the INFAMOUS "Hall-of-Fame" Credential-Holders, for the massive destruction and grave misery they brought upon the millions. They were the marauders who plundered and killed, raped and enslaved and tortured God's people (living peacefully, in the lands of their birth), with ruthlessness and dastardly-elan.

Human-Mentality and Psyche continues to follow the same dictum, today, while perpetrating cruelty on fellow-humans, in some parts of the world. The highest Spiritual Center of the Sikh-Faith (the GOLDEN- TEMPLE, in Amritsar, Punjab, India, became the target of a full-fledged Army Operation, in 1984, when Holy relics were desecrated, and precious pearls and diamonds confiscated. Thousands

120

of innocent pilgrims and devotees, including the old, infirm, ladies and children were massacred. The same year, several thousands of Sikhs were murdered in cold blood, in the veil of so-called riots, in scant violation of basic civilized-norms, with wild marauders burning the Sikhs alive, with tyres round their necks.

Religion has been misused as a "WEAPON" by fanatics and fundamentalists, for 'en-masse' conversions, from other faiths, to their own. If they could not force people to convert, they would, of course, as a matter of their "BIRTHRIGHT", resort to mass-genocide.

Discord, on account of community, caste, language or region, has been the root-cause of innumerable conflicts. In recent history, religious fanaticism has resulted in countless murders. Sikhs, as a community have been persecuted, right from the day they asserted their distinct identity, more than five centuries ago. And the same trend continues, today, when forces inimical to the Sikhs have adopted nefarious means to annihilate the followers of this religion, 'en masse'. But this martial race was born to resist oppression and tyranny, and no degree of cruelty, and no decree of authoritarian-regimes, would succeed in ulterior motives.

It is futile to pin hopes on a human-being (mortal). One must, instead, dwell upon the Giver, the Provider, God, the Only One.

Reliance on mortals is in vain — know this well. The Great Giver is the One Lord God. By His gifts, we are contented, and we suffer from thirst no longer. The One Lord (Himself, the Creator) destroys, and also preserves and sustains. Human-beings exercise no control, whatsoever, over any incident in life. Understanding His Order, there is peace. So take His Name, and wear it as your necklace. Remember God, and meditate. Guarantees NANAK : " NO obstacle shall deter you, during your victorious march, towards self-reliance ". [173]

The Lord is the Fulfiller of desires, the Giver of total peace; the Kaamadhaynaa (the mythological wish-fulfilling cow), is His slave. So meditate on such a Lord, O my soul. Then, you shall obtain total peace, O my mind, Chant the True Name (Sat Naam). In this world, and in the world beyond, your face shall be radiant, by meditating continually on the immaculate Lord. [174]

---

[173] ਮਾਨੁਖ ਕੀ ਟੇਕ ਬ੍ਰਿਥੀ ਸਭ ਜਾਨੁ ॥ ਦੇਵਨ ਕਉ ਏਕੈ ਭਗਵਾਨੁ ॥ ਜਿਸ ਕੈ ਦੀਐ ਰਹੈ ਅਘਾਇ ॥ ਬਹੁਰਿ ਨ ਤ੍ਰਿਸਨਾ ਲਾਗੈ ਆਇ ॥ ਮਾਰੈ ਰਾਖੈ ਏਕੋ ਆਪਿ ॥ ਮਾਨੁਖ ਕੈ ਕਿਛੁ ਨਾਹੀ ਹਾਥਿ ॥ ਤਿਸ ਕਾ ਹੁਕਮੁ ਬੂਝਿ ਸੁਖੁ ਹੋਇ ॥ ਤਿਸ ਕਾ ਨਾਮੁ ਰਖੁ ਕੰਠਿ ਪਰੋਇ ॥ ਸਿਮਰਿ ਸਿਮਰਿ ਸਿਮਰਿ ਪ੍ਰਭੁ ਸੋਇ ॥ ਨਾਨਕ ਬਿਘਨੁ ਨ ਲਾਗੈ ਕੋਇ ॥ ੧ ॥ (pg. 281 A.G.)

[174] ਇਛਾ ਪੂਰਕੁ ਸਰਬ ਸੁਖਦਾਤਾ ਹਰਿ ਜਾ ਕੈ ਵਸਿ ਹੈ ਕਾਮਧੇਨਾ ॥ ਸੋ ਐਸਾ ਹਰਿ ਧਿਆਈਐ ਰੇ ਜੀਅੜੇ ਤਾ ਸਰਬ ਸੁਖ ਪਾਵਹਿ ਮੇਰੇ ਮਨਾ ॥ ੧ ॥ ਜਪਿ ਮਨ ਸਤਿ ਨਾਮੁ ਸਦਾ ਸਤਿ ਨਾਮੁ ॥ ਹਲਤਿ ਪਲਤਿ ਮੁਖ ਊਜਲ ਹੋਈ ਹੈ ਨਿਤ ਧਿਆਈਐ ਹਰਿ ਪੁਰਖੁ ਨਿਰੰਜਨਾ ॥ (pg. 669 A.G.)

One person brings a full bottle, and another comes to fill his cup. Drinking it, his intelligence departs, and madness enters his mind. He cannot distinguish between his own and others' — he is struck down by his Lord and Master. Drinking it, he forgets his Lord and Master, and he is punished in the Court of the Lord. Don't drink the false wine at all, if it is in your power. Says Nanak : by His Grace, one obtains the true wine (of the ADDICTION OF GOD'S NATURE AND NAME), when the True Guru comes and meets him. He shall dwell forever in the Love of the Lord and Master, and obtain a seat in the Mansion of His Presence.[175]

Those who eat betel nuts and betel leaf and indulge in any kind of intoxicants; such as smoking and drugs etc., and do not contemplate the Lord, — the Messenger of Death will seize them and take them away.[176]

The Messenger of Death could arrive in the guise of any deadly disease, such as cancer or emphysema. Addiction of any kind is a vice that shall ruin the body and the mind. The ramifications of such deeds shall be far-reaching and horrific, at times. Gambling is another cruel vice that shatters the peace of households, and results in penury and hunger.

My Lord and Master is the Provider of the choicest fruits (those that the mind desires). He knows all the useless vanities and pains of the soul. Meditating on the Protector of weak souls, the Companion of all, your life shall not be lost in the GAMBLE (either the games of chance,

---

[175] ਮਾਣਸੁ ਭਰਿਆ ਆਣਿਆ ਮਾਣਸੁ ਭਰਿਆ ਆਇ ॥ ਜਿਤੁ ਪੀਤੈ ਮਤਿ ਦੂਰਿ ਹੋਇ ਬਰਲੁ ਪਵੈ ਵਿਚਿ ਆਇ ॥ ਆਪਣਾ ਪਰਾਇਆ ਨ ਪਛਾਣਈ ਖਸਮਹੁ ਧਕੇ ਖਾਇ ॥ ਜਿਤੁ ਪੀਤੈ ਖਸਮੁ ਵਿਸਰੈ ਦਰਗਹ ਮਿਲੈ ਸਜਾਇ ॥ ਝੂਠਾ ਮਦੁ ਮੂਲਿ ਨ ਪੀਚਈ ਜੇ ਕਾ ਪਾਰਿ ਵਸਾਇ ॥ ਨਾਨਕ ਨਦਰੀ ਸਚੁ ਮਦੁ ਪਾਈਐ ਸਤਿਗੁਰੁ ਮਿਲੈ ਜਿਸੁ mਨ ਆਇ ॥ ਸਦਾ ਸਾਹਿਬ ਕੈ ਰੰਗਿ ਰਹੈ ਮਹਲੀ ਪਾਵੈ ਥਾਉ ॥ ੧ ॥ (pg. 554 A.G.)
[176] ਪਾਨ ਸੁਪਾਰੀ ਖਾਤੀਆ ਮੁਖਿ ਬੀੜੀਆ ਲਾਈਆ ॥ ਹਰਿ ਹਰਿ ਕਦੇ ਨ ਚੇਤਿਓ ਜਮਿ ਪਕੜਿ ਚਲਾਈਆ ॥ ੧੩ ॥ (pg. 726 A.G.)

or the self-deceptive pleasures) . Nanak offers this prayer to God: Please shower me with Your Mercy, and carry me across the terrifying world-ocean. [177]

On being possessed by the addictive substances, one fails to comprehend the distinction between right and wrong, between life and death, and between Sin and Virtue.

When one is under these influences it is impossible to draw the line of demarcation, and one loses the faculty of thought, and all the acquired knowledge and intelligence is relegated to the back-benches. NOW, the DEVIL is in 'Total-Command', thereby awarding a Free-Reign to the addictive substances, who indulge in their passionate-play, designed to wreaking havoc, and reducing the consumer to a physical and mental wreck. One does not retain any control over the functions of the brain, and over the movements of the limbs. On a different and more significant plane, of Morality, one loses the power to differentiate between 'Love & Lust', between one's own spouse, and that of another. Under the demonish influences, one cannot realize whether one is acting sinfully and disgracefully, with one's daughter, sister or mother. Already, man and woman are infested with the menace of Lust, day in and day out, and when attacked by the additional forces of addictions, they succumb to the temptation of sexual indulgence and promiscuity. Incest, no longer, remains an improbability, and that is the most horrendous of all known SINS.

The conclusion, then, is that an extra thought needs to be given to searching for remedial measures, to tackle this 'epidemic', the aftermath of which is really torturous, physically, emotionally, and mentally.

'Addiction' is very essential in one's life. It lends a flavor of challenge and motivational-interest, to an otherwise dull and monotonous life. But, one should partake of such an addiction that does not harm oneself, and/or others, and such an addiction could ONLY be: the intoxication provided by God's Name, Selfless-Service towards

---

[177] ਮਨ ਬਾਂਛਤ ਫਲ ਦੇਤ ਹੈ ਸੁਆਮੀ ਜੀਅ ਕੀ ਬਿਰਥਾ ਸਾਰੇ ॥ ਅਨਾਥ ਕੇ ਨਾਥੇ ਸ੍ਰਬ ਕੈ ਸਾਥੇ ਜਪਿ ਜੂਐ ਜਨਮੁ ਨ ਹਾਰੀਐ ॥ ਨਾਨਕ ਕੀ ਬੇਨੰਤੀ ਪ੍ਰਭ ਪਹਿ ਕ੍ਰਿਪਾ ਕਰਿ ਭਵਜਲੁ ਤਾਰੀਐ ॥ ੨ ॥ (Pg.80 A.G.)

124

fellow-beings, and compassion towards all creatures. Creative and constructive contributions in other spheres of endeavour are exemplary 'Addictions', for instance: Academics, Business or the Arts.

The general tendency in some modern societies is to follow the dictum of 'enjoy life while you can', without bothering about the grave consequences of irresponsible acts of addictions and adultery. Those practitioners of this theory tend to ignore the simple mathematical calculation that if they consume any addictive substance, for instance, for even 8 hours out of 280 hours, in a week, it works out to give a percentage of about 3%. And this 3% of the time is bound to have serious ramifications on the remaining 97% of one's time, spent dealing with the significant aspects of one's life (moral, physical, social, financial, emotional, mental, and spiritual).

Those who meditate on You, Lord, those who meditate on You—those humble beings dwell in peace in this world. They are liberated, they are liberated—those who meditate on the Lord. For them, the noose of death is cut away. Those who meditate on the Fearless One, on the Fearless Lord—all their fears are dispelled. Those who serve, those who serve my Dear Lord, are absorbed into the Being of the Lord. Blessed are they, blessed are they, who meditate on their Dear Lord. Nanak is a sacrifice unto them.[178]

The wicked and the faithless cynics, do not know the Taste of the Lord's Sublime Essence. The thorn of egotism is embedded deep within them. The more they walk away, the deeper it pierces them, and the more they suffer in pain, until finally, the Messenger of Death smashes his club against their heads. The humble servants of the Lord are absorbed in the Name of the Lord. The pain of birth and the fear of death are eradicated. They have found the Imperishable Supreme Being, the Transcendent Lord, and they receive great honour, throughout, and in all the worlds and realms.[179]

The Gurus and Seers have equated the World and Life, with an "Ocean-of-Fire", and a "Turbulent-Sea", to be ferried across which, one is advised to dwell upon God's Name and Attributes.

Humans fear one another, but do NOT fear God, while committing SINS. Only if we start loving Him, by shunning SIN, shall we become

---

[178] ਹਰਿ ਧਿਆਵਹਿ ਹਰਿ ਧਿਆਵਹਿ ਤੁਧੁ ਜੀ ਸੇ ਜਨ ਜੁਗ ਮਹਿ ਸੁਖਵਾਸੀ ॥ ਸੇ ਮੁਕਤੁ ਸੇ ਮੁਕਤੁ ਭਏ ਜਿਨ ਹਰਿ ਧਿਆਇਆ ਜੀ ਤਿਨ ਤੂਟੀ ਜਮ ਕੀ ਫਾਸੀ ॥ ਜਿਨ ਨਿਰਭਉ ਜਿਨ ਹਰਿ ਨਿਰਭਉ ਧਿਆਇਆ ਜੀ ਤਿਨ ਕਾ ਭਉ ਸਭੁ ਗਵਾਸੀ ॥ ਜਿਨ ਸੇਵਿਆ ਜਿਨ ਸੇਵਿਆ ਮੇਰਾ ਹਰਿ ਜੀ ਤੇ ਹਰਿ ਹਰਿ ਰੂਪਿ ਸਮਾਸੀ ॥ ਸੇ ਧੰਨੁ ਸੇ ਧੰਨੁ ਜਿਨ ਹਰਿ ਧਿਆਇਆ ਜੀ ਜਨੁ ਨਾਨਕੁ ਤਿਨ ਬਲਿ ਜਾਸੀ ॥ ੩ ॥ (pg. 11 A.G.)

[179] ਸਾਕਤ ਹਰਿ ਰਸ ਸਾਦੁ ਨ ਜਾਣਿਆ ਤਿਨ ਅੰਤਰਿ ਹਉਮੈ ਕੰਡਾ ਹੇ ॥ ਜਿਉ ਜਿਉ ਚਲਹਿ ਚੁਭੈ ਦੁਖੁ ਪਾਵਹਿ ਜਮਕਾਲੁ ਸਹਹਿ ਸਿਰਿ ਡੰਡਾ ਹੇ ॥ ੨ ॥ ਹਰਿ ਜਨ ਹਰਿ ਹਰਿ ਨਾਮਿ ਸਮਾਣੇ ਦੁਖ ਜਨਮ ਮਰਣ ਭਵ ਖੰਡਾ ਹੇ ॥ ਅਬਿਨਾਸੀ ਪੁਰਖੁ ਪਾਇਆ ਪਰਮੇਸਰੁ ਬਹੁ ਸੋਭ ਖੰਡ ਬ੍ਰਹਮੰਡਾ ਹੇ ॥ ੩ ॥ (pg. 13 A.G.)

liberated forever. Radical reforms and discoveries and inventions have been possible, in human history, only by overcoming fears of all kinds. Lives have been staked for the espousal of cherished causes, for the sake of common human-welfare, dignity. The fortified citadels of democracy have been erected by fearless, courageous ones.

Fear is an obstacle in the route to the attainment of self-confidence. Imaginary fears or apprehensions could be devastatingly dangerous, for humanity. Wars have been thrust upon a nation, by another, that imagined a threat-perception. Cult-suicides (en masse) are the result of an imaginary thought of an imbalanced mind. Huge nuclear arsenals might be deployed for self-annihilation, some day, by an error, although they were meant to destroy others. This is FEAR at its peak.

The fickle consciousness does not remain stable. The deer secretly nibbles at the green sprouts. One who enshrines the Lord's lotus feet in his heart and consciousness lives long, always remembering the Lord. Everyone has worries and cares. He alone finds peace, who thinks of the One Lord. When the Lord dwells in the consciousness, and one is absorbed in the Lord's Name, one is liberated, and returns home with honor. [180]

My bed is adorned in splendor. My mind is filled with bliss, since I heard of God's arrival. Meeting God, the Lord and Master, I have entered the realm of peace; I am filled, to the brim, with joy and delight. Enjoying the blissful communion with my Master, all my sorrows have departed, and my body, mind and soul are all rejuvenated. I have obtained the fruits of my mind's desires, meditating on God; the day of my wedding is auspicious. Prays Nanak : when I met the Lord of excellence, I came to experience all pleasure and bliss. [181]

Amongst the diseases, 'Worry' is a very dreaded one, when it is in it's worst manifestations. The ramifications arising out of extreme worry are really serious. An extremely worried and tormented person could commit suicide, or could go insane. Worry is such a raging fire that destroys the mental-equilibrium and the physical-capabilities.

Worry pertains to past events, having possible repercussions, in the future. Very seldom does one, realistically, want to live in the present. And, NOT living in the present is a serious 'disease'. But, this style

---

[180] ਚੰਚਲੁ ਚੀਤੁ ਨ ਰਹਈ ਠਾਇ ॥ ਚੋਰੀ ਮਿਰਗੁ ਅੰਗੂਰੀ ਖਾਇ ॥ ਚਰਨ ਕਮਲ ਉਰ ਧਾਰੇ ਚੀਤ ॥ ਚਿਰੁ ਜੀਵਨੁ ਚੇਤਨੁ ਨਿਤ ਨੀਤ ॥ ਚਿੰਤਤ ਹੀ ਦੀਸੈ ਸਭੁ ਕੋਇ ॥ ਚੇਤਹਿ ਏਕੁ ਤਹੀ ਸੁਖੁ ਹੋਇ ॥ ਚਿਤਿ ਵਸੈ ਰਾਚੈ ਹਰਿ ਨਾਇ ॥ ਮੁਕਤਿ ਭਇਆ ਪਤਿ ਸਿਉ ਘਰਿ ਜਾਇ ॥ ੨੩ ॥ (pg. 932 A.G.)
[181] ਮੇਰੀ ਸੇਜੜੀਐ ਆਡੰਬਰੁ ਬਣਿਆ ॥ ਮਨਿ ਅਨਦੁ ਭਇਆ ਪ੍ਰਭੁ ਆਵਤ ਸੁਣਿਆ ॥ ਪ੍ਰਭ ਮਿਲੇ ਸੁਆਮੀ ਸੁਖਹ ਗਾਮੀ ਚਾਵ ਮੰਗਲ ਰਸ ਭਰੇ ॥ ਅੰਗ ਸੰਗਿ ਲਾਗੇ ਦੂਖ ਭਾਗੇ ਪ੍ਰਾਣ ਮਨ ਤਨ ਸਭਿ ਹਰੇ ॥ ਮਨ ਇਛ ਪਾਈ ਪ੍ਰਭ ਧਿਆਈ ਸੰਜੋਗੁ ਸਾਹਾ ਸੁਭ ਗਣਿਆ ॥ ਬਿਨਵੰਤਿ ਨਾਨਕ ਮਿਲੇ ਸ੍ਰੀਧਰ ਸਗਲ ਆਨੰਦ ਰਸੁ ਬਣਿਆ ॥ ੨ ॥ (pg. 459 A.G.)

128

and art of living cannot be mastered without serious inclination, tempered with meditation. Hence the vast multitudes continue to grope in the dark corridors, worrying about imaginary hallucinations. Furthermore, superstition and 'fear of the unknown' have an additional deliterious effect on the faculties of the mind. NOW, all of this seems and sounds to be (and rather, IT, ACTUALLY, IS) really absurd, considering the time-tested fact that man exercizes, absolutely, NO control over results. Hence, 'worry' is futile. Otherwise, if man had control over situations and results, or could rectify/remedy a situation, by worrying, nothing would ever go wrong, after one would implement a particular plan-of-action.

Happiness, joy, and the ULTIMATE CELESTIAL BLISS can be attained, only, by living in the present.

Pious thinking and Meditation upon God's Name are intertwined. Meditation and prayer could be performed in solitary-confinement, or even in Congregations. Attending spiritual-discourses and sermons, delivered by pious persons, whose vision and verbosity is capable of relieving the worried mind, and of providing it with the much-needed solace and stability.

In times of depression and distress, one must turn towards the Sanctuary of God's Name, and it's in HIS refuge that one would find peace and tranquility. The Redeemer shall destroy all forms of worry and misery. HIS Name yields Knowledge and Power, Peace and Joy.

When someone's household has no glory, the guests who come there depart still hungry. Deep within, there is no contentment, and he suffers and writhes, in pain. The 'bride' called Illusion has the tenacity to corrupt the consciousness of even the most dedicated ascetics and sages. This 'bride' is the daughter of a wretched miser. Abandoning the Lord's servant, she sleeps with the world (the wretched ones). Standing at the door of the holy man, she says, "I have come to your sanctuary; now save me!" [182]

Largesse of the heart is a great boon granted by God, to man. To talk to everyone with an open and clean heart, to donate magnanimously to charitable-causes, and to receive guests with a welcome smile are some of the noble attributes that a miser lacks, so very miserably and unfortunately.

Since God is gracious, Himself, His devotees, too, shall become like Him. Such people deal politely, always, with everyone. They have no enemies, no rivals. They consider others' problems and tears as being their very own. They would not shirk, while going out of their way, to resolve others' crisis, even at at the price of financial-loss, loss of prestige, or even at the cost of their lives.

On the contrary, a miser prefers to remain elusive and evasive, so very indifferent to the pain and misery of others. Such miserable beings do not wish to share their knowledge and skills with others, and would rather die, without imparting these talents to another.

Misers do not have any friends and admirers and confidantes. Because what one sows, does one reap. In such hearts there's no place and feeling for friendship and love, compassion and humility.

---

[182] ਗ੍ਰਿਹਿ ਸੋਭਾ ਜਾ ਕੈ ਰੇ ਨਾਹਿ ॥ ਆਵਤ ਪਹੀਆ ਖੁਧੇ ਜਾਹਿ ॥ ਵਾ ਕੈ ਅੰਤਰਿ ਨਹੀ ਸੰਤੋਖੁ ॥ ਬਿਨੁ ਸੋਹਾਗਨਿ ਲਾਗੈ ਦੋਖੁ ॥ ੧ ॥ ਧਨੁ ਸੋਹਾਗਨਿ ਮਹਾ ਪਵੀਤ ॥ ਤਪੇ ਤਪੀਸਰ ਡੋਲੈ ਚੀਤ ॥ ੧ ॥ ਰਹਾਉ ॥ ਸੋਹਾਗਨਿ ਕਿਰਪਨ ਕੀ ਪੂਤੀ ॥ ਸੇਵਕ ਤਜਿ ਜਗਤ ਸਿਉ ਸੂਤੀ ॥ ਸਾਧੂ ਕੈ ਠਾਢੀ ਦਰਬਾਰਿ ॥ ਸਰਨਿ ਤੇਰੀ ਮੋ ਕਉ ਨਿਸਤਾਰਿ ॥ ੨ ॥ (pg. 872 A.G.)

A miser would be a rude and crude person, with no sense of etiquette and hospitality. He loves isolation, so that none would get a chance to bother him with any request for monetary or other assistance.

The pain of separation is as unbearable as the pain of extreme hunger. The greatest, and unendurable, pain is the attack of the Messenger of Death. Another pain is the disease consuming my body. O doctor, don't administer me medicine. The pain persists, and the body continues to suffer. Your medicine has no effect on me. Forgetting his Lord and Master, the mortal enjoys sensual pleasures; then, disease wells up in his body. The blind (ignorant/foolish) mortal receives his punishment. The value of sandalwood lies in its fragrance. The value of a human lasts only as long as the breath in the body. When the breath is taken away, the body crumbles into dust. The mortal's body emanates a golden-aura, and the soul-swan is immaculate and pure, if even a tiny particle of the Immaculate Name resides within. Only then shall all pain and disease be eradicated. Says Nanak : the mortal is saved through the True Name.[183]

Worldly possessions are obtained by pain and suffering; when they are gone, they leave pain and suffering. Says Nanak : without the True Name, hunger is never satisfied. Beauty does not satisfy hunger; when the man sees beauty, he hungers even more. As many as are the pleasures of the body, so many are the pains, which afflict it.[184]

---

[183] ਦੁਖੁ ਵੇਛੋੜਾ ਇਕੁ ਦੁਖੁ ਭੂਖ ॥ ਇਕੁ ਦੁਖੁ ਸਕਤਵਾਰ ਜਮਦੂਤ ॥ ਇਕੁ ਦੁਖੁ ਰੋਗੁ ਲਗੈ ਤਨਿ ਧਾਇ ॥ ਵੈਦ ਨ ਭੋਲੇ ਦਾਰੂ ਲਾਇ ॥ ੧ ॥ ਵੈਦ ਨ ਭੋਲੇ ਦਾਰੂ ਲਾਇ ॥ ਦਰਦੁ ਹੋਵੈ ਦੁਖੁ ਰਹੈ ਸਰੀਰ ॥ ਐਸਾ ਦਾਰੂ ਲਗੈ ਨ ਬੀਰ ॥ ੧ ॥ ਰਹਾਉ ॥ ਖਸਮੁ ਵਿਸਾਰਿ ਕੀਏ ਰਸ ਭੋਗ ॥ ਤਾਂ ਤਨਿ ਉਠਿ ਖਲੋਏ ਰੋਗ ॥ ਮਨ ਅੰਧੇ ਕਉ ਮਿਲੈ ਸਜਾਇ ॥ ਵੈਦ ਨ ਭੋਲੇ ਦਾਰੂ ਲਾਇ ॥ ੨ ॥ ਚੰਦਨ ਕਾ ਫਲੁ ਚੰਦਨ ਵਾਸੁ ॥ ਮਾਣਸ ਕਾ ਫਲੁ ਘਟ ਮਹਿ ਸਾਸੁ ॥ ਸਾਸਿ ਗਇਐ ਕਾਇਆ ਢਲਿ ਪਾਇ ॥ ਤਾ ਕੇ ਪਾਛੈ ਕੋਇ ਨ ਖਾਇ ॥ ੩ ॥ ਕੰਚਨ ਕਾਇਆ ਨਿਰਮਲ ਹੰਸੁ ॥ ਜਿਸੁ ਮਹਿ ਨਾਮੁ ਨਿਰੰਜਨ ਅੰਸੁ ॥ ਦੂਖ ਰੋਗ ਸਭਿ ਗਇਆ ਗਵਾਇ ॥ ਨਾਨਕ ਛੂਟਸਿ ਸਾਚੈ ਨਾਇ ॥ ੪ ॥ ੨ ॥ ੭ ॥ (pg. 1256 A.G.)

[184] ਦੁਖੀ ਦੁਨੀ ਸਹੇੜੀਐ ਜਾਇ ਤ ਲਗਹਿ ਦੁਖ ॥ ਨਾਨਕ ਸਚੇ ਨਾਮ ਬਿਨੁ ਕਿਸੈ ਨ ਲਥੀ ਭੂਖ ॥ ਰੂਪੀ ਭੂਖ ਨ ਉਤਰੈ ਜਾਂ ਦੇਖਾਂ ਤਾਂ ਭੂਖ ॥ ਜੇਤੇ ਰਸ ਸਰੀਰ ਕੇ ਤੇਤੇ ਲਗਹਿ ਦੁਖ ॥ ੨ ॥ (pg. 1287 A.G.)

Millions of obstacles (innumerable problems) infest and afflict such a person, who forgets (rather, does NOT WANT TO remember) to meditate on God's Name and Grace. A state of ingratitude, thanklessness and shame.. Such a one shall live and die in pain and misery, like a crow trapped in a barren isolated house[185]

The TRUE GURU (Teacher, Guide, Philosopher) would help a serious and worthy disciple, who is spiritually inclined, to master the techniques required for remembering God, under all circumstances. In adversity, it is the natural tendency of human-beings, to pray, for help. But, one who retains the essence of the Lord's Sacred Name, in his soul, even in the season of prosperity, is the Redeemed one. And this would have the somber effect of destroying all obstacles and pain, miseries and tormentations, in the life of the devotee.[186]

---

[185] ਕੋਟਿ ਬਿਘਨ ਤਿਸੁ ਲਾਗਤੇ ਜਿਸ ਨੋ ਵਿਸਰੈ ਨਾਉ ॥ ਨਾਨਕ ਅਨਦਿਨੁ ਬਿਲਪਤੇ ਜਿਉ ਸੁੰਵੈ ਘਰਿ ਕਾਉ ॥ ੧ ॥ (pg. 522 A.G.)

[186] ਬਿਘਨ ਬਿਨਾਸਨ ਸਭਿ ਦੁਖ ਨਾਸਨ ਸਤਿਗੁਰਿ ਨਾਮੁ ਦ੍ਰਿੜਾਇਆ ॥ ਖੋਏ ਪਾਪ ਭਏ ਸਭਿ ਪਾਵਨ ਜਨ ਨਾਨਕ ਸੁਖਿ ਘਰਿ ਆਇਆ ॥ ੪ ॥ ੩ ॥ ੫੩ ॥ (pg. 622 A.G.)

The herons in their white feathers dwell in the sacred shrines of pilgrimage. They tear apart and eat the living beings, and so they are not called white. My body is like the simmal tree; seeing me, other people are fooled. Its fruits are useless — just like the qualities of my body. The blind man is carrying such a heavy load, and his journey through the mountains is so long and treacherous. My eyes can see, but I cannot find the Way. How can I climb up and cross over the mountain? What good does it do to serve, and be good, and be clever? Says Nanak : contemplate the Name of the Lord, and you shall be released from bondage.[187]

Oh my deceived Mind! Why did you not adhere to the teachings of the learned and accomplished GURU? What good is it that you shaved off your head, and donned an orange-colored attire, with the intention of conning people, into believing your word, and treating you as a pious soul. Is it a worthy and justifiable deed, to be masquerading in a disguise? Bidding adieu to Truth, you've been wasting your life by letting yourself be influenced by Falsehood. All you've done, so far, is to eat, sleep, and make merry, in gay- abandon, like a carefree-animal (your instincts are identical to those of animals). Remember that this form of life is lived at a baser-level, and not when one is granted the Great Human-Birth.[188]

---

[187] ਬਗਾ ਬਗੇ ਕਪੜੇ ਤੀਰਥ ਮੰਝਿ ਵਸੰਨਿ ॥ ਘੁਟਿ ਘੁਟਿ ਜੀਆ ਖਾਵਣੇ ਬਗੇ ਨਾ ਕਹੀਅਨਿ ॥ ੩ ॥ ਸਿੰਮਲ ਰੁਖੁ ਸਰੀਰੁ ਮੈ ਮੈਜਨ ਦੇਖਿ ਭੁਲੰਨਿ ॥ ਸੇ ਫਲ ਕੰਮਿ ਨ ਆਵਨੀ ਤੇ ਗੁਣ ਮੈ ਤਨਿ ਹੰਨਿ ॥ ੪ ॥ ਅੰਧੁਲੈ ਭਾਰੁ ਉਠਾਇਆ ਡੂਗਰ ਵਾਟ ਬਹੁਤੁ ॥ ਅਖੀ ਲੋੜੀ ਨਾ ਲਹਾ ਹਉ ਚੜਿ ਲੰਘਾ ਕਿਤੁ ॥ ੫ ॥ ਚਾਕਰੀਆ ਚੰਗਿਆਈਆ ਅਵਰ ਸਿਆਣਪ ਕਿਤੁ ॥ ਨਾਨਕ ਨਾਮੁ ਸਮਾਲਿ ਤੂੰ ਬਧਾ ਛੁਟਹਿ ਜਿਤੁ ॥ ੬ ॥ ੧ ॥ ੩ ॥ (Pg.729 A.G.)

[188] ਮਨ ਰੇ ਗਹਿਓ ਨ ਗੁਰ ਉਪਦੇਸੁ ॥ ਕਹਾ ਭਇਓ ਜਉ ਮੂੜ ਮੁਡਾਇਓ ਭਗਵਓ ਕੀਨੋ ਭੇਸੁ ॥ ੧ ॥ ਰਹਾਉ ॥ ਸਾਚ ਛਾਡਿ ਕੈ ਝੂਠਹ ਲਾਗਿਓ ਜਨਮੁ ਅਕਾਰਥੁ ਖੋਇਓ ॥ ਕਰਿ ਪਰਪੰਚ ਉਦਰ ਨਿਜ ਪੋਖਿਓ ਪਸੁ ਕੀ ਨਿਆਈ ਸੋਇਓ ॥ ੧ ॥ ਰਾਮ ਭਜਨ ਕੀ ਗਤਿ ਨਹੀ ਜਾਨੀ ਮਾਇਆ ਹਾਥਿ ਬਿਕਾਨਾ ॥ ਉਰਝਿ ਰਹਿਓ ਬਿਖਿਅਨ ਸੰਗਿ ਬਉਰਾ ਨਾਮੁ ਰਤਨੁ ਬਿਸਰਾਨਾ ॥ ੨ ॥ ਰਹਿਓ ਅਚੇਤੁ ਨ ਚੇਤਿਓ ਗੋਬਿੰਦ ਬਿਰਥਾ ਅਉਧ ਸਿਰਾਨੀ ॥ ਕਹੁ ਨਾਨਕ ਹਰਿ ਬਿਰਦੁ ਪਛਾਨਉ ਭੂਲੇ ਸਦਾ ਪਰਾਨੀ ॥ ੩ ॥ ੧੦ ॥ (pg 633 A.G.)

Your hypocricy shall be exposed, sooner or later. Therefore, pay heed, and listen to the beneficial advice of your Master, and take pre-emptive action, before falling deep into the darkest dungeons of death. Realization of your judgmental-errors and fallibilities and fallacies, should dawn upon you, while you are alive. Only then is there any probability of being rescued.

Egotism is opposed to the Name of the Lord; the two do not dwell in the same place. In egotism, selfless service cannot be performed, and so the mind goes unfulfilled. O my mind, think of the Lord, and practice the Word of the Guru's Shabad. If you submit to the Lord's Command, you shall meet with the Lord, and then egotism will depart from within. Egotism is within all bodies; through egotism, we come to be born. Egotism is utter darkness; under the influence of egotism, no one can understand anything. In egotism, devotional worship cannot be performed, and the Lord's Command cannot be understood. In egotism, the soul is in bondage, and the Name of the Lord does not come to abide in the mind. Says Nanak, meeting with the True Guru, egotism is eliminated, and then, the True One comes to dwell in the mind. Practicing Truth, abiding in Truth, and serving Truth, one is absorbed in the True One. [189]

"Egocentric-nature and God's Name (meditation) are opposing thoughts, extremely contradictory, to one another, and, hence, CAN'T, ever remain (stay) together, at one place (can never reside in one human-being).

The GURUS made it amply, emphatically, and abundantly clear that an egoistic person can never be an ideal devotee, or believer, because he lacks the Nectar of HUMILITY, a prerequisite for, and an essential ingredient of the Twin Paths of Meditation and Devotion.`

---

[189] ਹਉਮੈ ਨਾਵੈ ਨਾਲਿ ਵਿਰੋਧੁ ਹੈ ਦੁਇ ਨ ਵਸਹਿ ਇਕ ਠਾਇ ॥ ਹਉਮੈ ਵਿਚਿ ਸੇਵਾ ਨ ਹੋਵਈ ਤਾ ਮਨੁ ਬਿਰਥਾ ਜਾਇ ॥ ੧ ॥ ਹਰਿ ਚੇਤਿ ਮਨ ਮੇਰੇ ਤੂ ਗੁਰ ਕਾ ਸਬਦੁ ਕਮਾਇ ॥ ਹੁਕਮੁ ਮੰਨਹਿ ਤਾ ਹਰਿ ਮਿਲੈ ਤਾ ਵਿਚਹੁ ਹਉਮੈ ਜਾਇ ॥ ਰਹਾਉ ॥ ਹਉਮੈ ਸਭੁ ਸਰੀਰੁ ਹੈ ਹਉਮੈ ਉਪਤਿ ਹੋਇ ॥ ਹਉਮੈ ਵਡਾ ਗੁਬਾਰੁ ਹੈ ਹਉਮੈ ਵਿਚਿ ਬੁਝਿ ਨ ਸਕੈ ਕੋਇ ॥ ੨ ॥ ਹਉਮੈ ਵਿਚਿ ਭਗਤਿ ਨ ਹੋਵਈ ਹੁਕਮੁ ਨ ਬੁਝਿਆ ਜਾਇ ॥ ਹਉਮੈ ਵਿਚਿ ਜੀਉ ਬੰਧੁ ਹੈ ਨਾਮੁ ਨ ਵਸੈ ਮਨਿ ਆਇ ॥ ੩ ॥ ਨਾਨਕ ਸਤਗੁਰਿ ਮਿਲਿਐ ਹਉਮੈ ਗਈ ਤਾ ਸਚੁ ਵਸਿਆ ਮਨਿ ਆਇ ॥ ਸਚੁ ਕਮਾਵੈ ਸਚਿ ਰਹੈ ਸਚੇ ਸੇਵਿ ਸਮਾਇ ॥ ੪ ॥ ੮ ॥ ੧੨ ॥ (pg. 560 A.G.)

Guru Nanak laments :

In ego they come, and in ego they go. In ego they are born, and in ego they die. In ego they give, and in ego they take. In ego they earn, and in ego they lose. In ego they become truthful or false. In ego they go to heaven or hell. In ego they laugh, and in ego they weep. In ego they become dirty, and in ego they are washed clean. In ego they lose social status and class. In ego they are ignorant, and in ego they are wise. They do not know the value of salvation and liberation. In ego they love Illusion, and in ego they are kept in darkness by it. Living in ego, mortal beings are created. When one understands ego, then the Lord's gate is known. Without spiritual wisdom, they babble and argue. Says Nanak : by the Lord's Command, destiny is pre-ordained. The Lord watches us, always, so be warned that you are under surveillance, therefore mend your ways.[190]

Elucidates the Second Nanak, Guru Angad Dev :

This is the nature of ego, that people perform their actions in ego. This is the bondage of ego, that time and time again, they are reborn. Where does ego come from? How can it be removed? This ego exists by the Lord's Order; people wander according to their past actions. Ego is a chronic disease, but it contains its own cure as well. If the Lord grants His Grace, one acts according to the Teachings of the Guru's Shabad. Nanak says, listen, people: in this way, troubles depart.[191]

---

[190] ਹਉ ਵਿਚਿ ਆਇਆ ਹਉ ਵਿਚਿ ਗਇਆ ॥ ਹਉ ਵਿਚਿ ਜੰਮਿਆ ਹਉ ਵਿਚਿ ਮੁਆ ॥ ਹਉ ਵਿਚਿ ਦਿਤਾ ਹਉ ਵਿਚਿ ਲਇਆ ॥ ਹਉ ਵਿਚਿ ਖਟਿਆ ਹਉ ਵਿਚਿ ਗਇਆ ॥ ਹਉ ਵਿਚਿ ਸਚਿਆਰੁ ਕੁੜਿਆਰੁ ॥ ਹਉ ਵਿਚਿ ਪਾਪ ਪੁੰਨ ਵੀਚਾਰੁ ॥ ਹਉ ਵਿਚਿ ਨਰਕਿ ਸੁਰਗਿ ਅਵਤਾਰੁ ॥ ਹਉ ਵਿਚਿ ਹਸੈ ਹਉ ਵਿਚਿ ਰੋਵੈ ॥ ਹਉ ਵਿਚਿ ਭਰੀਐ ਹਉ ਵਿਚਿ ਧੋਵੈ ॥ ਹਉ ਵਿਚਿ ਜਾਤੀ ਜਿਨਸੀ ਖੋਵੈ ॥ ਹਉ ਵਿਚਿ ਮੂਰਖੁ ਹਉ ਵਿਚਿ ਸਿਆਣਾ ॥ ਮੋਖ ਮੁਕਤਿ ਕੀ ਸਾਰ ਨ ਜਾਣਾ ॥ ਹਉ ਵਿਚਿ ਮਾਇਆ ਹਉ ਵਿਚਿ ਛਾਇਆ ॥ ਹਉਮੈ ਕਰਿ ਕਰਿ ਜੰਤ ਉਪਾਇਆ ॥ ਹਉਮੈ ਬੂਝੈ ਤਾ ਦਰੁ ਸੂਝੈ ॥ ਗਿਆਨ ਵਿਹੂਣਾ ਕਥਿ ਕਥਿ ਲੂਝੈ ॥ ਨਾਨਕ ਹੁਕਮੀ ਲਿਖੀਐ ਲੇਖੁ ॥ ਜੇਹਾ ਵੇਖਹਿ ਤੇਹਾ ਵੇਖੁ ॥ ੧ ॥ (pg. 466 A.G.)

[191] ਹਉਮੈ ਏਹਾ ਜਾਤਿ ਹੈ ਹਉਮੈ ਕਰਮ ਕਮਾਹਿ ॥ ਹਉਮੈ ਏਈ ਬੰਧਨਾ ਫਿਰਿ ਫਿਰਿ ਜੋਨੀ ਪਾਹਿ ॥ ਹਉਮੈ ਕਿਥਹੁ ਉਪਜੈ ਕਿਤੁ ਸੰਜਮਿ ਇਹ ਜਾਇ ॥ ਹਉਮੈ ਏਹੋ ਹੁਕਮੁ ਹੈ ਪਇਐ ਕਿਰਤਿ ਫਿਰਾਹਿ ॥ ਹਉਮੈ ਦੀਰਘ ਰੋਗੁ ਹੈ ਦਾਰੂ ਭੀ ਇਸੁ ਮਾਹਿ ॥ ਕਿਰਪਾ ਕਰੇ ਜੇ ਆਪਣੀ ਤਾ ਗੁਰ ਕਾ ਸਬਦੁ ਕਮਾਹਿ ॥ ਨਾਨਕੁ ਕਹੈ ਸੁਣਹੁ ਜਨਹੁ ਇਤੁ ਸੰਜਮਿ ਦੁਖ ਜਾਹਿ ॥ ੨ ॥ (pg. 466 A.G.)

The remedial measure, suggested for the extinction or extermination of EGO, is the time-tested Principle of Meditation, wherein no intermediary is required: It has to be, quintessentially, a one-to-one Relationship, between God and Creation. This, then, is the ONLY route or via media to avoid Ego.

The potentially strong Vice, called Ego, is, always, present, in a variety, and varying degrees, of subtle forms, in the human psyche.

Enquires Guru Arjan Dev (the 5th Nanak) :
Is there anyone, who can shatter his ego, and turn his mind away from this sweet Illusion? Humanity is in spiritual ignorance; people see things that do not exist. The night is dark and gloomy; how will the morning dawn? Wandering, wandering all around, I have grown weary; trying all sorts of things, I have been searching. A rejoicing and jubilant Nanak thanks God, while paying obeisance, for bestowing His merciful glance ; and sings thus, in gay abandon: I have found the treasure of the Saadh Sangat, the Company of the Holy.[192]

When the Supreme Benevolent Grace is bestowed on a chosen one, it is only then that the Beneficiary seeks the company and blessings and advice of the BLESSED ONES (the Saintly and Pious Souls), and, thus, in the process, secures redemption, and is, now, beyond the domain of the octopus-like tentacles of EGO.

---

[192] ਹੈ ਕੋਈ ਐਸਾ ਹਉਮੈ ਤੋਰੈ ॥ ਇਸੁ ਮੀਠੀ ਤੇ ਇਹੁ ਮਨੁ ਹੋਰੈ ॥ ੧ ॥ ਰਹਾਉ ॥ ਅਗਿਆਨੀ ਮਾਨੁਖੁ ਭਇਆ ਜੋ ਨਾਹੀ ਸੋ ਲੋਰੈ ॥ ਰੈਣਿ ਅੰਧਾਰੀ ਕਾਰੀਆ ਕਵਨ ਜੁਗਤਿ ਜਿਤੁ ਭੋਰੈ ॥ ੧ ॥ ਭੁਮਤੋ ਭੁਮਤੋ ਹਾਰਿਆ ਅਨਿਕ ਬਿਧੀ ਕਰਿ ਟੋਰੈ ॥ ਕਹੁ ਨਾਨਕ ਕਿਰਪਾ ਭਈ ਸਾਧਸੰਗਤਿ ਨਿਧਿ ਮੋਰੈ ॥ ੨ ॥ ੧੨ ॥ ੧੪੦ ॥ (pg. 212 A.G.)

Beauty and sexual desire are friends; hunger and tasty food are tied together. Greed is bound up in its search for wealth, and sleep will use even a tiny space as a bed. Anger barks and brings ruin on itself, blindly pursuing useless conflicts. It is good to be silent, because without the Name of the Lord, one's mouth spews forth only filth. Royal power, wealth, beauty, social status and youth are the five thieves. These thieves have plundered the world; no one's honour has been spared. But these thieves themselves are robbed, by those who fall at the Guru's Feet.[193]

You are overflowing with sexual desire, and your intellect is stained with darkness; In the heat of youthful passion, you look with desire upon the faces of other men's wives; you do not distinguish between good and evil. Drunk with sexual desire and other great sins, you go astray, and do not distinguish between vice and virtue.[194]

O my Lord and Master, I know nothing, in my ignorance and indifference. My mind is sold out, and is, now, in Illusion's hands. You are called the Lord and Master, the Guru of the World. I am called a lustful being of the Dark Iron-Age (Kali-Yuga). The five vices have corrupted my mind. Moment by moment, they lead me further away from the Lord. Wherever I look, I see loads of pain and suffering.[195]

---

[193] ਰੂਪੈ ਕਾਮੈ ਦੋਸਤੀ ਭੁਖੈ ਸਾਦੈ ਗੰਢੁ ॥ ਲਬੈ ਮਾਲੈ ਘੁਲਿ ਮਿਲਿ ਮਿਚਲਿ ਉਂਘੈ ਸਉੜਿ ਪਲੰਘੁ ॥ ਭੰਉਕੈ ਕੋਪੁ ਖੁਆਰੁ ਹੋਇ ਫਕੜੁ ਪਿਟੇ ਅੰਧੁ ॥ ਚੁਪੈ ਚੰਗਾ ਨਾਨਕਾ ਵਿਣੁ ਨਾਵੈ ਮੁਹਿ ਗੰਧੁ ॥ ੧ ॥ ਮਃ ੧ ॥ ਰਾਜੁ ਮਾਲੁ ਰੂਪੁ ਜਾਤਿ ਜੋਬਨੁ ਪੰਜੇ ਠਗ ॥ ਏਨੀ ਠਗੀਂ ਜਗੁ ਠਗਿਆ ਕਿਨੈ ਨ ਰਖੀ ਲਜ ॥ ਏਨਾ ਠਗਨਿ੍ ਠਗ ਸੇ ਜਿ ਗੁਰ ਕੀ ਪੈਰੀ ਪਾਹਿ ॥ (pg. 1288 A.G.)

[194] ਉਡਲਿਆ ਕਾਮੁ ਕਾਲ ਮਤਿ ਲਾਗੀ ਤਉ ਆਨਿ ਸਕਤਿ ਗਲਿ ਬਾਂਧਿਆ ॥ ੨ ॥ ਤਰੁਣ ਤੇਜੁ ਪਰ ਤ੍ਰਿਅ ਮੁਖੁ ਜੋਹਹਿ ਸਰੁ ਅਪਸਰੁ ਨ ਪਛਾਣਿਆ ॥ ਉਨਮਤ ਕਾਮਿ ਮਹਾ ਬਿਖੁ ਭੂਲੈ ਪਾਪੁ ਪੁੰਨੁ ਨ ਪਛਾਣਿਆ ॥ (pg. 93 A.G.)

[195] ਨਾਥ ਕਛੂਅ ਨ ਜਾਨਉ ॥ ਮਨੁ ਮਾਇਆ ਕੈ ਹਾਥਿ ਬਿਕਾਨਉ ॥ ੧ ॥ ਰਹਾਉ ॥ ਤੁਮ ਕਹੀਅਤ ਹੌ ਜਗਤ ਗੁਰ ਸੁਆਮੀ ॥ ਹਮ ਕਹੀਅਤ ਕਲਿਜੁਗ ਕੇ ਕਾਮੀ ॥ ੧ ॥ ਇਨ ਪੰਚਨ ਮੇਰੋ ਮਨੁ ਜੁ ਬਿਗਾਰਿਓ ॥ ਪਲੁ ਪਲੁ ਹਰਿ ਜੀ ਤੇ ਅੰਤਰੁ ਪਾਰਿਓ ॥ ੨ ॥ ਜਤ ਦੇਖਿਓ ਤਤ ਦੁਖ ਕੀ ਰਾਸੀ ॥ ਅਜੌਂ ਨ ਪਤ੍ਯਾਇ ਨਿਗਮ ਭਏ ਸਾਖੀ ॥ ੩ ॥ (pg. 710 A.G.)

Others' spouses, others' wealth, greed, egotism, corruption, evil passions, slander of others, sexual desire and anger — all of these are like venom; give up all these.[196]

Unbridled sexual indulgence and promiscuity have been the sole cause of the spread of the deadly epidemic called AIDS, along with several other life-endangering diseases.

---

[196] ਪਰ ਦਾਰਾ ਪਰ ਧਨੁ ਪਰ ਲੋਭਾ ਹਉਮੈ ਬਿਖੈ ਬਿਕਾਰ ॥ ਦੁਸਟ ਭਾਉ ਤਜਿ ਨਿੰਦ ਪਰਾਈ ਕਾਮੁ ਕ੍ਰੋਧੁ ਚੰਡਾਰ ॥ ੧ ॥ (pg. 1255 A.G.)

Sheikh Fareed advises: answer evil with goodness; do not fill your mind with anger. Your body shall not suffer from any disease, and you shall obtain everything. [197]

One who has an abiding faith in the Holy-Word, God resides within him (body and soul). He does not come or go in reincarnation, and he is rescued. Through the Word of the Guru, his heart-lotus blossoms forth. Whoever is seen, is driven by hope and despair, by sexual desire, anger, corruption, hunger and thirst. Says Nanak: those detached recluses who meet the Lord are so very rare. [198]

There is no real chanting, meditation, penance or self-control, as long as one does not live, in consonance with the Word and Spirit of the Guru's Command. Accepting the Word of the Guru, one obtains Truth; through Truth, one merges in the True Lord. Sexual desire and anger are very powerful in the world. They lead to all sorts of actions, but these only add to all the pain. Those who serve the True Guru find peace; they are united with the True Word. [199]

The meek and humble beggars stand begging at Your Door. Please be generous and give to those who are yearning. Save me, O God — I have come to Your Sanctuary. Please implant the Guru's Teachings, and Your Name, within me. Sexual desire and anger are very powerful in the body; Bless me with courage and fortitude that I may rise to wage war against them, and that I may emerge victorious.

---

[197] ਫਰੀਦਾ ਬੁਰੇ ਦਾ ਭਲਾ ਕਰਿ ਗੁਸਾ ਮਨਿ ਨ ਹਢਾਇ ॥ ਦੇਹੀ ਰੋਗੁ ਨ ਲਗਈ ਪਲੈ ਸਭੁ ਕਿਛੁ ਪਾਇ ॥ ੭੮ (Pg 1381-1382 A.G.)

[198] ਸਬਦਿ ਮਰੈ ਤਿਸੁ ਨਿਜ ਘਰਿ ਵਾਸਾ ॥ ਆਵੈ ਨ ਜਾਵੈ ਚੂਕੈ ਆਸਾ ॥ ਗੁਰ ਕੈ ਸਬਦਿ ਕਮਲੁ ਪਰਗਾਸਾ ॥ ੨ ॥ ਜੋ ਦੀਸੈ ਸੋ ਆਸ ਨਿਰਾਸਾ ॥ ਕਾਮ ਕਰੋਧ ਬਿਖੁ ਭੂਖ ਪਿਆਸਾ ॥ ਨਾਨਕ ਬਿਰਲੇ ਮਿਲਹਿ ਉਦਾਸਾ ॥ ੮ ॥ ੨ ॥ (pg. 224 A.G.)

[199] ਜਪੁ ਤਪੁ ਸੰਜਮੁ ਹੋਰੁ ਕੋਈ ਨਾਹੀ ॥ ਜਬ ਲਗੁ ਗੁਰ ਕਾ ਸਬਦੁ ਨ ਕਮਾਹੀ ॥ ਗੁਰ ਕੈ ਸਬਦਿ ਮਿਲਿਆ ਸਚੁ ਪਾਇਆ ਸਚੇ ਸਚਿ ਸਮਾਇਦਾ ॥ ੧੨ ॥ ਕਾਮ ਕਰੋਧੁ ਸਬਲ ਸੰਸਾਰਾ ॥ ਬਹੁ ਕਰਮ ਕਮਾਵਹਿ ਸਭੁ ਦੁਖ ਕਾ ਪਸਾਰਾ ॥ ਸਤਿਗੁਰ ਸੇਵਹਿ ਸੇ ਸੁਖੁ ਪਾਵਹਿ ਸਚੈ ਸਬਦਿ ਮਿਲਾਇਦਾ ॥ ੧੩ ॥ (pg. 1060 A.G.)

*Please treat me as Your Own and save me; through the Perfect Guru,
I drive them out. The powerful fire of corruption is raging violently
within; the Word of the Immaculate Guru is the icy-water which
soothes my body, and provides solace to my mind. My mind and body
are calm and tranquil; the disease has been cured, and now I sleep in
peace. As the rays of the sun spread out everywhere, the Lord
pervades each and every heart. Meeting the Holy Saint, one drinks in
the Sublime Essence of the Lord; sitting in the home of your own inner
being, drink in the essence.*[200]

Anger could be the consequence of a array of feelings and emotions,
including victimization and betrayal, powerlessness, insecurity, failure
in communication, and a host of related causes. To keep the demonic-
force of Anger, at bay, one could deploy the technique of ' stepping-
back ', or even think in terms of adopting a novel-method of self-
imposition of a penal-action, for each defeat at the hands of Anger.

The penalty could be having to set aside a substantial amount of
monetary-donation to a non-profit organization (you may include
"DIVINE POWER, Inc., in your list; just kidding).

---

[200] ਮੰਗਤ ਜਨ ਦੀਨ ਖਰੇ ਦਰਿ ਠਾਢੇ ਅਤਿ ਤਰਸਨ ਕਉ ਦਾਨੁ ਦੀਜੈ ॥ ਤੁਹਿ ਤੁਹਿ ਸਰਨਿ ਪ੍ਰਭ ਆਏ
ਮੋ ਕਉ ਗੁਰਮਤਿ ਨਾਮੁ ਦ੍ਰਿੜੀਜੈ ॥ ੧ ॥ ਕਾਮ ਕ੍ਰੋਧੁ ਨਗਰ ਮਹਿ ਸਬਲਾ ਨਿਤ ਉਠਿ ਉਠਿ ਜੁਝੁ ਕਰੀਜੈ
॥ ਅੰਗੀਕਾਰੁ ਕਰਹੁ ਰਖਿ ਲੇਵਹੁ ਗੁਰ ਪੂਰਾ ਕਾਢਿ ਕਢੀਜੈ ॥ ੨ ॥ ਅੰਤਰਿ ਅਗਨਿ ਸਬਲ ਅਤਿ
ਬਿਖਿਆ ਹਿਵ ਸੀਤਲੁ ਸਬਦੁ ਗੁਰ ਦੀਜੈ ॥ ਤਨਿ ਮਨਿ ਸਾਂਤਿ ਹੋਇ ਅਧਿਕਾਈ ਰੋਗੁ ਕਾਟੈ ਸੂਖਿ ਸਵੀਜੈ
॥ ੩ ॥ ਜਿਉ ਸੂਰਜੁ ਕਿਰਣਿ ਰਵਿਆ ਸਰਬ ਠਾਈ ਸਭ ਘਟਿ ਘਟਿ ਰਾਮੁ ਰਵੀਜੈ ॥ ਸਾਧੂ ਸਾਧ ਮਿਲੇ
ਰਸੁ ਪਾਵੈ ਤਤੁ ਨਿਜ ਘਰਿ ਬੈਠਿਆ ਪੀਜੈ ॥ ੪ ॥ (pg. 1325 A.G.)

They may live in heavenly realms, and conquer the nine regions of the world, but if they forget the Lord of the world, they are just wanderers in the wilderness. In the midst of millions of games and entertainment, the Lord's Name does not come to reside in their minds and hearts. Their home is like a wilderness, in the depths of hell. He sees the terrible, awful wilderness as a city. Gazing upon the false objects, he believes them to be real. Engrossed in sexual desire, anger and egotism, he wanders around insane. When the Messenger of Death hits him on the head with his club, then he regrets and repents. Without the Perfect, Divine Guru, he roams around like Satan.[201]

Cruelty is the handiwork of devilish tendencies, which have resulted in massive spillage of blood on the face of the earth. Although there is no such entity as a devil, all the negative vices have been considered to be the manifestations of the devil. The existence of 'ghosts' has been negated.

---

[201] ਬਸੰਤਿ ਸੁਰਗ ਲੋਕਹ ਜਿਤਤੇ ਪ੍ਰਿਥਵੀ ਨਵ ਖੰਡਣਹ ॥ ਬਿਸਰੰਤ ਹਰਿ ਗੋਪਾਲਹ ਨਾਨਕ ਤੇ ਪ੍ਰਾਣੀ ਉਦਿਆਨ ਭਰਮਣਹ ॥ ੧ ॥ ਕਉਤਕ ਕੋਡ ਤਮਾਸਿਆ ਚਿਤਿ ਨ ਆਵਸੁ ਨਾਉ ॥ ਨਾਨਕ ਕੋੜੀ ਨਰਕ ਬਰਾਬਰੇ ਉਜੜੁ ਸੋਈ ਥਾਉ ॥ ੨ ॥ ਪਉੜੀ ॥ ਮਹਾ ਭਇਆਨ ਉਦਿਆਨ ਨਗਰ ਕਰਿ ਮਾਨਿਆ ॥ ਝੂਠ ਸਮਗ੍ਰੀ ਪੇਖਿ ਸਚੁ ਕਰਿ ਜਾਨਿਆ ॥ ਕਾਮ ਕ੍ਰੋਧਿ ਅਹੰਕਾਰਿ ਫਿਰਹਿ ਦੇਵਾਨਿਆ ॥ ਸਿਰਿ ਲਗਾ ਜਮ ਡੰਡੁ ਤਾ ਪਛੁਤਾਨਿਆ ॥ ਬਿਨੁ ਪੂਰੇ ਗੁਰਦੇਵ ਫਿਰੈ ਸੈਤਾਨਿਆ ॥ ੮ ॥ (pg. 707 A.G.)

143

A Note from the Publisher

****

It was inspiring to read about the manifesta-
tion of the 'power of prayer', in a couple of
newspapers, very recently. In order to generate the readers' faith in such power, the
author reluctantly agreed to permit us to
append the following three pages, from one
such press-clipping in an abridged form.

We are sincerely grateful to God, for having
provided us this opportunity, of being
associated with the publication of this work,
for the service to humanity.
****

COMMUNITY

PRAYERS SAVE MILLIONS OF DOLLARS

Singh Sahib Jagtar Singh 'Jaachak' honoring Mayor Suozzi with a plaque

A well attended gathering was organized at Raj Palace, Great Neck, on Friday, Jan. 30th. The dinner was held to express a deep sense of gratitude to all those "Instruments who were commanded by God" to get the mission accomplished, pertaining to the Gurdwara and School, at 100 Lattingtown Road, Glen Cove, N.Y. The atmosphere was one of rejoicing and thankfulness.

The sprawling complex is spread over 15.43 acres, and has a palatial mansion, having a built-up area of 30,000+ sq. ft., and is located in a serene environment. Just across the road is a golf course, and there is a beach, only a 5-minutes drive away. Unibank took a loss of $7 million when selling the complex to Sikh Forum, Inc., Plainview, N.Y., for $1.2 million.
Amazingly, all the other links in the chain leading to the final approvals, including the Real Estate Broker, the Attorneys, and the Architect, contributed up to 90% of their consultancy fee, towards the donations for the Gurdwara.

Dr. Harsimran Singh Sabharwal set the tone for the evening when he emphasized upon the Power of Prayer, and the occurrence of Miracles. The audience heard this zealous orator with rapt attention. He remarked that the esteemed Honorees were the people who practiced Religion and Humanism, in the true sense of the words, and were God's chosen few.

Dr. Sabharwal then introduced Ms. Tracy Peddy, of Siegel, Fenchel & Peddy, P.C., Attorneys-at-Law, who fought the legal-battle, for years, against the City of Glen Cove.

Tracie Peddy, Attorney at Law

Michael Tassis

The County, City, and School Taxes, totaling approximately $ 200,000 were reduced by about 70% as a result of her sincere efforts and legal acumen. Additionally, as per the laws of the City of Glen Cove, the Sikh Forum was required to pay School Taxes, for the year 1996-97, to the tune of $ 115,000 ($35,000 on a reduced basis). The audience heartily applauded when Dr. Sabharwal revealed that the taxes have now been completely waived. This, he said, was another major legal victory. The audience continued to cheer Ms. Peddy, when the speaker announced that the Attorney's fee demand of $ 57,000 (based on 1/3 of the total taxes reduced, as per the contractual agreement) was brought down to $3,000, when Ms. Peddy graciously accepted Dr. Sabharwal's telephonic request that she accept that amount. She did not require more than a couple of seconds to agree. This could only be God's Miracle.

Next to be introduced was Mr. Dean Tassis, the broker, in absentia. He was unable to attend, as he is suffering from lung cancer. His son, who read a note written by him, addressed to Dr. Sabharwal, and other Sikh-community members, represented him.

The note read as follows : "I am very much obliged that you considered to give me this honor, and to be part of this major achievement. I feel so bad that I could not come personally, because of my sickness. Dr. Sabharwal, you may be wondering why I kept working so hard with you, even after having sold the property. Trust me, it was your integrity that you were proving to your God, and I wanted to be part of it. When you got the contract to purchase this property for $ 1.2 million in your name, I had brought you many offers, where you could have made double your purchase price, but you wouldn't consider it. The world may think that you are a crazy man, because money is everything, but it is not. I had the same values in my life, and they have even become stronger, as I am suffering from this sickness. During these years of working with you, I have learned that

146

Dr Harsimran S. Sabharwal addressing the gathering

Thomas Joseph Pirlk, Architect;

prayer to God works. If there is anything you can give me as a reward, I want you and your community to pray for me. Thank you, and God bless you". Sd/- Dean Tassis.

Mr. Thomas Joseph Pirkel, the Architect, who was responsible for the work on the parking lot, interiors, electrical and mechanical jobs, was heartily cheered, when it was announced that he had kindly accepted only $5,000, whereas the entire job could actually cost many times over. Mr. Pirkel did not hesitate, over the phone, while accepting Dr. Sabharwal's offer, saying that he was doing this for God's house.

Dr. Sabharwal praised the Honorable Thomas R. Suozzi,

Mayor of Glen Cove, for his continuous help and guidance pertaining to the permissions for the Gurdwara. The Mayor drew a repeated round of applause for his far-sighted approach, wonderful sense of humor and courteous nature.

The Mayor remarked that Dr. Sabharwal is a very humble man. He does not want to take credit for anything. But the fact remains that God made him the means to achieve all this. It wasn't easy for him to achieve all the successes right from acquisition of the property, to getting the taxes reduced to nothing, and then getting all the requisite permissions.

(an abridged version)

147

NOTES